We have only one choice to make, now and always: to open ourselves to embrace truth and its constant companion, love; or to withdraw from truth and love, defining ourselves through contraction and resistance. This choice is placed before us relentlessly, with exquisite precision, in our close relationships. . . .

There is no better place to practice all this than right where we are, every moment of every day: in a relationship with our own hearts and souls, and with the hearts and souls of people around us. This is why close relationship opens the conscious heart.

—From the Introduction

"Gay and Kathlyn's most vulnerable and powerful book yet. If you want a real loving relationship, study this book. It's all here, and it works."

—Kenny and Julia Loggins, co-authors of *The Unimaginable Life*

"I consider Gay and Kathlyn Hendricks to be my teachers."

—John Bradshaw

"Kathlyn and Gay Hendricks are masters in the art of intimate relationships."

—John Gray, author of *Men Are from Mars, Women Are from Venus*

THE
CONSCIOUS
HEART

SEVEN SOUL-CHOICES THAT INSPIRE

CREATIVE PARTNERSHIP

Kathlyn Hendricks, Ph.D., and
Gay Hendricks, Ph.D.

BANTAM BOOKS

New York   Toronto   London   Sydney   Auckland

THE CONSCIOUS HEART
A Bantam Book

PUBLISHING HISTORY
Bantam hardcover edition / September 1997
Bantam trade paperback edition / February 1999

Grateful acknowledgment is made for permission to reprint the following:
Excerpt from the *Tao Te Ching* by Lao Tzu. Translation copyright © 1990 by Victor H. Mair.
Reprinted by permission of Bantam Books, a division of Random House, Inc.

Author photo by Clint Weisman.

Book design by Richard Oriolo.

Library of Congress Catalog Card Number: 96-52282

ISBN 0-553-37491-5

Published simultaneously in the United States and Canada

Bantam Books are published by Bantam Books, a division of Random House, Inc. Its trademark,
consisting of the words "Bantam Books" and the portrayal of a rooster, is Registered in U.S.
Patent and Trademark Office and in other countries. Marca Registrada. Bantam Books, 1540
Broadway, New York, New York 10036.

PRINTED IN THE UNITED STATES OF AMERICA

FFG 10 9 8 7 6 5

Contents

PART FOUR

THE ESSENTIAL PRACTICES

Introduction / 259
Six Exercises in Transformation

THE TABLECLOTH TRICK

Love says
let's get down
in the pit of your fears
and wrestle
hip to hip.
Let's swing
the maypole of lust
through your butterflies and
free their belly dust.

Love says
let's pry
your dirty fingernails
from the antic box
where howls and yelps
flutter and scratch.
Let's pull the thread
that unravels
your naked source.

Love says
let's slide
through the rollercoaster
of your heart
upsidedown
and run our toes
through the muck.
Let's bowl
in your mind
and scatter the knobby pins
of your fort.

Love says
let's do the tablecloth trick.

Let's pull
out the smooth assumptions
you squat over and see what's left.

Love says
let's tickle,
let's scuffle,
let's go eyelash to eyelash
and see who blinks first.

Love says
I want
everything.
I'll devour you to
the last earlobe.
Then,
we'll play.

KATHLYN HENDRICKS

Acknowledgments
and Gratitude

◆❧

We are grateful to the couples and individuals who have worked with us in therapy and workshops over the past twenty years. They are the laboratory of the human heart out of which our work has developed. Their contribution to the work is immense: Through them we have discovered what is most essential in relationships and in human transformation. We are also grateful to the several hundred graduates of our professional training programs for helping us refine the practical application of our work.

We feel deep gratitude to friends and family who have been with us on our incredible journey: Alex Merrin, Mary Manin Morrissey, Amanda Hendricks, Chris and Helen Hendricks, Mike and Lou Hendricks, Bonnie Raitt, Pamela Polland and Bill Ernst, Julia and Kenny Loggins, Polly and Bob Swift, Rod and Sandy Wells, Steve Sisgold, David Hubbard, Gary Zukav and Linda Francis. There are many others, too numerous to name, but you know who you are, and we thank you in our hearts.

After our children left for college in the mid-eighties, we decided to use our newfound freedom to take our work more into the public forum. Thanks to the many people who were there with helping hands:

- Oprah Winfrey, a great spirit, who first gave us a large national audience

- Bob Berkowitz
- Sally Jessy Raphael
- John Bradshaw
- Deepak Chopra

We are blessed with the finest literary agent in the land, Sandy Dijkstra, and an editor, Toni Burbank, who is not only masterful in her work but also an extraordinary human being. To both of them our gratitude is absolute.

A Personal Welcome

❧

Welcome to the path of the conscious heart. This path invites you to create your relationships by design instead of by default. It shows you a set of stepping-stones that will carry you to the rich and magnificent feeling we call *essence*. Essence is your deeply felt sense of who you truly are, accompanied by a feeling of unity, clarity, and love. Essence is known in your mind and experienced in your body. It is always just a breath away and can be yours in every moment. Once you have embraced essence in yourself—through the practices we call the path of the conscious heart—you have a place to come home to in yourself. Then you can invite another person into your home, if you desire loving partnership.

Nothing can reveal essence like a close relationship, and nothing can obscure it more thoroughly. The unconscious heart would have us reject essence and cling to our old wounds and defenses. To open the conscious heart and embrace this essence-feeling, you have to master a handful of skills and attitudes that are wonderfully simple yet that require benign vigilance of the highest order. Life gives you repeated opportunities to make choices that lead you closer to or farther away from your essence. In every moment you are choosing either to embrace essence or to shun it. In our own relationship we came to recognize the choices that took us toward essence, such as appreciating each other or genuinely wondering. Other choices, such as insisting on being right, buried essence in the unconscious heart. We then had to patiently work to reopen the conscious heart for minutes, hours, and sometimes days.

We continue to be our own best customers in these practices. Every day we find ways to refine and deepen the practice of supporting and revealing essence in each other and in ourselves. The effort has been most worthwhile.

We have two main goals in this book. We want to help create a world of relationships in which the essence and creativity of each person is nurtured and brought to full flower. Second, we want to show how the evolutionary speed bumps of close relationships can be dealt with in a new way that allows for maximum growth in each person.

Let's put our conviction squarely on the line here at the outset: The purpose of revealing essence is to produce a certain body-feeling, not a set of abstractions. If this path of the conscious heart is worthwhile, you will feel an easeful streaming feeling of well-being in your body, accompanied by a sense of connection to other people and the universe around you. This is what essence is all about, and don't let anyone talk you out of it. Many of us have been brainwashed to think this feeling is unobtainable or that it must come from outside ourselves by the power of some authority. We hope to show you otherwise. Particularly we will ask you to reclaim your natural birthright—your own organic essence-feelings in your body—and to see that they are produced when you follow certain guideposts on the path.

All relationships are sacred. Relationships are the sacred space in which we live out our full development. Essence lives in the spaces between us, as well as in ourselves and in the universe at large. If essence does not live in our relations with others, it does not live at all. A thousand sermons or a hundred meditations lose all their meaning when the preacher or the meditator utters an abusive word to a loved one. The way we treat others is the measure of how conscious our hearts have become. It cannot be otherwise.

In this book we will ask you to set aside your psychological theories and religious beliefs and instead focus on your actual body-sense of essence. We do this for a particular reason. Beliefs occur in the mind—they are cognitive, abstract, and arguable. Beliefs divide. In some places in the world, people have been fighting for hundreds of years simply over their beliefs.

We seek an experience that unifies rather than divides. What unifies us, what lets us know we are deeply, consciously well, are our body-feelings. Our body-sense of our essence occurs at a level deeper than our beliefs. We can celebrate an authentic, organic feeling of resonance in the body at every moment; there we can actually celebrate the unity of humanity. Relationship—the practice of the conscious heart—is the best way we have found to produce and keep that feeling. In our own daily lives, we meditate every day, get frequent exercise, and do our best to eat fresh, healthy food. All these things are important, even crucial. But relationships are in a class by themselves. If essence does not live in our relationships, it does not live at all.

In our work with several thousand couples, we have discovered a set of attitudes and simple skills that allow all our relationships to deepen essence-contact with ourselves and the universe. If we know these skills, we can enjoy our close relationships and employ them to bring us deeper into unity with ourselves, our loved ones, our community, and the universe itself. If you embrace essence with a conscious heart, you can tap a transcendental energy-source through the vehicle of your everyday experiences with people. This transcendental energy can bring you into a rich embrace of your own nature and that of your partner, and an appreciation of the essence of the universe. This is the possibility of the conscious heart.

Speaking personally, our own relationship brings us joy and rich learnings every day because we treat it as our main evolutionary path. We did not always see it this way. In fact, nearly two decades ago we came into the relationship with about as much unconscious baggage as everyone else. But as we worked through the deep fears and conflicts that divided us from true intimacy, we discovered that embracing and supporting essence in our relationship gave us a large enough context to handle all the exhilarating highs and soul-despairing lows that came our way as our relationship matured.

Close relationships are the greatest source of pain that most of us ever feel in our lives. When people are on their deathbeds, they do not regret the mansions not lived in or the cars not driven. Instead, they weep for love not given or received. They regret the unspoken words of love and forgiveness to the people closest to them. People who have endured the pain of difficult childbirth or the crushing grip of a heart attack have told us that these pains, awful as they are, are not equal to watching a beloved child make a destructive life decision or to feeling contempt pouring from eyes that once beheld us with love. Physical pain has a focal point, and it usually has a beginning, a middle, and an end. But the pain of a close relationship often expands in waves and spirals that seem to have no end.

At the same time close relationships are our greatest source of joy. Most of us have felt the deep soul-connection with a new baby or a new romantic partner: This is life on earth at its finest. We melt into union with another person, and we feel real, complete, whole. In transcendent relationship moments we do not merely understand the meaning of life—we feel it. We know deep in our cells that the whole purpose of the universe is served through surrendering to the resonant union with ourselves, others, and the universe itself.

Our view of relationship is very different now from what it was twenty years ago. Our book *Conscious Loving* was our own Relationships 101. We wrote it because we were interested in finding answers to common problems that we and our clients experienced in close relationships. Now we are interested in moving to a deeper level. Our clients and workshop participants come up with magnificent questions: "How will I know if I'm seeing what's real or just what I'm imagining or want to see?" "Is it possible to live in a new way, a way that honors who each of us really is?" "My habits are so strong—they just seem to take over. Is fundamental change really possible?" The exploration seemed to point to another dimension, one that had more to do with subtle, profound corrections that can have huge positive effects. We became very interested in underlying shifts of attitude that affect being and, through being, actions.

Conscious Loving talked about doing things differently. We have sometimes referred to it as practical magic—the openings that occur when we change patterns or communicate differently. We could almost say that in that book we worked from outside relationship patterns into the core. By changing practices, we changed the fundamental quality of relationship. In this book, however, we are moving from the inside out. By shifting our deepest intentions, attitudes, and purposes, we are shifting the emerging choices and actions that shape the flow and future of a relationship.

Readers of *Conscious Loving* consistently told us that four principles stood out: the six co-commitments, telling the microscopic truth, taking 100 percent responsibility, and the Upper Limits Problem.

The six co-commitments provide a solid, safe foundation for change. They also expose the counter-commitments, or barriers that aren't apparent prior to stepping into commitment. Our readers have also used the co-commitments to *recommit* when they got stuck, rather than give up or struggle to do it perfectly the first time. We have changed the wording in the years since we published *Conscious Loving*. Here is our current version of the co-commitments, with their counter-commitments (we think humor is an important part of conscious relationships):

- *I commit to being close, and I commit to clearing up anything in the way of doing so.*
  Counter-commitment: I commit to holding back and to keeping hidden my barriers to closeness.

- *I commit to my own complete development as an individual.*
  Counter-commitment: I commit to holding back from expressing my full development as an individual.
- *I commit to the full empowerment of people around me.*
  Counter-commitment: I commit to holding back those around me, so they won't leave, so they'll need me, because I'm comfortable.
- *I commit to taking full, healthy responsibility in my close relationships.*
  Counter-commitment: I commit to a lifelong search to find who's to blame for this fix I'm in.
- *I commit to revealing rather than concealing.*
  Counter-commitment: I commit to hiding.
- *I commit to having a good time in my close relationships.*
  Counter-commitment: I commit to suffering, to finding out how much pain I can endure without flinching.

These commitments have been used in wedding ceremonies, and even in business contracts and organizational design.

The principle of *telling the microscopic truth* has embroiled us in more controversy than any other aspect of *Conscious Loving.* People either expand with joy or explode in outrage at the suggestion that they tell their partner the truth about everything. We recommend telling the truth about facts, such as affairs and broken agreements; about fantasies, such as imagining a different partner during sex; and about feelings, such as fear or anger. We have been encouraged by the number of readers who have contacted us to tell us that the truth really has set them free from jealousy, competition, and power struggles. Renewed passion and creative juice seem to flow for those courageous enough to practice our definition of the truth: *that which cannot be argued about.*

Most people associate *responsibility* with blame or burden. They either take it on as duty, or they point the finger of blame at their partner, themselves, or the world. We have learned from our readers and clients that the moment either partner steps out of 100 percent responsibility and makes a run for the victim position, power struggles begin. They end only when each person chooses to take full, healthy responsibility for creating the conflict. The heart of responsibility is genuine wondering, and we've witnessed thousands of people reap the benefits of making the shift from blame to wonder. We got so much feedback about the importance of this principle that we have expanded our exploration of responsibility in this book.

The Upper Limits Problem strikes people as *obvious,* both literally and metaphorically, once they understand the dynamics. Here is the Upper Limits Problem in brief: We each have a thermostat setting for how much love and positive energy our nervous system can handle. When we exceed that limit, our unconscious patterns and behaviors bring us back to a more familiar, safe level. Readers have documented Upper Limits vignettes for us, some hilarious and some poignant. Some people have Friday-night fights on the verge of an intimate weekend. Others worry, get busy, or wreck their car. Sometimes whole families participate in Upper Limits patterns: When one member gets really successful, someone else gets very ill, starts a fight at school, or loses the dog.

We began to see that the Upper Limits Problem is actually about our relationship with essence. Will something bad happen if I feel too good? Is it selfish or immoral to be happy? Can I actually expand into a larger version of myself? How? Can I express my essence fully and still be in a relationship, and can being in relationship accelerate that process? We began to explore the possibility that relationship itself is a medium to grow an expanded sense of purpose and contribution in the world.

Enhanced creativity is the ultimate reward for choosing the path of the conscious heart. Both of us came into our relationship as creative people, but our relationship has liberated unimaginably greater creativity than either of us could have attained on our own. Embracing essence has opened a deeper collaborative exchange between us, as you will see in this book. We have each brought our individual experiences to certain parts but have written much of the book together. Many of the ideas came effortlessly while we were riding bikes or conducting seminars together. As we encountered differences in our growth and interests, we solved them using principles that we'll suggest to you.

For many years our conscious intention was to create "one voice," to speak from a unified experience. Now our intention is to speak as two full voices in complete harmony, honoring and supporting each other's contribution. So you will sometimes hear us speaking together and sometimes hear our individual perspectives woven throughout the book.

The issues we address in this book seem to be timeless. Human beings seem to have been struggling with intimacy since the beginning of recorded time. If you are reading these words a thousand years from now, perhaps on the other side of a dark age, you are likely to have exactly the same issues as we face now: how to live in authenticity, equality, and appreciation. You may have possibilities and challenges that are undreamed of now, but you will surely have the most awesome task of all still at hand: You will still be learning to live in a way that honors your own essence and honors the essence of those around you.

As these words are being created on the computer screen, the soaring depths of Gorecki's Third Symphony are in the background, and the writer is crying tears of grief and joy. The tears are for what has been seen, for what has been felt, for the losses endured and the glories attained in this quest. Whether you stand facing the twenty-first century or the thirty-first, we ask you to pause for a moment to honor yourself for keeping the spark of awareness alive, to honor the lineage of those wonderers who have come before you, and to honor the quest of human spirit to live in harmony and celebration of itself and our creator.

Although we have stood together atop Himalayan peaks, strolled the Taj Mahal at sunset, and tasted many of the world's glories, we can say without hesitation that relationship itself—opening the conscious heart—is the ultimate adventure. It is a journey that truly contains infinity: Every moment is charged with the potential for learning and transcendence. If you are drawn to this journey, you know deep in your heart that you will never be satisfied with anything else. For this we salute you, as partners and equals in the quest, and we welcome you to share our journey.

PART ONE

THE PATH
OF THE CONSCIOUS
HEART

Plum-Blossom Courage

The path of the conscious heart is sacred to us, and we treat it as the ultimate spiritual path. Only through relationship, we have found, can we see our shadows, the parts of ourselves that most deeply need to be embraced. Relationships are always bringing to us the very thing that most needs our urgent attention. "Life is fired at us point-blank," said the philosopher Miguel de Unamuno, and nowhere is that more true than in relationship. In relationships we are always having the experience we are supposed to be having, in spite of how we protest our innocence and victimhood.

When we speak of relationship in this book, we are talking

3

about all types of relationships. We refer not only to couple-unions and romantic love but to relationships at work, with family members, and with the universe itself. The principles and practices we explore work equally well in the boardroom and the bedroom, between parent and child, in a busy group, and by yourself on a deserted stretch of beach at sunset. Although we have used them most frequently with couples in therapy, we have also used them in consultations with corporations and families.

Drawing on these diverse relationships, this book primarily explores the nature and issues of committed, long-term relationships. Long-term commitment, better than anything else, can open the doors for mutual growth and creativity. In our own lifetimes we have seen an enormous change in cultural attitudes about long-term relationships. We were both born in the 1940s, when long-term relationships were simply taken for granted; anything that differed from this pattern was odd and somewhat rare. When we were in elementary school, no one in our neighborhood was from a divorced family. Then everything changed. By the time our own children were in elementary school, they and most of their friends came from families in which divorces had taken place. Long-term relationships had almost become a rarity.

Now the pendulum has swung again. Many people are finding that changing partners is not the solution to their problems. They have come to see value in the depth and richness that a long-term commitment can bring. And they are asking questions like "How do we handle our diverging goals after twenty years of mutual focus on childrearing and work?" "How do we rekindle sexual passion?" "How do we deal with one of us being more committed to solving problems than the other?"

As a relationship matures, the partners have the opportunity to embrace aspects of themselves that were latent in the early years of the relationship. The early years are often full of career and family decisions, hard work, and struggles to juggle societal roles and expectations with individual desires. Both men's and women's essence can be overshadowed by these demands.

As the years pass, however, the drive toward wholeness in each partner grows stronger and presses for expression. If this drive is acknowledged, the partners begin to live in the question: "What aspects of me need to be developed in order for me to be whole?" If this drive is not consciously embraced, they may sink into the unconscious heart and defend themselves against the very learnings that could liberate them. But in a relationship that supports and embraces essence, both partners open up to learning what they most need to learn.

In the majority of couples with whom we have worked, a role reversal occurs as the relationship matures. Typically the men, who have been trained to be outer-directed, open up to the inner aspects of themselves. They become more attuned to feelings, dreams, and needs, developing a nurturing quality that may have been only latent earlier in their lives. Women, whose nurturing aspects are usually more highly developed earlier, become more focused on their own needs and creativity. In mythological terms the woman who was a martyr in her youth steps forward into the hero role. As one of our colleagues, Barbara Marx Hubbard, puts it, "she becomes vocationally aroused." Her mate, who played hero to her martyr when he was young, now is saved by learning to adopt the ways of being and feeling that she has already mastered.

These issues go beyond the psychological into the realm of the conscious heart and the possibility of embracing essence. Through our therapy practice we have had the opportunity to work with many spiritual seekers and their close relationships. We can testify that many beautiful, well-intentioned people struggle with applying their spiritual knowledge in the point-blank world of relationship life. "The great failure of my life," one renowned author-lecturer said in our office, "is that I cannot seem to practice what I preach." This is a problem that resonates with almost everyone, and the only solution that we have found is through the practices of the conscious heart.

Another problem that many people encounter is that they come into relationship with an expectation that nearly guarantees misery: the expectation that conflict is a sign of failure and there-fore should be avoided. Lack of meaningful education about rela-tionship, coupled with fairy-tale programming from childhood, may lead us to expect that if the relationship is sound, we will not feel ruffled, either inside or out. But the exact opposite is true: In a sound relationship that is opening your conscious heart, you will be bringing to the light the deepest feelings and ancient patterns that are stored inside you. They come to the light to be welcomed into yourself, to be bathed in the radiance of the spirit. They *are* the path, and how you handle them determines your progress on the path.

In our own relationship we discovered that much was required of us if we wanted to go all the way to having open, conscious hearts. We had to make a commitment to the relationship that was bigger than our respective needs to be right. In fact, the act of making that commitment was the only thing that could reveal to us our deepest patterns of resistance.

Each moment requires us to choose either commitment or complacency. As we've encountered that choice-point daily, we've learned something valuable each time we've chosen commitment over righteousness. It was in those moments of going beyond the power struggle—of surrendering the need to be right in favor of the authentic experience of wonder and not-knowing—that we first felt the clear, open, spacious warmth, the essence-connection with our own inner being and that of our beloved.

To experience this essence-feeling all day every day! That is the great reward of the practices of the conscious heart. To start with only a glimpse of it and then keep it flowing all day for years: that is, we think, the true miracle of co-creation.

Following this path requires considerable courage. We must overcome many layers of programming. Deeply embedded in our cells is an ancient prejudice against our own bodies and the sacred-ness of relationship. Many of us in the West have inherited a crippling split between relationship and essence. Our clerics have often railed against a harmonious relationship with the body, projecting their own misery about their feelings and their sexuality onto the rest of us. They have withdrawn from the hot and unpredictable world of close relationships into the safer, cloistered boundaries of inner and outer monkhood. We have inherited centuries of mistrust of our own organic feelings, along with a tendency toward a sheeplike relationship to authority. This is costly. We settle for someone else's boundaries for our relationships, rather than asking ourselves how we would like to design them.

Lack of self-knowledge, particularly in the deepest areas of intimacy, can actually make people sick. The body will not be lied to. No matter how much we distract ourselves with overwork or numb ourselves with alcohol and drugs, no matter how tightly we regulate the flow of our deeper feelings, our bodies will always be speaking to us until we listen to them or kill them in order to silence them. We may think we can lie to our bodies by trying to hide our anger, our fear, or our sexual feelings. But the throbbing temples or the painful low back at the end of the day will remind us not to lie to ourselves about something so sacred.

Many scientific studies have now discovered that good relationships contribute to good health. One study found that the only thing that increased the life-spans of cancer patients was the quality of their relationships with their loved ones. Just as we cannot lie to our bodies, we cannot lie to our relationships. Relationships are the living body seen in three dimensions. When we are at home in ourselves, we are at home in our relationships.

There is ultimately only one relationship, and it's where you are right now: The universe itself is the sum of all our relationships. Whatever we withdraw from—or whatever we go toward and embrace—becomes the universe that we have created. If we feel angry at a loved one, we have a choice to embrace that anger and tell the truth about it, or to hide it. We may think this choice is simple, with few ramifications, but it is actually the cosmic moment that defines the universe we will live in. When we withdraw from any experience—love, anger, sexuality—we condemn ourselves to repeating the lesson until we learn it: the lesson that everything in ourselves must be bathed in the light of truth and love. The ultimate learning at the beginning and the end of the journey is: Love everything and yourself with exactly the same embrace, and you and everything are forever changed.

We have only one choice to make, now and always: to open ourselves to embrace truth and its constant companion, love; or to withdraw from truth and love, defining ourselves through contraction and resistance. This choice is placed before us relentlessly, with exquisite precision, in our close relationships.

Zen masters speak of the development of plum-blossom courage. The plum blossom appears soft and glowing, even when the winter winds still blow. It knows, deep in its essence, that spring is almost here, even without outside agreement. The plum blossom symbolizes the resilience of the human spirit, its ability to open again to love and to go forward into another opportunity for celebration. In close relationships we gradually develop plum-blossom courage through coming back, time and again, to fundamental skills like telling the truth, taking responsibility, and holding ourselves and our significant others in a space of loving acceptance.

There is no better place to practice all this than right where we are, every moment of every day: in a relationship with our own hearts and souls, and with the hearts and souls of people around us. This is why close relationship opens the conscious heart.

How We Found the Conscious Heart of Our Own Relationship

Love demands all, and has a right to it.

—BEETHOVEN

Our relationship began in a crystalline moment of essence-recognition. Since its evolution mirrors themes we will develop in this book, we would like to share our story with you.

Our moment of recognition cut through years of baggage that we both carried from our childhood and our previous adult relationships. Both of us had come from families where, although basic needs were met, emotional closeness was absent. We survived the relationship experiments of the sixties and seventies with a few scars and some rich stories. By the time we met, each of us had weathered a previous marriage and divorce and the roller coaster of relationships that had foundered. Each of us had a teenage child, and both of them were accustomed to the rights and privileges of being only children. One of our cars was near death, and the other spent considerable time with a mechanic under it. One of us had just enough money to move to Colorado, and the other's American Express card had just been repossessed. On the surface it wouldn't seem fertile soil, but essence has a way of growing even from humble beginnings, when there is a willingness to make commitments and live authentically.

Gay begins the story: "In 1974 I was about to start my job as a professor of counseling at a university, and I felt like a fraud. I was a knowledgeable fraud, but a fraud nonetheless. My master's degree and Ph.D. had given me credentials and a useful toolkit of therapy techniques, but there was nothing I knew deep in my soul that I could call my own. There was nothing I knew for sure that would produce transformation in myself or others; I felt the lack of a deeply felt organizing principle.

"I wondered where I could go to get such a principle or experience. I had already been through all the formal education I could stand, and if I didn't have it yet, where would I get it? In a moment that changed the course of my life, I decided not to go anywhere outside myself, but to ask myself and the universe what I most needed to know. It seemed a radical and even ridiculous idea, but I decided to try it. I simply paused under the trees and asked out loud what I wanted to know. What was the one thing I needed to know or experience to give me unshakable confidence in my ability to transform myself in every moment? Was there something I was doing wrong that, if I did it right, would smooth everything out in my life? Seconds later the answer roared through my body in the form of an ecstatic energy-rush that left in its wake a deep wellspring of knowledge.

"The answer was nothing like what I had expected: I was keeping myself distant from my feelings and my joy-in-the-moment with the keenly developed mechanisms of my thought. I was filtering everything through my intellect. Like Mr. Duffy, in James Joyce's *Dubliners*, I was 'living at a little distance from my body.' The answer continued: 'Let yourself feel deeply, let yourself open up to who you truly are, and you will have the unity you seek. If you simply feel and express what is unarguably authentic, you will always be grounded in a space of integrity.'

"Standing under the trees, I took this advice, and for the next thirty to forty-five minutes, I felt every feeling I had repressed for my whole life. I opened myself to whatever was true in me, and I was surprised by what emerged. I cried tears for my absent father, quaked in fear of my powerhouse mother, felt waves of grief and cascades of love. It was all there for me to feel—the misery and the ecstasy—and with every deep breath, I opened to it more.

"The answer continued: 'The real problem is that you do not love yourself and the world exactly as it is. Every moment is an opportunity to expand in love; your job is to love yourself and all your experiences as they are, then make new choices from that space of love.' Again I took the advice: I loved myself for everything I felt, and I embraced others—even those with whom I had deep conflicts—exactly as they were. The process of loving myself and the universe around me brought intensely pleasurable waves of bliss, which swept through my body with each breath. When the waves subsided, I felt cleansed, brand new, and whole.

"This new knowledge gave me the organizing principle not only for my life but for my therapy practice. When people would talk to me about a problem, I would help them lovingly embrace anything about themselves or their problem that they had not accepted. Once they were grounded in a sense of loving acceptance, I would ask them to make new choices and brainstorm the required action steps. Every day of my life, using this new learning, I saw miracles unfold in my clients. But while my therapy practice bloomed, my own intimate relationships were more challenging. Although I had discovered a map, I sometimes forgot how to use it and had to rediscover the territory all over again."

Kathlyn's journey to our first meeting began when she was nine: "I remember standing in the dining room watching my mother and grandmother argue in the kitchen. I don't remember the content of their disagreement—just their pain, frustration, and longing to love and be loved. That moment set the course of my quest. I saw that their conflict wasn't personal or unique. I ached for the generations of misunderstanding and lack of connection. I spun inside with an archetypal yearning and confusion. My mind formed a primal question: 'What's wrong, and how can we fix it?' I saw that I come from a line of sensitive women who long to be seen and treasured for their intuition and soul-seeing, but who also create thorny barriers to intimacy.

"All of this swirling recognition happened in a minute or so of unarticulated feelings that took me years to understand and express fully. I did know absolutely, at nine, that I would stop that pattern and not pass that heritage to another generation. I think that most children see clearly what is going on in their families and then make up stories to explain the dynamics. Since family myths are so often based on secrets and incomplete issues going back many generations, nobody really knows what's going on or where it started. Rather than try to understand the complexities of family history, I decided to do whatever I needed to do to create harmonious relationships in my own life. I promptly forgot that decision—at least consciously. But my body and internal director remembered, giving me tasks and lessons to shape a new course.

"I embarked on a quest in which I read everything I could find on the archetypes and myths of relationships: *The Thousand and One Nights, Bluebeard*, the Arthurian legends, the Greek gods and their messy alliances with one another and humans, the Norse myths, Native American tales, Sufi tales, and Hasidic stories. By the time I was thirteen, I was very well read and incredibly inexperienced in my own relationship life. I had also picked up some distortions from my literary sources: I came into my early relationship years with lots of romantic and idealistic myths. I thought that men were more interested in adventure than in intimacy. I imagined that women needed to keep their sexuality and passion hidden or they would get into cataclysmic trouble. All my novels proved that there is a vast gap between the first flush of love and its fulfillment, and that true love is racked with suffering and huge obstacles. Early rock 'n' roll repeated the message: Love doesn't last, but the memory of what might have been does, haunting every subsequent alliance. I carried these myths in my mind while appearing on the surface to be a fairly normal adolescent.

"This passion of my childhood desire shaped my life-decisions even when it looked as if I were making huge mistakes. I developed an incredibly accurate bullshit detector and was incapable of lying about what I saw around me. After several episodes when I was subjected to outraged punishment simply for making observations, I learned to make them in my mind— except when other people were being treated unfairly. Other students were drawn to talk to me about their deepest feelings, and teachers were surprised when this quiet student would suddenly bolt to her feet to denounce some injustice perpetrated on a fellow student.

"I realize now that I was already looking for my Beloved, and knew intuitively that this was a heart-centered, not a head-centered, quest. I observed interactions between my parents and their friends to try to find The Answer but was often disappointed at their level of communion. I looked to the Christian tradition for basic nourishment—a feeling of unity and deep connection—and became a youth group counselor and Sunday school teacher, only to crash when I read 'The Grand Inquisitor' chapter of *The Brothers Karamazov*. I could not reconcile a God of love with the suffering of innocents. I knew I needed to look further."

Gay continues: "Practically as soon as I had this soul-shifting experience of loving myself, I entered a relationship in which the magic I'd learned was put to the test—by far the most intense relationship of my life. It was my first adult experience of 'falling in love,' complete with all the symptoms I had chuckled at when I heard about them in pop songs. I wasn't chuckling anymore. Now I knew firsthand about being in a jealous rage and being unable to sleep at night and dropping ten pounds in three days because I forgot to eat. Looking back on it, I can now appreciate that I had ordered up the perfect relationship to test my ability to love all my feelings. I didn't always feel so appreciative at the time, however. Half the time I reeled around in the dazed ecstasy of love, while I spent the other half wondering why the universe was making me so miserable.

"This relationship continued on an on-again-off-again basis for about five years. One day in 1979 I 'woke up' and realized that she and I had been having the same argument over and over again. The theme was always the same: I would complain that she was too critical, too demanding of my time, and too concerned about 'communicating feelings.' In our worst moments I would accuse her of lying to me about significant issues. Her complaint was that I wasn't committed to her, that I had my eye on other women, and that I never really let down my guard. We would vigorously defend our positions through various escalations until we were exhausted. Then, somehow, we would make up, and all would be well for another month. The arguments seemed to last three days, with a few days of recovery time afterward. All in all, about one week per month was taken up by this drama.

"One day, after being away at a two-week meditation retreat, I came out of this five-year trance and decided to put an end to the drama. I sat down on the floor of my office and confronted myself unflinchingly: What was it about me that caused me to repeat this pattern? Within a few seconds of asking this question from an undefensive place of responsibility, I was flooded with awarenesses and answers.

"I saw that I had created my relationship with this woman out of the pattern of my relationship with my mother. In addition to her many wonderful characteristics, my mother was possibly the most critical person I have ever known. She was also a consummate stonewaller when it came to telling the truth about significant issues in her life. She would hide her feelings until she boiled over, then she would blow up in a major escalation. Oddly enough, this would happen about once a month. My own withheld truths usually revolved around some bad thing I'd done and was hiding from her. Eventually, of course, I would get caught. Then I would

14

get punished, sometimes physically, sometimes with restrictions, or my mother would go into a tearful funk for a couple of days. A subconscious part of me must have decided that this is the way intimate relationships are supposed to be—so I created one critical relationship after another as an adult. She was also a very powerful person, and I feared being engulfed by her, of losing myself if I didn't stand on constant guard against her. Here I was, years later, in my thirties, playing out this same drama.

"It was very enlightening and sobering to see how powerfully able I was to create my reality. I remember thinking: If only I could harness this power to my conscious, creative goals, I could put a few Nobel prizes in my pocket."

Kathlyn continues her journey: "That moment in the dining room when I was nine also opened my life work. I grew adept at observing body language to discover what was really going on underneath what people were saying. My closest friend and I played all sorts of mimicking and acting games. One of my favorite pastimes was guessing the feelings behind people's gestures when I was walking or waiting for the bus. In my late teens I discovered that a profession called dance/movement therapy actually existed; it used nonverbal communication and movement to heal individuals and groups. The more I explored this medium, the more my conviction grew about the need to ground decisions in the body. When I was confused or troubled, I would move until clarity surfaced. And I added 'energetic,' 'aware of his body,' and 'good dancer' to my wish list for my ideal mate. I wanted someone who was as passionately absorbed by human behavior and potential as I was.

"This choice, which I would now call the Short Path, required me to make decisions that superficially looked ruthless. My inner voice would demand that I leave a relationship—even if it seemed as if I were jumping off a cliff. Sometimes I wondered about my own judgment. I left my son's father when Chris was a year old, even though my mother, and others, warned me, 'You could do worse.' But it had become clear that he wasn't interested in the kind of evolving path we had originally talked about and united from, so I decided it was better to be alone. I was twenty-one, still in college, and had about two hundred dollars a month to live on and an infant to raise. I knew I would rather navigate single parenting and juggle day care with school than continue to live in a dead end where the most that was demanded of me was to keep the refrigerator stocked with beer.

"The moments when relationships end seem so much clearer in retrospect than they do at the time. The night before Chris was born, his father had been taken out drinking by his buddies for his twenty-first birthday. So when we got to the hospital in the early morning hours, he was tipsy, tired, and somewhat lacking in social proprieties, in my opinion. I had really followed the happily-ever-after script as best I could, complete with embroidered hand towels, coupon-cutting, and homemade German chocolate cake for the big birthday. I went to the hospital with my hair in curlers because labor was scheduled to be induced the next day and I wanted to look as pretty as possible. I was in strong labor, three and a half weeks overdue with what turned out to be a ten-and-a-half-pound baby, in an unfamiliar atmosphere—and my husband was either asleep or flirting with the nurses.

"Today I can admit that when Chris was born—with forceps and considerable loss of blood—my first thought was 'Oh, now I have two children to raise.' I felt totally abandoned during the event where I most needed support. If I had known how angry I was, I might have been able to reach out and reconnect. But in that moment I had already left, although it took me another year to make the move. One afternoon I came home from college after picking up Chris from day care. I was very excited about a new book I was reading in my sociology class, and I had bubbled on about it for a couple of minutes, when Chris's father said, 'I'm not interested in reading, and I'm not interested in hearing about all these theories.' That was it; my inner voice said, 'Get out of here or die.' I got out.

"Chris journeyed with me through those early turbulent years of short-term relationships with a variety of men, many of whom bailed out at the prospect of having a young child around full-time. I knew that if I wasn't growing, I couldn't give anything of value to Chris, and I wasn't ready to give up before I'd even lived. The challenge of essentially raising both of us forged independence, resilience, and innovation out of unformed potential. It was with Chris that I first practiced the relationship skills that have evolved into *The Conscious Heart*. Many times I had conversations with him about what I was feeling and asked him what he was feeling. He helped me stop smoking when he was five. By the time he entered school, he could easily ask, 'Mommy, are you sad today?' or talk about how his friends sounded when they were hiding something or needing a hug.

"What saved us in many frustrating situations was sharing what was true for each of us. Chris could call my bluff and demand to be heard with great courage and vulnerability. He became interested in body language and the nuances of behavior, parallel with Dungeons and Dragons and martial arts. Until I met Gay, Chris was my primary relationship, the one I protected and nurtured with every faculty I possessed. I had adult partners, but until I found my essence-partner, I hadn't committed to a primary relationship where Chris could revolve as a constellation. Until Gay, there had been no choice; Chris was the hub.

"My relationship mythology didn't fall away quickly. I had learned, as many women do, to look for others' approval to validate my worth. I had consolidated my early reading, experiences, and observations into a personal comic-book version of Superwoman: the heroine who can do everything and still be feminine and totally responsive to her mate's every need. My fierce independence contained a trap, though. I was raising Chris, maintaining a private practice in movement therapy, going to graduate school, cleaning the house, making gourmet meals, and sewing original creations—all without looking too closely at what I really wanted. No wonder I sometimes got resentful, but I would turn my anger against myself for not living up to my personal myth.

"Gradually I learned that I could want, that I could ask for what I wanted and could learn from that choice. I love to be stretched emotionally, cognitively, physically, all ways, and I turned toward lessons like a heliotrope. Each one of my relationship decisions, even the steps backward, led me closer to the moment in that graduate school class when Gay and I recognized each other and I came home."

Gay continues: "It was the truth-withholding pattern that finally brought my five-year relationship to a crisis point. Often my partner would not tell me the truth about some significant issue, then would start finding fault with me. I would get rattled, trying to figure out what I'd done wrong, only to find out later that her hypercriticalness was coming from a withheld truth on her part. I realized that I had encountered this pattern before, in one of my first significant relationships, when I was in my early twenties. My partner had suddenly one day become suspicious—to the point of paranoia—that I was having an affair with another woman. This went on for the better part of a month, with many heated denials on my part. Later it turned out that she had indulged in a one-nighter while she was away at a conference and had not confessed this to me. The guilt had eaten away at her, inspiring her suspiciousness, until the truth came out.

"Shortly before my moment of 'waking up' in 1979, my partner had become erratic and critical, which was puzzling to me because we had been getting along quite well. Then, by accident, I learned that she had started smoking again on the sly—an addiction that had previously caused many a rift between us. She had hidden it from me for several months. When the truth came out, I discovered that her smoking coincided with her erratic and critical behavior toward me. This was indeed a hot-button: My mother's tobacco addiction had eventually killed her.

"For my part, I had indulged in some sex play in my office with a graduate student late one night. Naturally, I had failed to mention this to my partner, justifying my withholding of the truth because the woman and I hadn't 'gone all the way.' Could it be, I wondered, that all our problems stemmed from truths we were withholding from each other?

"As I sat on the floor of my office thinking all of this over, I decided to do something radical. Instead of blaming my partner or defending myself in any way, I decided to accept responsibility for everything. Instead of thinking of myself as the victim of a world full of cheating, lying, smoking women, I simply accepted that I had created, chosen, and perpetuated these relationships through the power of my programming.

"I made a vow: I would tell the truth from then on in my close relationships, and I would take full responsibility for any problem that was occurring. Rather than argue about whose fault any problem was, I would take responsibility for it and ask the other person to do the same. If the other person was not willing to tell the truth and take responsibility, I would get out immediately.

"I stood up a changed man. I felt years younger, pounds lighter. I put my decision into action immediately. I walked to my partner's house and said we needed to talk. I told her of my experience and asked her if she would be interested in having a relationship in which we told the truth, took full personal responsibility, and turned our attention to creative expression rather than quarreling. I felt calm, clear, energized, and full of confidence.

"I was shocked when she said no. No? It seemed like such a great idea! How could she say no? Then she told me why, and the reason shook me deeply then and still saddens me nearly two decades later. She told me that we could have a successful relationship only if I were willing not only to take all the responsibility for our problems but also to admit that she was right and I was wrong. She said she had no responsibility, that it was all my fault, that she saw no connection between her lying and our problems, and that given a choice between me and smoking, she would take the Marlboros and not the man. 'Why?' I asked. 'Why would you choose being right over the relationship?'

"Softening a little, she said that she was afraid to look at the pattern in herself. It felt like looking into the abyss. If she had to choose between confronting this fear and sacrificing the relationship, she would let the relationship go. She didn't feel that she had the courage to do it. 'That's the way it is,' she said. I felt a wave of grief but also a surge of elation and relief. In that moment every cell in my body said good-bye.

"I ran back to my room and sat down on the floor again. I spent a few minutes quieting myself with slow, deep breaths. Then I had an exhilarating thought: I could design the kind of relationship I wanted! I could think up what I wanted, and if my commitment was strong enough, it would come into being. I quickly sketched out my desires on a piece of paper. I wanted someone who was honest and loving, someone for whom taking responsibility was no struggle. I wanted a woman who would be willing and able to join me in a relationship where both of us expressed our full creativity. I didn't have any requirements as to size, shape, or age: All I was really interested in was the quality of our ongoing interactions. If there was honesty, if there was responsibility, if there was a mutual commitment to creativity and spiritual growth, I would be happy. I really wanted a spiritual partner for the journey, someone for whom relationship itself could be integral to our unfolding evolution.

"It took me less than ten minutes to clarify what I wanted. Then I added a radical clause: If it was not in the cosmic plan for me to have this high-quality relationship, I would gladly be alone. I vowed never to settle for anything less than what I really wanted, no matter how lonely I might feel. I figured I would be better off by myself than I would be replaying these old dramas for the next fifty years. I vowed this deep in my soul. It was a done deal. I was thirty-four at the time of this decision.

"Within a day or two my commitment was put to the challenge. My former partner appeared at my door and begged me to take her back. She said she would do anything if I would reconsider. She would stop smoking, admit she was wrong, tell the truth—whatever I wanted. She turned on her soul-stirring sexual charms, which had always affected me like a deer in the headlights. But although I was physically turned on, I felt only sadness inside. I knew her change of heart was not authentic, that it was simply a manipulation driven by the fear of loss. I said no and meant it. I made good on my commitment not to settle for less, and perhaps as a reward and a wink from the universe, a month later I met Kathlyn.

"Our first meeting shines in my memory as one of the most treasured experiences of my life. I had gone to California to teach a workshop for a group of graduate students, about fifty in all. As we began, I looked around the circle to make contact. I have a way of softening my eyes so that I can see the energy-configurations of people rather than their physical appearance. In first meeting people, I can tell more about them from the shimmering of their energy-fields than from anything they may say. In a workshop setting, in which we are going to be dealing with emotional catharsis and other life-changing events, I find this skill very helpful in showing me who will need extra attention, who might be physically sick, and other bits of information.

"As I scanned the circle, my eyes lit on Kathlyn, and she stopped me in my tracks. The pure radiance around her let me know that she had kept her love alive throughout her life. The energy danced vibrantly around her and through her with an exuberance I'd never seen before. I paused to enjoy it for a few seconds. Then I nodded slightly to her as if to say, 'Well done,' and moved on around the circle. Using my regular vision, I sneaked another peek and saw to my great pleasure that she was also gorgeous and dressed in a creative, colorful, flowing style that appealed to me. As the morning unfolded, I also found that she laughed at all my jokes, even the obscure ones. Hmm, I thought: 'She's beautiful, she has pure energy, and she laughs at my jokes. I need to get to know her a little better.' "

Kathlyn recalls meeting Gay: "In January 1980 Gay came to my graduate school to teach a weekend seminar. Before the workshop actually began, I noticed him looking around the circle and was immediately intrigued with his presence and the laserlike quality of his attention. As he glanced at each person around the circle, I could see that he was looking at people's energy. I sense energy kinesthetically through moving with or taking on people's postures, and I was very interested to discover another energy sensor. Gay looked at me and continued past, then came back. So much transpired in those few seconds of eye contact. We exchanged nonverbal acknowledgments of our passion for understanding how human beings work. I recognized in him a similar curiosity and a similar fierceness.

"As we gazed at each other, I felt a bone-level shift in me, as if he were looking into my poet's soul. My protected and dormant essence vibrated and expanded infinitely in that moment. The Superwoman myth began to melt, and the quest I began at nine came into reality. I had constructed a maze for potential lovers that no one had ever penetrated until Gay saw so easily into my essence-desire to live whole and in harmony. And I saw the most energetic, funny, spacious being that I'd ever encountered. The resonance of his voice touched and opened my heart and delighted me—still does."

Gay remembers the next interaction: "During one activity I told her about my experience of her energy-glow during the circle. When she came up to ask a question during a break, I said I'd like to spend some time with her."

Kathlyn adds: "It sounded like Gay was asking to spend some time with me, but I knew what he was really asking. I immediately forgot my question. It took me about fifteen seconds to respond, 'How about lunch?' "

Gay continues: "She had perceived the connection too and agreed to get sandwiches and deviled eggs from a deli we both liked—Draeger's, in Menlo Park (which is still thriving and producing the best deviled eggs in the known universe). Over lunch and a subsequent tea a day or two later, I poured out my story and the realizations I had come to. I told her that I had made a total commitment to honesty in every moment, accompanied by a willingness to take full responsibility for any conflict I found myself in. I said that I wanted a relationship in which both people were fully engaged with their creativity and committed to empowering each other to reach their full potential. I asked her if she was interested. She said yes, without hesitation, and in that moment our essence-partnership began. I felt something relax deep inside me that I think had been tense since I was a child. I had always had a sense that my destiny was a soul-connection with someone, yet part of me feared that I would never have it. Now I had a home to settle into—not a physical home but a home inside myself. And I had someone to share it with."

Kathlyn says: "I remember how funny you were, how you seemed to turn perceptions askew and show the absurd underside of each. I remember the breadth of your vision, your hunger for possibilities. You were outrageous, saying things I had maybe thought but didn't dare say and lots of things I didn't dare think. I remember how big and solid you felt when I first hugged you.

"As we sat having tea in the English Tea House in Palo Alto, I heard that you were interested in a relationship that ran on continuous positive energy, no time wasted in conflict. All my carefully constructed patterns and familiar concepts about relationships just exploded out of my mind. I remember the thrill of a real adventure, of thinking, 'I am launching the most powerful rocket I can imagine. This is my moon voyage, and I am ready.'

"It was dusk in the winter when we had tea. The shop had wrought-iron filigree on the windows and lots of English goodies like cookies and tea cozies. A fire was dancing behind you and framed a particularly animated, embracing gesture that I would come to see often. For the first time since I was six and tried to launch off the garage roof, I knew that flight was really possible. When you touched me, I knew you wanted nothing and everything, even those dusty aspects of me that I'd carefully folded up in my personal attic. When you first looked at me, just at me, the ocean in your eyes told me I was home. I've always loved water and feel right at home even in the deepest midnight-blue waves. I've dived in, swung on rope swings, and jumped in from parachutes. But your blue-green eyes with gold flecks of mischief beckoned me, with infinite peace and play, to a new ocean. Over the years of uncovering and healing old wounds and projections, the vista of space and the vision of wholeness has always held us."

There were many details to sort out before we could be

together. We both had entanglements in other relationships, and Gay was just leaving for a two-month tour of Asia and Europe. But compared to the deep soul-satisfaction we felt inside, these details of time and space meant nothing. Within six months of meeting, we were settled into a rental house in Colorado, complete with children and cat. Then the real work began: turning our aspirations and intentions into real-world skills that would allow us to live in harmony in the hot moments of relationship.

A KEY DECISION

Gay recalls a watershed moment during a lecture by J. Krishnamurti in 1973: "Sitting on a bare stage in a straight-backed chair, he addressed several thousand of us in his precise Oxford English. His message was radical, then and now: He invited us to do away with all teachers and gurus, himself included. He said that if we paid attention, life itself would teach us what we needed to know. At first this idea confused and disappointed me; I was in the stage of spiritual immaturity where I thought some magical guru out there could give me the keys to the kingdom. But the more I resonated with it, the idea of trusting myself and the universe as my teacher profoundly changed my life.

"One way of applying this idea is something I still do every day: When I felt unhappy or confused, I began to look for what I was thinking or doing just when I started experiencing the unpleasant feelings. It worked marvelously, teaching me the specific dynamics of how we go about making ourselves unhappy. For some reason, though, it never occurred to me to do this in relationship until I met Kathlyn."

Soon, though, we caught on. We committed ourselves to learning from every issue and conflict, turning each moment, even the ones of deep stress, into learning opportunities. We found that if we accepted our relationship itself as a valid path to reveal and embrace essence, we could make great advances in learning about ourselves and the life of the spirit even in the moments of conflict. As we embraced this commitment—what we call the master commitment in the next chapter—everything shifted. Moments of conflict, formerly dreaded, now became learning opportunities.

Both of us had a set of internal sensations that let us know we were operating in a state of clarity and integrity. For Kathlyn it was "a feeling of ease and comfort in my movements, a sense of being at home in myself. When I didn't feel that, I knew I had done something to block it. I would turn my attention to finding out what I'd done to interfere with this feeling. Sometimes it was something I ate that messed up the feeling, other times it was some communication glitch. The important thing, though, was noticing that the feeling wasn't there and sorting back through the preceding seconds or minutes until I could find where it had disappeared."

Gay's internal sense of well-being was "a streaming feeling of flow, mostly along the front of my body between my pelvis and my throat. It felt like a breeze blowing softly through my chest and belly. When I lost touch with that feeling, I would run a quick check: 'What had I said just before it stopped? What had I thought? What had I done?' I noticed that I often had a series of negative thoughts just before the flow-feeling disappeared. Mentally I had judged myself wrong or compared myself unfavorably with someone else. These thoughts, especially if I entertained them for a while, would stop the flow of pleasant sensations in my body."

We began to apply this same principle to our relationship. We noticed that delight and wonder characterized the flow of feeling and communication when we were at our best with each other. It didn't matter whether we were talking about the weather, a movie, or our income tax return: When that feeling of delight was there, we knew we were in harmony with each other. When it disappeared, we would look for what we had been doing, saying, or thinking just before it departed. This guidance system became a powerful teacher for us, helping us develop the major commitments that we now teach.

For example, the sweet feeling disappeared if we did not consciously take space from each other now and then. If we didn't spend alone-time on a regular basis, we could not enjoy our close-time. Perhaps like all human beings, we have needs for both closeness and autonomy. These deep drives for intimacy and separate development can take us through the gateway of relationship to great spiritual heights, but when denied or resisted, they can become the fuel for a great deal of dissatisfaction.

The sweet feeling disappeared in the wink of an eye if one of us hid some feeling from the other. When we were angry or scared or hurt, we learned to speak out clearly and quickly, because if we didn't, the sweet feeling would be replaced with strain and distance. We discovered that the physical energy that one of us uses to withhold something separates us from a deep feeling of connectedness, both inside and with each other. Now we saw that even the subtlest, most trivial withheld feeling created static. This static-filled distance felt completely different from the easeful feeling of space that we experienced when we were close to ourselves and each other at the same time. When we spoke up about our feelings, we could feel close, even if we were engaged in different activities at opposite ends of the house and even if one of us was traveling.

We also found, to our great surprise and pleasure, that once we were in a relationship together, we had even more and stronger experiences of essence than we had had before we met. Both of us were accustomed to opening our hearts in solitary activities like meditation, yoga, breathwork, and dance. What we hadn't known was that even greater essence-feelings are available through relationship, if we followed certain guideposts. That's not to say we didn't confront barriers galore. Both of us are very strong people, with strong opinions, and so our barriers had those same grandiose qualities at times.

THE HARDEST BARRIERS
WE'VE HAD TO CONFRONT

Looking back at the first few years of our relationship, it seems that life was administering us pop quizzes every week or two to find out if we were serious about our commitment. It was a time of rich learning, of being forged in the fire. In the long run it was an incredibly productive time because it gave us an unshakable sense of what is possible in close relationships. It also gave us a toolkit of reliable skills that we could use not only in our own lives but with the people who came to us for therapy. But in the short run the challenges of this period sometimes seemed overwhelming.

Letting Go of Controlling the Other Person

Gay comes from a wild and crazy creative family, where house-cleaning, dinnertime, and the routines of daily life were secondary to the whims and passions of his single-parent writer-mother. Kathlyn comes from a Betty Crocker family, with two parents, three kids, and a tidy house in the suburbs. Life was very predictable; Thursday was always Spanish rice night, with ice cream for dessert. As we were learning to live together, these two polar-opposite styles brought us into conflict frequently. "Do you have to be so messy?" was a question that frequently occupied Kathlyn's mind, while "Couldn't you focus more on your creativity and lighten up on polishing the kitchen counters?" occupied Gay's. If only the other person could be more like us, we'd be happy!

Soon we became frustrated with our total lack of success in getting the other person to see we were right. Fortunately this frustration inspired us to give up on our improvement projects sooner rather than later. Kathlyn came to accept that Gay might live and die as a terminally untidy person, while Gay got used to Kathlyn's desire to have the kitchen clean before she could start work on her creative projects each day. As if by magic, when we let go of trying to control each other, we began to see evidence of change. Gay became tidier; Kathlyn put a higher priority on her creativity; and we both pitched in to do more housework. Letting go of trying to control and reshape each other gave us a lot more energy to spend on having a good time together.

Going Through Complete Cycles of Feeling

Early in our time together, we noticed that we each had our favorite ways of stopping the other from feeling things we didn't want them to feel. Gay was very afraid of women getting angry at him, so if he saw Kathlyn starting to get angry, he would distract her by saying something complimentary or getting her to laugh. Kathlyn's family was organized partly around keeping her father from going into rages, so she was a master of being hypervigilant to the early warning signs of Gay's displeasure and finding some way to please him. As she describes it, "Often this involved getting very quiet and still, disappearing so as to make myself invisible. It took me a couple of years to separate Gay from my father. I laid an unconscious picture of my father's face on him practically every day, but as I got more clear, I realized that I had nothing to fear from Gay's feelings. If I didn't stop him from feeling them, he would communicate them, usually in a straightforward way, and he would be done with it. I was afraid that he was going to be like my father, storming around the house, snorting like an enraged bull, and I danced around his feelings to keep this from happening. But in fifteen years I've never seen Gay do anything like that. My fears were something I made up out of unresolved feelings about my father."

Once we caught on, we stopped interrupting each other's feeling-cycles. If one of us saw the other getting upset, we would encourage them to feel and express the anger or whatever was in the air. We might say, "It looks like you're mad. I'd like to hear about it." Then we would do our best not to interrupt until they had thoroughly aired their grievance. In order to do this, we found we had to be genuinely committed to helping each other be completely whole.

As we learned to be with and for each other's feelings, our love and attention actually deepened our feelings and allowed us access to levels of emotion that wouldn't have been possible on our own. Kathlyn, feeling into her anger, safely explored depths of rage that seemed to extend back into early childhood. Gay opened to feelings of sadness and loss that he had previously successfully channeled into work.

In those early days Kathlyn was terrified of flying. On milder occasions she would dream she had missed her flight or become very agitated about getting to the airport on time. On other occasions it was worse: She spent many flights with her head between her knees or holding the plane up with white knuckles and held breath. Before he got wise, Gay would try to talk her out of it by saying things like "It's safer than driving" and "There's nothing to be afraid of with flying; it's falling you've got to be concerned with." None of these ministrations helped. But later he learned to let her go through complete feeling-cycles, saying, "Go ahead and let yourself feel scared. There must be something to it, or it wouldn't be an issue for you." Kathlyn let herself feel it deeply, breathing with it and turning it into fear-dances in the living room. As she breathed and moved with her fear, she went through nausea, headache, dizziness, and several periods of unpleasantness. But when the cycle was complete, so was the fear. Fear of flying disappeared for her as an issue, and she has logged nearly a million miles since then, circling the globe to teach our work. The point is that resisting or interrupting feeling-cycles prolongs them; when we made a safe space for ourselves and each other to feel them completely, their unpleasantness disappeared.

Achieving Transparency

Although we are both deeply committed to revealing our feelings, the barriers to telling the truth about them sometimes seemed insurmountable. We both came from backgrounds where the last thing anyone would do was to say how they were actually feeling. Both of us can be great stonewallers, and from time to time we locked into a stubborn standoff where each of us thought the other should apologize for some inconsiderate act, like interrupting a phone conversation or lecturing. When we got stuck, it was often because there was some fact or feeling we weren't sharing. Kathlyn has a great deal of difficulty saying when she's angry, while Gay has trouble with fear and sadness. Many's the time we got hopelessly mired in conflict, only to free ourselves with a ten-second burst of authenticity like "I'm scared you're going to get mad and leave me." We would create a whole drama on top of a simple truth like "I'm mad you didn't pick up Chris on time yesterday." And you know what? No matter how many thousands of times we've tasted the power of authenticity, and no matter how many times we've seen it work miracles in therapy, telling the truth is still a challenge. Hardly a week goes by that we don't overlook some truth, usually a feeling, that we should be communicating to the other person. Practice has made us more nimble, though. We've cut down our stuck-time to a matter of seconds or minutes before we remember to tell the truth and get the flow going again.

Taking Healthy Responsibility

In our original families responsibility meant asking, "Whose fault is it?" It was associated with blame, punishment, and burden. Both of us were well trained to run for the victim position in any conflict. We both had siblings with whom we were in constant conflict, and often the issue was "whose fault it was." Who broke the glass, who burned a hole in the rug, or who left the dirty dishes in the sink after eating the last of the pie occupied a lot of the daily conversation.

In our relationship we have learned that true responsibility is not about finding fault or accepting blame. It is about a genuine insight into the causes of an action or event. If you drop a heavy object on your mate's foot, as happened in our kitchen once, it does no good simply to apologize or make yourself wrong. Taking responsibility is the ability to make a real connection with the cause—perhaps seeing that you were thinking of something else and weren't paying attention. When true responsibility is taken, learning can take place. Instead of stopping with an apology, we learned to keep the inquiry open: to wonder out loud what was occurring just before the event. Kathlyn said at the time, "I realize that I was mad at you for leaving a bunch of coffee grounds on the counter, and I didn't say anything. I feel sad that I hurt you and sad that I was more interested in being mad than in being aware of your presence in the kitchen so I could move around you. I make a new commitment to telling you when I'm angry directly so I don't act it out in ways that cause pain."

But to this day taking healthy responsibility remains a challenge for us. Even though we are a thousand times better at it now than we were fifteen years ago, we still get stuck in places where it really looks like it's the other person's fault. On occasion we still make mental lists of the other's shortcomings, correct each other's grammar, accuse each other of sloth, huff about broken agreements like not taking out the trash, and so on. But it never is the other person's fault; in a relationship there is always an interlock between both people's programming. There are no victims and villains in the real world of relationship, only people who have not yet learned to operate from a place of true empowerment. We're still learning—often in the heat of conflict, while we're making a mad dash for the victim position—to ask ourselves, "What am I bringing to this conflict? How is this my creation?"

Learning Integrity

We're still learning how to make and keep meaningful agreements. As Tom Peters once said, "There's no such thing as a minor lapse of integrity," and in our relationship we have found those words truer than we would like them to be. We discovered that even the smallest unclear or broken agreement, when swept under the rug, always came back to haunt us.

For example, in the first years of our relationship, Kathlyn would ask Gay to complete some household task or take care of making a travel arrangement. A couple of days later she would proceed, thinking that that task had been handled, only to discover that Gay had forgotten. We both learned about our habits from examining our reactions to this kind of small-agreement snafu. Kathlyn learned that she would often ask Gay to do something just when he was in the middle of a creative project and his mind was immersed in layers of thought. That timing almost guaranteed that he'd mumble, "Uhhuh," and go back to his work, having filed the information under Later. Gay, for his part, learned that he needed to make time to hear about the trivial but essential elements of daily life and to stop assuming that Kathlyn would be the exclusive organizer.

In our most recent agreement uproar, Gay asked Kathlyn to call a mutual friend who had said she missed having Kathlyn's attention. He understood that Kathlyn had agreed to do it on a Monday night, so he asked Tuesday morning how the conversation had gone. Kathlyn hadn't made the call, not having understood that it was Gay's perception that they had an agreement. Gay got angry about it. It sounds trivial, and many agreements are, but Gay's mind ran away with it. "I soon found myself thinking," he recalls, "that Kathlyn didn't like Mary, whom I wanted Kathlyn to like because I liked her. I realized I was trying to control Kathlyn's feelings toward Mary. Then I started wondering if I could trust Kathlyn, which led to wondering what I was doing to create lack of trust in our relationship. And all of this because we hadn't been clear with each other about when a phone call would be made."

Overcoming Inertia

The inertia of the routines, distractions, and pulls of daily life is one of the biggest barriers to embracing essence. Early on we noticed that our relationship worked well when we remembered to nurture it—by taking walks together, bike riding, communicating our feelings, meditating together, and dancing, among other things. A well-known psychiatrist once said that if people spent an hour a day dancing, we could close down all the mental health clinics because there'd be no need for them. We certainly agree and would add meditation, breathwork, and stretching, along with a daily touch-in of intimate communication.

We found that we had to make a priority of nurturing the relationship, then guard that priority zealously. Otherwise, the busy-ness of life would take over, we would lose our connection with each other. Then, of course, conflict would happen. When we sorted it out, we realized that we had been forgetting to take walks, meditate together, dance, and have our times of intimacy in front of the fireplace.

In our hectic first years together, we had two young teenagers to nurture as well as our relationship. Amanda, Gay's daughter, was in boarding school and came to visit on holidays and for longer periods over the summer. Chris lived with us full-time. A typical day in our lives involved the multiple merry-go-rounds of our various commitments and work. Gay juggled classes and office hours at the university with several therapy groups and private clients per week. Kathlyn coordinated her growing private practice with Chris's school schedule, since for a few years sessions took place in our living room. Chris needed daily support for one school project or another and transportation to his beloved martial arts classes. We also had the daily chores of cooking, cleaning, shopping, doing laundry, and paying bills that all households face, and the challenge of blending two families.

Several times a week the phone lines hummed between Amanda and Gay. Amanda often had crises at boarding school or with her mother and counted on Gay to rescue and liberate her.

She first saw Kathlyn as an enemy to disdain or ignore, and for several years her visits were punctuated by sullen outbursts or utter silences. Kathlyn gradually chipped away at her armor and made herself available whenever Amanda was open to contact with her. (Now Amanda calls Kathlyn "Katie-Mom" and counts her among her best friends.)

For a year or so, Chris felt rather displaced from California, where he had had close friends, good schools, and soccer. He knew immediately that Gay wasn't a pushover, as some of Kathlyn's previous relationships had been. He also sensed that at some intimate level our bond didn't include him, and he resented having to share Kathlyn for the first time in his life. Kathlyn remembers the afternoon of our wedding: "Gay said to Chris, 'Look, just because I love your mother, you're not going to lose anything. There's plenty of love for us and for you. You can have the kind of relationship you want with your mom and the kind of relationship you want with me, and I want you to ask directly for what you want.' I was so relieved to have the game called and a simple solution offered, rather than go through years of covert power struggles and diverted possibilities."

Interwoven in this mix were Chris's pets—snakes, gerbils, and hamsters—and a neurotic but treasured cat who didn't take to the move graciously and would hurl herself at the screen door for hours whenever we attempted to put her outside. We went to school plays and Boy Scouts, on camping and skiing trips, to the swimming pool and the video arcade. Finding time for our personal relationship was a daily challenge.

This problem has become much more extreme in our present lives. Fortunately our sensitivity to it has also grown. We're much busier now than we were in those days, even though our kids are grown and we are no longer full-time chauffeurs for young soccer players, ice skaters, and martial artists. Nowadays we average one air trip a week and more than a hundred presentations a year—which sometimes keep us apart for days at a time. This means that we have to be much more vigilant about nurturing the relationship. In the early days we compared developing our relationship skills to learning to drive an oxcart: We didn't have a lot of skills, but we weren't moving very fast, either. Now we feel like we're moving at 120 in a Ferrari. It's exhilarating, but it means we have to keep our unwavering attention on the path.

Giving Up Being Right

Sometimes we say that our relationship works well because we've added one word: We've progressed from valuing Being Right to valuing Being Right There. Hundreds of times in our first few years together, we would get stuck because we were choosing being right over being present in the relationship. Being right is one of the most powerful addictions human beings face. Being wrong is not far behind, but it is really a twisted version of being right, in which we get to be right by making ourselves wrong. It has the same effect—withdrawing into a shell of defensiveness instead of being fully revealed in the relationship.

We noticed that when we got stuck in our conviction of our own rightness, we were always scared. As we caught on that fear drives the conviction of rightness, we began to make progress. Instead of swaggering around being right or whimpering around feeling wrong, we started seeing and saying what we were scared about. Sometimes we were afraid of being left; other times we were afraid of being alone or losing control or being engulfed. Whatever the fear, we found that when we could express it clearly to the other person, our need to be right would melt into intimacy.

It really came down to choosing and rechoosing a thousand times to be present rather than to be right, to be intimate rather than protect our own cherished patterns of defensiveness. After making a few hundred sticky choices like this, we found that the short-term glee of being right was nothing compared with the deep, resonant satisfaction of harmonious essence-communication with each other.

We began to see that in our relationship we could create a spiral of flowing essence rather than get caught in the push-pull of a power struggle. When we both focused on supporting each other to experience and express who we really are, that support set up an exchange of possibility. We began to actively choose seeing each other clearly and wholly rather than focus on what was wrong. We found that we could build the essence-connection between us as well as uncover it in ourselves. As one of us listened consciously to the other's expression of a real want or a deep feeling, the other would feel a surge of aliveness and deeper intimacy.

We could also choose to notice and appreciate each other's essence-qualities. For example, as Gay acknowledged Kathlyn's unconditional loving, she felt more at ease about expressing herself spontaneously and following her intuition. Later, when she might notice his furrowed brow, she could follow her impulse to give him some space. Her recognition of his need for alone-time increased his trust that his essence was being seen and appreciated. The heart of this path is to look for and support each other's essence. When each partner actively looks for opportunities to support the other's essence while also supporting their own deepest self, essence overflows in a growing spiral that includes both.

Most couples could use a set of practices to apply to the ongoing flow of a close relationship. We've touched already on what many of these practices are, and the rest will be clear by the end of the book. For ourselves, through the practice of embracing and supporting essence in our relationship, clarity and bliss are there almost all the time now. And when they're not, we know how to get them flowing again.

TWO

The Master Commitment That Opens the Conscious Heart

The most wonderful of all things in life, I believe, is the discovery of another human being with whom one's relationship has a glowing depth, beauty and joy as the years increase.

—SIR HUGH WALPOLE

The way to get started on the path of the conscious heart is to make a commitment at the level of the soul. People who are thriving on the path are doing so because of the power of the specific commitments they have made in the deepest part of themselves. One particular commitment opens the path. In order to invoke its full power, you must make it deep down in your cells.

A soul-level commitment is one into which you surrender with your whole being. It must be something you really want. The moment you make this master commitment, you activate a force-field of energy that carries you with it and arranges learnings for you that you could not have gotten otherwise. We are dealing here with a very powerful force, and the universe seems to have arranged things so that you have to invoke its support, through making your commitment, before it is granted you. No doubt this is a protective measure to keep ambivalent, uncommitted people from hurting themselves.

The word *commitment* originates from Latin words that mean "to bring together" and "to send forth." The modern definition includes the idea of "pledging and binding yourself to a chosen course of action." A genuine commitment, then, comes from bringing yourself together body and soul, then sending forth your unified being into a chosen path of action. Are you willing to make this kind of commitment to your relationship? Are you willing to unify yourselves and be taken into the zone of the unknown?

By *unknown*, we mean the territory of embracing and supporting in relationship. Even though other adventurers have walked this path, no one can walk it for you. To walk it you must be willing to open up a zone of yourself that is unknown to you at present.

Imagine that there are three zones of yourself. The first zone is what you know that you know. This is an easy zone to navigate: You know how to type, and you know how you like your hair to look. You are comfortable there; you can almost travel this zone in your sleep. You know it, and you know you know it.

Then there is the second zone—what you know you don't know. This is also an easy zone to navigate: You know you don't know how to fly a helicopter, perhaps, so you don't even try. Of course, you may be learning new things as self-improvement projects. If you know that you don't know how to enjoy an orgasm or communicate effectively with your teenager, you may be working to improve in those areas. But you know that you don't know enough about these things now.

Finally, the third zone: what you don't know that you don't know. This is the zone that can, will, and must be enlightened if you are to embrace essence. The barriers that keep us stuck in old patterns in relationship all lie in this third zone.

Bill gets angry at Marilyn for dawdling over her coffee while he is champing at the bit to go out. Ask him about his anger, and he will tell you more than you want to know about why he's right and Marilyn is wrong. He thinks that her behavior is what upsets him. But the truth lies in the third zone. The real source of his upset is that he was trapped in the birth canal for thirty-six hours, building up a lifetime charge of "gotta get outta here." When Marilyn dawdles, enjoying her easygoing rhythm, Bill is triggered into what feels like a life-and-death struggle. And he doesn't know what it is. Worse, he doesn't know that he doesn't know it.

This true example from therapy is one of several thousand we've collected in which people were able to disappear their problem by opening themselves up to the third zone. As soon as Bill let go of thinking he knew what his problem was—Marilyn's daw-dling—he got to find out something that he didn't know that he didn't know. It changed his life, enabling him to truly enjoy his daughter's erratic progress on the violin, to draw more creativity from his employees, and to make his way through eighteen holes on the golf course without bending a club around a tree. The third zone will change all of our lives when we open up to it.

The moment you make a soul-level commitment to embrac-ing essence, you begin to shine a light on the third zone.

HOW TO MAKE A SOUL-LEVEL COMMITMENT

You surrender into a soul-level commitment with the intention of participating in every cell in your body. You make a con-scious decision to hold nothing back. The decision is radical, but in order to travel the path of conscious relationship safely, radical commitment is required. We call it radical for two reasons: because it produces a truly revolutionary effect on people's lives, and be-cause the original Latin word—*radix*—refers to the core or root of something. We must make this special commitment at the very core of ourselves if we are to arrive safely at the goal—the transformation of ourselves in our close relationships.

You also go public with a soul-level commitment. If there is someone close by you right now, say clearly to that person what your commitment is. In fact, a commitment gains power by being declared openly. In our trainings and workshops, we often have participants declare their chosen commitment to another person. Some friends of ours who were exploring commitment found that saying it out loud allowed them to feel its power as a tangible, even scary, force rather than merely as an interesting idea.

There is one primal commitment that opens up the path. Once you have made this master commitment, you can move on to seven soul-level commitments that move you safely and rapidly forward on the path.

THE MASTER COMMITMENT

The master commitment is a diamond with several facets. It begins in this way:

- *I accept relationship itself as my primary teacher about myself, other people, and the mysteries of the universe. I open myself to letting every relationship interaction, no matter how seemingly trivial, deepen my connection with my essence and the essence of others. I invite all healing powers in myself and the universe to remove any obstacles to my relationships being a source of joyful fulfillment to me in all my depths.*

The master commitment continues:

- *I commit to clearing up anything in me that keeps me from full loving unity with myself and my loved ones.*
- *I make a commitment to intimacy that is greater than my*

> commitment to being right and perpetuating my conditioned patterns.

The master commitment will change at every moment of your life, and as you deepen your embrace of it, it will heal parts of you that you cannot heal otherwise. Conflict becomes a gift that reveals your current learning edge. Problems come to be viewed as signs of what you most need to learn, not as evidence that there's something wrong with you, other people, or the world. What you once regarded as moments of pain and strain become powerful teachers of your most crucial life-lessons.

As teachers and therapists, we have seen miracles of transformation occur once the master commitment is embraced. A graduate of one of our workshops gave us a beautiful example: "As my relationship with my wife deepened over our first year together, I kept repeating a pattern that I'd seen happen a lot in past relationships. I would get close to her, then I would do something to mess it up. Usually this would mean forgetting to do something I'd promised to do. I would forget to do an errand, or I'd leave a sink of dirty dishes when it was my turn to wash them. When she would criticize me, I would get busy defending myself and not do anything about the pattern. I would withdraw and do a lot of meditation and exercise. These practices would get me to feeling better, and eventually I'd reconnect with her. But the pattern wouldn't budge.

"Finally, after one particularly bad time, I woke up. I saw that I had not accepted this relationship event as my teacher. I was using it as an opportunity to feel bad about myself and defend myself. I paused, closed my eyes, and said the master commitment a few times in my mind—I accepted relationship, and this pattern in particular, as my teacher. Within seconds I felt a big shift in my body. Something dropped away down in my belly, as if I had dropped my defenses. A few seconds later I had a major realization: that the pattern was a replay of my 'naughty boy' programming as a child, when I had played out the rebel role in my family. I was simply being the naughty rebel in my new family. But I didn't see that until I let this pattern be my teacher instead of my righteously defended way of operating."

Read the master commitment, and say it aloud a few times until you get the feel of it in your body. Think carefully about what you are committing to. You are agreeing to have all relationships—lover, spouse, boss—enable you to learn things that will advance your journey toward essence, who you really are.

You are agreeing to drop the barrier between what you might previously have thought of as essence-practices—such as prayer, meditation, or churchgoing—and the ongoing, moment-to-moment interactions that make up your relationships. These are now equal aspects of your path. If you previously thought going to meditation retreat was a more enlightened activity than speaking to one of your children, this inequality is now erased by virtue of your commitment.

You either commit or you don't. It is not possible to be 12 percent committed or even 98 percent committed. What many people think of as commitment is a percentage plus a compelling story about noncommitment. One of our students recently said he had thought commitment "was a razor blade to stand on." When he stepped into full commitment, he discovered a safety and ease that he said would have been impossible to imagine from his can't-commit stance.

Further, in making the master commitment, you are agreeing to let a transcendental energy-force assist you in removing barriers to enjoying the path. You are committing to enjoyment. And why not? What is the use of meaningful relationships unless they are joyful?

Here we part company from conventional wisdom and a host of other relationship experts. We say that essence and relationship are designed to produce joy and creativity: We are committed to living all of life in expanding waves of happiness. But some people think enlightenment and relationship are very serious business, perhaps even that they are about suffering. In some places in the world people still flagellate their bodies in the name of religion, and in many other places people beat their partners in the name of relationship. Certainly most of us still beat up on ourselves with our critical thoughts and words, in the name of both relationship and spirituality. It is time for the suffering to stop. The first stand we can take against suffering is to commit ourselves to joy.

One of our life-goals is to be happy all the time. Other feelings—grief, anger, fear, sexuality—are important and are certainly not to be denied. Nor is the path of the conscious heart merely about positive thinking, a false cheer that covers pain. True happiness is a large enough container to allow you to feel angry or sad without disturbing the underlying context of happiness. You are agreeing to clear the barriers to a deep and lasting happiness. In our trainings participants agree to have their learning occur in ways that are friendly and fun. Initially most people are startled at the juxtaposition of learning and fun. But we want to support people in experiencing joy even within painful emotions and memories. We have heard hundreds of delighted exclamations as people discover that they can be happy even in the midst of fear or the memory of an old loss.

By making the master commitment, you are agreeing to receive each experience in your relationship as a learning gift. Many people ruin their lives and relationships by ignoring the learning potential of the events that befall them. They tend to run for the victim position when relationship energy gets ruffled. In a close relationship the act of learning about commitment is really an act of constant recommitment. Unless you're superhuman, you'll find yourself wobbling and falling off your commitments from time to time. It is what you do when you fall off that makes or breaks your close relationship.

New monks in a monastery are told that their deepest doubts will not even come up until they have made a soul-level commitment to their path. When the doubts come up they regard them as part of the path, not as a sign that their commitment was a mistake. Some difficulties emerge *because* of the commitment, not in spite of it.

During the 1970s Gay had a life-changing experience practicing meditation at a Zen monastery: "Our teacher gave us our first instruction one morning about five A.M. He said to count our breaths until we got to ten, then to go 'back to one' and start all over again. If we lost the count somewhere on the way to ten, we were not to judge ourselves but simply to go 'back to one' and begin again. He said that if we got to ten without our minds wandering, we should not stop to pat ourselves on the back, but just go 'back to one.' 'No praise, no blame' was how he put it. Before he left, he said to practice until nine-thirty, when we would have breakfast!

"Needless to say, it was a long and often frustrating four hours. By breakfast I thought I had been through both heaven and hell. My mind went through every possible flip-flop to keep me from getting to ten and going back to one. I saw how committed I'd been all my life to judging myself and others, a judgmentalness that kept me from focusing on the task at hand. After a few hours, though, my mind had a major meltdown. Everything was clarified and purified. I quit judging myself and just focused on counting my breaths. When I lost it, I would simply go 'back to one,' making it no big deal. By the end of the week, we were doing this practice about fourteen hours a day. But by then, living in this state of no praise and no blame, the hours melted into each other, to the extent that I was always surprised when the meditation period was up."

That's the way commitment works. You start by making a master commitment as best you can, with your whole being. The act of making this commitment flushes to the surface any places in your being where you are not yet capable of living up to it. You fall off. Then you go "back to one" and start again. You look at the issue that threw you off, then remake your commitment and get back on again.

THREE

Seven Soul-Commitments That Allow the Conscious Heart to Thrive

*Any time not spent on love
is wasted.*

—TASSO

I n the first two years of our own relationship, we spent much time finding out what true commitment was all about. We had no models to follow. Our parents had married into traditional relationship that emphasized duty and hard work. They had lived through the hardships of the Depression and the war and had firsthand familiarity with scarcity and sacrifice. Both our families lost lands and businesses in the political and economic upheavals of those times. Afterward they valued stability and lifetime commitment. As of this writing, Kathlyn's parents are approaching their fifty-first wedding anniversary. As we were growing up, it was difficult to see *how* a lifetime commitment could work except by denying feelings, settling into unquestioned roles, or sliding into sleepwalking.

As we began to inquire into it, we saw that most people were focusing on the wrong kind of commitment. They were making *outcome* commitments rather than *process* commitments. An example of an outcome commitment is: "I will stick by you through thick and thin until death do us part." It focuses on the outcome, on the goal rather than the journey, ignoring the fact that outcomes can't be controlled. In a process commitment two people make an agreement about how they will travel together, not about where they are going. Process commitments focus on things that are absolutely within their control, such as telling the truth, keeping agreements, and listening nonjudgmentally.

By making soul-level commitments to seven specific processes—each of which is completely within your control—you take ownership of a reliable map of the path. Then reaching the destination becomes a real possibility.

THE SEVEN SOUL-COMMITMENTS

As our relationship grew in depth and understanding, we found that there were seven major process commitments that really made a difference. We took years to develop, understand, and embrace these commitments in our souls. Once we did, however, the heart-level satisfaction of our relationship became much more profound. Here are the commitments that we discovered to be essential:

The First Soul-Commitment

I commit to realizing my full potential for both closeness and autonomy. I open myself to learning about and honoring my essence-rhythms of closeness and separateness, and to learning about and honoring those rhythms in others.

The Second Soul-Commitment

I commit to full expression, to holding back nothing. This means telling the truth about everything, including my feelings, my fantasies, and my actions. I commit to telling the unarguable truth—truth that no one can argue with—instead of giving my opinions, beliefs, and prejudices. I also commit to listening, nonjudgmentally, to what people say to me.

The Third Soul-Commitment

I commit to becoming the source of full responsibility for my life, including my happiness, my well-being, and my life-goals. I absolve everyone, living or dead, past or present, from any implication that they cause my feelings or actions in any way.

The Fourth Soul-Commitment

When faced with the choice between being happy and being defensive, I commit to choosing happiness. I commit to doing this especially in those situations when my defensiveness seems most warranted and when it is totally obvious to me that I am right and the other person is wrong.

The Fifth Soul-Commitment

I commit to learning to love and appreciate myself and others in my close relationships.

The Sixth Soul-Commitment

I commit to the full expression of my creativity, and to inspiring the full creative expression of those around me.

The Seventh Soul-Commitment

I commit to celebration as the dominant emotional tone of my relationships. Particularly, I commit to celebrating the essence of myself and those close to me.

As you step into these soul-commitments, you may find, as we did, that you have stepped off the shore and into a vast ocean of possibilities and currents. As we learned to appreciate the daily challenges of riding the waves of discovery, we sometimes tumbled and rolled with an unexpected swell.

COMMITTING TO CLOSENESS AND AUTONOMY

We came from very different places on the autonomy spectrum: Gay was from the "don't fence me in" school of autonomy, while Kathlyn was from the "devoted to the point of self-sacrifice" school. At first each of us thought our own path was the only correct one. If only the other could be like me, each of us would wistfully think. As we matured, though, we saw that our real growth came from accepting each other's way of being as our teacher. For Gay, one of the key learnings of his life was to let go of some of his go-it-aloneness: "I had always been a loner ever since my childhood. There were few other kids in the neighborhood and they were mostly older, so I spent a lot of time playing by myself. As I got into close relationships in high school and college, I still held back a large part of myself. One time I took my girlfriend and a friend of hers to my dorm room to get something, and the friend exclaimed, 'There's nothing on the walls—no posters or anything! There's no personality.' My girlfriend replied dryly, 'That *is* his personality.' It stung, but I knew what she meant.

"When I started my relationship with Kathlyn, I was thirty-five and ready to make some major revisions in my personality. I realized that my loner script, which had worked well for me as a survival strategy growing up, was now costing me. The more I defended myself with it, the less intimacy I enjoyed. I began to study Kathlyn's style of being with people. She touched them a lot, listened to their feelings, cared for them in ways that I felt were mushy. But as I tried on some of her ways of being, I found I liked them. They gave me a softer, more tolerant way of connecting with other people."

Meanwhile, Kathlyn was studying Gay's style: "I noticed that Gay was completely comfortable being by himself, whereas I often got scared when alone and kept myself busy to avoid the fear. Gay could go into a room by himself, write for several hours, and come out feeling happier than when he went in. That was tough for me, and I could see that my discomfort was keeping me from being as creative as I could be. On the other hand, he avoided parties, small talk, and schmoozing, often feeling drained and grouchy if he had to make more than a polite appearance at a party. At first I criticized him for being a lone wolf, but later I began to admire him for it. I tried creating boundaries for myself. Instead of saying yes to every demand on my time, I adopted Gay's ways of saying no to the dozens of people who were always trying to get his attention. I feel like I am so much more of a whole person now that I have more of a balance between my autonomy and being close."

Then we began to question whether our adapted rhythms were our essence-rhythms. In other words, did Gay's essence really thrive when he was alone, and did Kathlyn feel most in touch with herself around other people? Or had these styles evolved in response to our early familial contexts? Gay spent much of his childhood around adults who carried on their grownup routines. He learned to create a rich inner life while on car trips with his mother and aunts. Kathlyn, on the other hand, was the middle child between two boys, who did pretty typical boy activities like building forts and racing around the neighborhood on bicycles. Kathlyn particularly adored her older brother and adopted a "me too" style in order to be included.

Probably our essential natures led us toward these adaptations. Certainly Gay requires a certain amount of alone-time to feel in touch with himself that Kathlyn doesn't require. But we have found, as have our clients and workshop participants, that the dance of unity-autonomy is the baseline in all relationships. It is such a strong pulsation in the relationship that everything else is built on the subtle exchanges and tides of moving closer and getting separate.

Once we had clarified the source of our particular rhythms, we could give more attention to our day-to-day dance of closeness and separateness. We realized that we had been expecting this dance to be symmetrical, like a minuet. We had imagined that if we really cared for each other, we would want to be close and then alone in a completely harmonious rhythm. We were startled, to say the least, to discover that the dance is almost always asymmetrical. We almost never operated at exactly the same pace. For example, one of us would swirl in for some closeness just as the other was withdrawing into a book.

Subtle changes in breathing and expression that we unconsciously read in each other give us clues about each other's needs. Sometimes we read them accurately and sometimes not, based on our ability to see essence clearly. We've found it's a lot more effective for each of us to tell the truth about the sensations and thoughts that signal our own preferences as they occur. A simple communication like "I notice I'm feeling some pressure in my forehead, and I'd like to take some time to sit out in the garden alone" can save days of mind-reading, sabotaging, and distancing.

The important thing to remember is that all of us have needs both for closeness and for alone-time. If you come from a background where you developed an ease for being by yourself, your learning edge may be to cultivate that same ease for being with people. If you are by nature comfortable with closeness, your learning edge may be to get comfortable with yourself as your only company.

COMMITTING TO FULL EXPRESSION AND TRUTH-TELLING

In our families of origin, people did not tell the truth about their feelings. Instead of speaking about their fears, sadnesses, dreams, and desires, they often hid them inside. Like most people, they had had no education or modeling about telling the truth about feelings, and they probably didn't know how. Many family members turned to addictions such as smoking to mask these hidden feelings, and many died from these addictions.

A participant in one of our workshops described the power of her commitment to authenticity and how it changed her relationships. "I was abused as a child, both sexually and physically," Rosemary told us, "a pattern that repeated in my marriage. After two years and my first black eye, we went for short-term counseling. But I went into complete denial in spite of nonstop verbal battering, continued beatings, and my husband's threats to kill me.

"I had numerous affairs during my fourteen-year marriage. The affairs stopped prior to my becoming pregnant with my daughter. Then seven years later I met someone and wanted to have another affair. I began to question why I was having affairs. The answer was: I was looking for an escape from the battering without having to change myself. I wanted the situation to change and for me to stay the same. I wanted my house, my routine, my perceived sense of security, and my projection of a successful marriage to all remain the same. Most of all, I'd always viewed myself as a happy person, and I wanted that to remain the same. I was very afraid that if I started to cry, I wouldn't be able to stop. I was afraid of the cost of getting out, and the benefits did not seem worth it.

"Several years ago some girlfriends encouraged me to start a women's group with them. The purpose of the group was for us to look at ourselves as women completely honestly. I joined the group for camaraderie, not realizing I had any issues.

"I told the group I was interested in having an affair with someone I had met. I expressed concern about that wish. I had thought that kind of behavior was behind me. The group encouraged me to look at my reasons for wanting an affair.

"My disclosure was followed by another member coming out about her bulimia. I was impressed by her bravery and honesty. It made it very safe for me. I felt that her truth allowed me to come out, both to myself and to the group, about my battering.

"I did it on a Tuesday night. On Wednesday morning I called a domestic violence program and got myself into it. Getting out of the battering did involve giving up my house and my luxurious lifestyle. I also spent two years crying and feeling a lack of joy in my heart. Reading *Conscious Loving* as part of my healing, I began taking responsibility and telling the truth to myself and to everyone else I came into contact with. I am still amazed at the benefits. The joy is back. I believe I am capable of achieving anything. I no longer walk on eggshells, constantly fearful of what is going to cause the next blowup. More than once I thought I might not survive a choking. That is no longer a concern."

Rosemary's situation was extreme, and her response courageous. Many of us are concerned that telling the truth will get us into trouble, not realizing that the lack of truth has already stirred up a storm of debris. When Rosemary told the truth, to herself and to others with whom she felt safe, she began to unwind the barbed wire of her pattern. We do not promise you that you will have no fallout from telling the truth. But we do promise, as Rosemary experienced, the fresh breath of joy, the power of making a free choice.

COMMITTING TO LISTENING

In our original families nonjudgmental listening was virtually unheard of. Gay recalls an insight in his first counseling class in 1968, when he was twenty-three: "We did an exercise where we simply listened and paraphrased what the other person was saying for five minutes of conversation. Sometimes called active listening, the intent is to summarize what the other person is saying without putting your own opinions or spin on it. It was one of the most illuminating and difficult five minutes of my life. When it was my turn to listen, I had a very hard time summarizing what the other guy was saying without giving my opinion. I realized that my listening was so contaminated with judgments and criticisms that I had little free space to hear what the other person was saying. When it was my turn to speak, though, I felt a surge of exhilaration in my body after a couple of minutes. In fact, I felt slightly dizzy. I think it was the first time in my life I'd ever been listened to consciously for five minutes. In my childhood we didn't ever 'just listen.' We listened in order to criticize, to give opinions, to poke holes in the logic. But we didn't ever just listen. I found it incredibly liberating."

Learning to listen became very important to our relationship. It probably took us the better part of five years to master listening, to the extent that we could do it even in the heat of differing opinions. We consider it so important to the conscious heart of relationship that it is the first skill we teach in Part Four.

COMMITTING TO FULL, HEALTHY RESPONSIBILITY

Sourcing responsibility was perhaps the toughest commitment for us to honor. In spite of our good intentions, education, and native intelligence, we still had a strong tendency to run for the victim position when we felt threatened. When we were upset, it always looked like the other person's fault.

It took us a long time to realize that relationships only exist between equals. Each of us has 100 percent responsibility to create our connection because we are each whole beings. People get into trouble when they stop acting from full creative participation. If you take less than 100 percent responsibility, it's easy to feel that other people are at fault. As one of our clients said to his wife, "If you'd just stand still for a moment, I wouldn't feel so chaotic!"

It's usually easier for us to recognize what we call a victim role, taking less than 100 percent responsibility, than it is to acknowledge the problems caused by taking more than 100 percent responsibility. If you're drawn to criticize or correct your partner, especially if it's for their own good, it may be difficult to see your actions as an attempt to control. The truly uncomfortable confrontation with yourself comes from recognizing the helpful suggestions and debris collection as the disrespectful gestures they are. When we take more than 100 percent responsibility, we communicate to our partners, "You are not capable, and I need to take over here because I'm right."

We found only three maddening role possibilities if we weren't taking full, healthy responsibility: persecutor, rescuer, or victim. Only three choices—but the combinations, skirmishes, and escalations they generate can look at first like real connecting. Some people even mistake the dramas caused by playing these roles for a relationship.

Relationship is not possible within these roles, only entanglement and encumbrance. As Edna St. Vincent Millay once said,

"It's not one thing after another. It's the same damn thing over and over." In our own relationship, we would interlock around one major theme and then repeat endless variations of it before we caught on. Our pattern looks like this: During surges of expansion or growth, we sometimes both get scared and don't realize it immediately. We know this is the Upper Limits Problem, but that intellectual knowledge alone doesn't break the pattern. It's as if the adrenaline rush knocks out the capacity to name feelings. As we roll along in the pattern, Gay handles his fear by getting more controlling, taking a persecutor role. Kathlyn deals with hers by adapting and trying to please; by taking the rescuer role, she ignores her own needs. Neither of these strategies allows room for a different point of view; both presuppose mind-reading and interpret behavior without checking out the assumptions. We also crowd each other with these strategies, so each of us feels our freedom is limited by the other.

Then Gay will say or do something that Kathlyn interprets as criticism, but she won't say she's angry until hours or days of withdrawal later. After a heated exchange of accusations, we both make the move to wonder, finally saying, "Hmm, what does this have to do with me?" We have also extended that to "What do we still have to learn from this pattern?" As soon as we make the wonder move, the other person starts looking like a friend again, and the logjam breaks up.

Each time this happens, we learn a deeper respect for the original perspectives that the other adopted early in life and continues to revert to under stress. We learn to love the old wounds of feeling unlovable and the old fears of having our creativity limited. Living in these process commitments over time has created a solid sense of safety during the big waves in our relationship. They have been unflippable rafts to rest in. Committing to sourcing healthy, full responsibility removes us from the life-and-death zone of close combat. It allows us to say, "Oh, we're doing this pattern again," rather than, "You're ruining my life," and to proceed to: "What about this needs to be loved right now?"

Recently a colleague who's been married for thirty-seven years publicly stated that she had not finally committed to the relationship until about twenty years into it. "I'm in now," she said quite peacefully, and her commitment was clear in the resonance of her voice and in her steady gaze at her husband. At first, we were astounded—twenty years seemed an awfully long time to waffle. But then her candid observation made sense. We ourselves had each held the ultimate trump card for many years, secretly or openly: "I can always leave. I can call off the game." Only by choosing, committing, to be here right now could we begin to flow into bigger questions: "How can I use this conflict as an opportunity to support my partner's essence? How can I remember who we really are as these ripples of heated feeling flow through?"

Committing to full, healthy responsibility is a path, not a single event or a mark on a chart. It always reveals our learning edge. Each time we step into full responsibility for a situation, we discover more creativity in ourselves. As one of our clients once exclaimed to us, "I'm creativity waiting to happen, and I'm also the cop waiting to stop me!" For us, taking responsibility frees the energy that has been tied up in the power struggle and makes it available to create projects, to make up stories for our granddaughter, to play with our cat, Lucy. Now, whenever our creative juice wanes, we ask ourselves: "Where am I not taking 100 percent responsibility right now?" We actively search for the places where we've slipped into victim or rescuer. Sure enough, as soon as the imbalance is corrected, creativity flows again, immediately.

COMMITTING TO HAPPINESS

Choosing happiness and harmony in our relationship was the most radical thing either of us could have done. It was truly setting forth into the unknown: To our knowledge, it had never been done before in either of our genetic histories. Once we regarded it as a thrilling adventure—a spiritual path of the most sacred kind—we began to savor even its challenges and adversities. As Barry Targan once said, "Adventure is hardship aesthetically considered." The founders of the United States created this country as a place for the "pursuit of happiness." When we first heard this idea in school, we did not understand it fully because we thought of "pursuit" as chasing after something. It brought to mind the image of millions of people running after happiness, which was trying to elude them like a scared rabbit. But in the days of the founders, the word *pursuit* meant a job or profession; it was common to say you were taking up the "pursuit" of law or medicine. So in America happiness is our profession, and we all have to ask ourselves if we are doing our job.

When we look into our granddaughter Elsie's eyes, it's absolutely clear that the essence of human beings is happiness. We are meant to express our deepest selves, and our children remind us that the pure expression of joy is at our very center. We pursue happiness on a daily basis. When a wave of happiness crests, we like to say so out loud to each other: "I'm happy!" (When one or the other of us is traveling, we sometimes forget that our usual audience is missing. Recently Gay was down in the locker room after working out at the gym. As he and a bunch of guys were changing clothes, he exclaimed, "I'm happy!" without editing himself. Several people gave him slightly strained smiles and more space, but several others said, "Yeah, me too!")

COMMITTING TO EMBRACING OURSELVES WITH LOVE

Learning to love ourselves is one of the key lessons of the conscious heart. One reason that traditional religions have lost favor today is that shame pervades their teachings. People now seem to be tired of feeling bad about themselves. Over the past few decades, a new wave of psychology and spirituality has swept the world, a wave that is cleansing the old shame-based spirituality from our minds and bodies. The shame-based model is still firmly in control in much of the world, however, and if we look deeply enough, most of us can find it in the cells of our own beings. To love ourselves, and to become a space in which others can love themselves, is a high calling and a foundation stone of the path.

Psychologist John Gottman's extensive marital research indicates that in relationships that thrive, the ratio of appreciations to criticisms is at least five to one. We like to invite our workshop participants to practice that ratio in their close relationships. One of our friends, Liz Barrow, taught her daughter Mary about appreciations and shared with us recently her daughter's use of the game.

"I worry about my weight, which bothers Mary, because she loves me and thinks I am beautiful. If she finds me looking critically at my image in the mirror, she demands that I state five appreciations about my fat. When I get stuck trying to think of *anything* to appreciate about fat, she prompts me. 'Mom, I love the way it jiggles when you dance. Feel how soft it is. Here's what Miss Greenfield [her large teacher] told me: She was swimming in the ocean and got stung by some jellyfish, and it didn't even hurt her because her fat protected her! Your fat will help you if you get stung by jellyfish.' "

COMMITTING TO CREATIVITY

Many relationships are transformed when both partners make soul-level commitments to their creativity. The greatest source of pain on our planet is untapped creativity and wasted potential. In the Third World untapped potential may be seen in the squalor of a Brazilian squatters' town or in the haunted eyes of a veiled woman in a Tehran marketplace. In Europe and America the same pain may be seen in a shopping mall, where the creative potential of millions is squandered to fuel the hungry machinery of a consumer society.

When you commit to the full expression of creativity and to facilitating the creativity of people around you, a major shift happens in your relationship. For one thing, making this commitment ends control. As therapists, we have been amazed at the amount of energy people spend trying to control things and people that are outside their control. Many people seem to think that others are there only to be controlled by them. The key to any spiritual path is to release control. It is fine and wise to have goals and plans, but if you think you can control exactly where you are going and how you are going to get there, you are thumbing your nose at God. If you think you know where your partner should go, look out.

COMMITTING TO CELEBRATION

L ife works better when we commit to living in waves of learning and appreciation rather than in contractions of control. This commitment won't stop the occasional spasm of control, but it will let you and the universe know that you do not plan to take them as seriously.

When you commit to celebration as an operating principle, you set a high emotional tone for your relationship. The dictionary tells us that to *celebrate* is "to praise and honor publicly" and "to have a convivial good time." *Convivial*, by the way, comes from the Latin word *convivium*, "a banquet or feast." Both of these intentions are important to a spiritual path. When we can praise and honor publicly our close relationships and live in them as an ongoing feast, we are using our relationships fully.

Celebration moves happiness into a higher gear by bringing more people to the feast. When you publicly appreciate your relationship, you inspire the heartfelt participation of your larger community. You widen the circle of essence by sharing the full expression of yourselves. We can all remember to source joy more easily when we are in committed company.

Making these soul-commitments has put us on the right path. They have not prevented us from slipping into our painful old patterns, but they have given us a place to come home to. A soul-commitment is like a destination to an airline pilot on a long journey: You will always have a tendency to drift away from your course, but the drift and its correction are both built into the plan. When the drift occurs—and it occurred for us a hundred times a week in our early days—you have a plan for coming back into alignment with the destination.

FOUR

❧

How to Keep from Sabotaging Your Commitments

*Most of our energy goes into upholding our importance. If we were
capable of losing some of that importance, two extraordinary things would
happen to us. One, we would free our energy from trying to maintain the
illusion of our grandeur, and two, we would provide ourselves with
enough energy to catch a glimpse of the actual grandeur of the universe.*

—CARLOS CASTANEDA

We all sabotage our commitments in one way or another, and
we all need to find out how and why. If we see the reasons
clearly, we are less likely to act them out. There are four main
reasons we break commitments: We make insincere commitments;
we commit to things we cannot control; we leave a back door
open; and we make unconscious commitments that contradict the
original commitment. Ultimately all of these reasons are rooted in
the same problem, fear.

FEAR: THE ULTIMATE SABOTEUR

The power of commitment is so great that it flushes our deepest fears from out of the depths of ourselves. On a Sunday afternoon one client couple made a commitment to financial equality in their relationship, but on Monday morning they were close to calling their lawyers about divorce. After several sweaty days and a couple of conference calls, they realized that they had gotten caught (again!) in their fear of being overpowered. Both had had intrusive, dominating parents and had learned to shoot from the hip at the slightest hint of unfairness. Her request that they control the business assets equally set off a storm of accusations and justifications. This is the power of unconscious commitment: It wants to keep you in the first zone—the familiar zone of the known. When your conscious commitments take off, you soar into the third zone of the unknown, the expression of your true potential. Then fear kicks in, and we either fall prey to it or soar beyond it. To help you soar beyond it, understanding how fear works is crucial.

Fear is the real issue underneath questions like "Can I get my needs met?" and "Is it safe to grow toward autonomy in this relationship?" When you're afraid in close relationships, you are usually feeling one of the following fears:

- I'm afraid I'm inadequate and unworthy of love.
- I'm scared of losing your love.
- I'm afraid of dying.
- I'm afraid of letting go of control.
- I'm scared of getting old.
- I'm scared of not being able to take care of myself.
- I'm afraid of losing my connection with my creative energy.
- I'm afraid of being alone.
- I'm scared there's something fundamentally wrong with me.

Fear causes contraction. When we're scared, we contract the muscles around the navel, fold in around the core, steel ourselves to survive, and cut off the flow of energy to our own essence and to the hearts of those close to us. Failing to see that we have cut ourselves off from our own experience and essence, we assume that others have cut us off.

When we get scared, we forget how to love ourselves, and we certainly forget that others love us. As for our loving others, forget it entirely—in those moments they're the enemy. Adults who are afraid can instantly revert to ancient survival patterns that they learned before they entered school. The veneer of adult life can peel off very quickly in the face of big fear. One moment you're in love; the next you're going for the jugular as a rampaging two- or three-year-old, if not as a raging infant.

When we're in the grip of fear, we can contract in several styles, some of which don't look like contractions on the surface. Anger, for example, can be a cover-up for fear. When you're angry, go ahead and say it, but don't be surprised if it doesn't solve the problem. You can pound a pillow to discharge the physical energy of anger, but you will never really get rid of it that way because the real issue is fear. Many people come out swinging at each other when they're really afraid of losing each other.

We worked with a couple recently who were on the verge of separation after a weeklong battle. On the surface it looked like it was his fault. He had broken their agreement that he would not see an old girlfriend. He had seen her in a social situation but had withheld that information from his fiancée for several days until she guessed that something was wrong and confronted him. Then he reluctantly told her about this incident, which he sarcastically said "didn't mean anything." She was making a big deal out of nothing, he declared. He expounded loudly and at some length about how he and his friends allowed each other some "basic humanness"—an allowance for mistakes that she, "Ms. High Standards for Everybody," obviously didn't. She spit back that what really galled her was that he had stonewalled when she had sensed distance between them and repeatedly asked him what was wrong. Her arms windmilling, she yelled that his withholding drove her "crazy."

We blew the metaphoric whistle and asked each of them to take a breath. What fear was their anger covering? we asked. Both of them quickly saw that just prior to the broken agreement, they had decided to live together after a particularly sweet and intimate weekend retreat. He saw that he had been afraid to give up the freedom of a separate residence and had retreated into righteous anger about her controlling behavior. She realized that she had climbed to the high ground of moral superiority out of her fear that she would lose herself if they got closer. They shifted back into seeing and supporting each other's essence only when they identified and expressed their fears.

Because we can get something out of our bodies by spitting, coughing, or sputtering, we believe that if we spit our anger out, it will help. But anger is only an expression of fear. The real issue is to get to what you are afraid of and say it clearly.

FEAR HAS FOUR EXPRESSIONS

When we are in the grip of fear, we are programmed to do one of four things: flee, fight, freeze, or faint. These four moves are all survival-oriented, ingrained in us through hundreds of thousands of years of threatening situations. We still respond in the same way, if not to the same degree, that our animal relatives do when threatened. Each of these four survival moves heightens our ability to deal with the unknown. Our bodies release adrenaline, which alerts many systems in the body. This heightened state of arousal originates in areas of the brain more primitive than the problem-solving cerebral cortex, and it can arise so quickly that we're already defensive before the problem-solving brain even knows anything is wrong. Unless we defuse these fear defenses, reconnecting in essence is very difficult. Without understanding our wiring, we may try to reason ourselves or others out of fear, but this never seems to work very well. The admonition "There's nothing to be scared of" generally has little impact except to annoy the receiver.

Two of our relationship-training participants got into such a vivid fear-tangle during a movement activity that they later shared their experience with the whole group. They were amazed to discover the repercussions of assuming what the other was feeling and not checking their perceptions.

DANA: I had a strong desire to hug Samantha because she looked afraid. Then I got scared because I thought if I tried to hug her, she wouldn't appreciate it and would reject my hug. Then I would feel abandoned. So I backed up so Samantha would feel safe, and I could then reapproach her as I so strongly desired. I realized later that I was afraid of her fear, and I was also keeping myself safe by backing up.

SAMANTHA: Dana could see I was afraid when we were close, so she backed up to give me space. What she didn't know was that I wanted to be close, and it's okay with me to feel the fear. One of my relationship complaints is not being close enough to people. Now I suspect that people's interpretations about my fearful expressions have gotten in the way of creating closeness.

The Four F's (as we call them around our house) have a great deal of power to cause problems of intimacy in close relationships. Let's look at each one separately.

Fleeing

Thousands of years ago, when human beings were in the wild, we absolutely needed to have programs in us to get us out of dangerous situations. Life, in Hobbes's memorable phrase, was "nasty, brutish, and short." Fear, with its heightened arousal and hypervigilance, was of great help in keeping us ready to run. Nowadays, when commitment arouses our fears, we have different ways to run: We flounce off to the beauty parlor or roar off in our car or stay very late at the office. We slam a door as we exit, or we sprint around the running track to try and get distance from our fear. Other fleeing moves are much subtler. We withdraw into ourselves, we sulk and play hard to get, we pout. Sometimes people are unaware that they are fleeing, but their partners almost always register the blank look or the mechanical gestures of fear.

Fleeing involves withdrawing energy from the relationship and pulling it into ourselves. We may not run physically, but most of us flee from essence on a regular basis. It is important to make a distinction between fleeing from intimacy, which is driven by fear, and consciously taking space, out of the desire to rest, rejuvenate, and get grounded. Taking space nurtures the spirit, while fleeing obscures it.

Fleers need to learn to stand their ground. They need to learn to say no out loud rather than let their flight speak for them. When fleers learn to make requests consciously, to say what they want and what they don't want, the automatic fleeing response loosens its grip on them.

Fighting

When we get scared, some of us run, while others stand and fight. The runner and the fighter are equally scared. The sooner they both recognize it, the sooner the problem can be solved.

The style of our original families usually determines whether we fight or flee. In some families shouting and hollering are favored styles of interaction, while others strictly prohibit loud expressions. In both our families the shout-'n'-holler style was off limits—at least for the children—while the "hide it and get back at the adversary later" style was favored and practiced daily.

The energy of fighting is so close to the experience of sexual arousal that these responses are often confused. In many relationships partners need to fight before they can have sex, or they create ever more dramatic scenes as foreplay. Our society seems to promote a great deal of confusion between anxiety and arousal, between fear and fighting. Consider action and horror films: The heroine is being threatened by the bad guys; lots of things blow up in adrenaline-packed chase scenes; then at the end the hero and damsel-in-distress lock in an embrace. If people learned to distinguish between sexual charge and anger, they could express themselves much more freely and have more rewarding sexual experiences.

True anger is useful and necessary in situations that are fundamentally unfair. Anger can clearly define boundaries. It can communicate, "No, you may not treat me this way. This is not all right with me, and I will protect myself." But if we use anger primarily as a self-defensive cover-up for our fears, we lose our ability to express this genuine anger. Many people blossom when they learn to identify their authentic feeling of anger and express it straightforwardly.

Freezing

In our lectures we sometimes survey our audiences and ask them which of the Four F's is most typical of them. The majority of audience members, about two-thirds, usually say they are either fighters or fleers. The other third will say they are freezers or fainters. Of course, sometimes there is an overlap, but most of us, if we look deeply enough, will find that we have a favored move and a couple of backups.

People who freeze become immobilized when they get scared. They can't think of anything to say or do. In Richard Adams's magical masterpiece *Watership Down*, rabbits become "tharn" when extremely scared: frozen, immobile, locked into place like a deer in the headlights. One of our friends, a freezer, describes her experience: "I'm just stunned when my husband yells about something, even if it's not about me. I can't move. My breath freezes, and my legs feel like stumps. All my thoughts are erased as I lock in on this seemingly huge threat. I guess I'm trying to be invisible, something that usually worked when my father was raging around the house. I noticed that my brothers and sisters who fought back got punished, while Dad seemed to ignore me."

Freezers need to thaw out. Just moving, stretching, or changing position can unlock the paralysis and restore flow and a feeling of connection. Taking a deep, centered breath often shifts the frozen person back into their experience of essence.

Fainting

Full-scale, falling-down fainting may occur on rare occasions, but here we are talking about a milder type. When they are scared, fainters get spaced out and confused. They fog over in the heat of conflict. While the fleer is busy retreating and the fighter is shouting nasty things, fainters are standing there with goofy looks on their faces. They may be feeling light-headed and "out of their bodies." Louise, a friend, is a fainter: "I get stupid. It's as if my thoughts are submerged underwater and get very slow. I totally lose my breath, my whole sense that the world works. Everything looks foreign and fuzzy, as if nothing fits anymore or makes any sense. And that all happens in a split second." Fainters space out until the danger passes.

Fainters need to come back into their bodies. Simply shifting their attention to a physical sensation will help them to reconnect. Tensing and releasing muscles, bouncing up and down, or stretching the jaw can return a fainter to the present moment and the possibility of flowing with feeling again.

COMMITMENT MISTAKES

Fear leads us to make four mistakes around commitment, mistakes that lead to self-sabotage.

Making Insincere Commitments

In therapy we have worked with hundreds of people who were sorting through the damage caused by sabotaged commitments. The most important factor leading to sabotage, we found, was that one partner had not really wanted to make the commitment in the first place. They had "gone along with" the commitment but had not embraced it at their essence level.

Make sure the commitments you make are ones you have freely chosen. Commitments made under duress or threat—"Promise never to do it again or else"—are seldom useful because they are not chosen freely at a soul level. Forced commitments are ripe for sabotage from the moment they are made. In our therapy sessions we get very pointed when people are making commitments. "Are you really sure," we ask, "that you want a relationship where both you and your partner tell the truth?" We pursue, badgerlike, a whole-body yes—a spoken yes accompanied by congruent body language. When commitment is chosen both verbally and physically, the energy of the room shifts dramatically. So when you have sabotaged a commitment, the first thing to do is to ask yourself, "Did I really want to commit in the first place?"

Committing to Things We Cannot Control

Many people set themselves up for failure by making commitments to things that are far outside their control. Outcome commitments, for example, attempt to control events and feelings that are beyond control. You may promise to love, honor, and obey another person forever but overlook the fact that at times you may not want to obey or even love the other. You may also overlook a host of variables that could impact the outcome "forever," such as an accident or illness, or a political or economic upheaval. So many people live in the future of the question "Will you love me forever?" that they neglect the essence-exchanges that make love real right now. A more meaningful commitment to intimacy would be an agreement about how to handle situations when you're *not* feeling loving—by telling the truth, for example.

In order to serve yourself well, make commitments only to things that are within your control, like process commitments. You can control whether you tell the truth when you are frightened or ambivalent.

Sexual commitments are a good place to practice distinguishing what you can and can't control. Hundreds of people have shared with us their confusion about what sexual commitments they should make and how to keep them. Their most common mistake is to try to commit to having sexual feelings only toward their mates. Human beings do not come factory-wired that way; thousands of generations of sexy ancestors have predisposed us otherwise. No one has total control over their sexual feelings, so it's meaningless to try to make a commitment that implies we do. But we do have control over whether we're aware of them and tell the truth about them. And we do have control—although some may argue this—over how we act on our sexual feelings.

A truly useful sexual commitment is to tell your partner the truth when you feel sexual feelings for someone else and to listen nonjudgmentally to their reaction. In our relationship we've established a criterion for what we share with each other. If either of us has done something that would probably not have occurred if we were both in the room, we tell the truth about it. For example, if we were flirting more intensely or dancing more closely than we would have if we were both at the party, we tell each other the truth about that. You can also commit to certain ways of expressing your sexual feelings, such as having sexual intercourse only with your partner.

Our clients have told us repeatedly that they experience freedom when they let themselves feel all their sexual feelings and, at the same time, commit to express them in ways that support an essence-connection with their primary partner. This action grows not only a conscious heart but a smart body. These people let themselves enjoy their sexual feelings as they move easily through aerobics class infatuations, office flirtations, and other daily fluctuations in the sexual thermometer. By feeling their feelings and telling the truth about them, they actually cycle more sexual excitement back into the primary relationship.

Leaving a Back Door Open

Many of us try to leave open a back door through which we can sneak out if a commitment becomes inconvenient. But we've found that the possibilities of growing the conscious heart of relationship really take off only if we close that door. Eliminating the escape routes contains the relationship energy that was leaking out the back door. This energy is fuel for changing the patterns that must be altered if the relationship is to grow.

As therapists, we pay attention to people's body language as they are making commitments to each other. Halfway through making a commitment to tell the truth, one person may scratch a shoulder. Another person, when making a commitment to take responsibility for his or her life, may cock their head to one side. These body-reactions *always* mean something. Your body will always tell you where you are blocking the true soul-level embrace of the commitment—and when you have left a back door open.

We remember one couple with whom we worked on the issue of wholehearted commitment to an exclusive relationship. On the surface it looked as if she was committed and he was not. In many of their arguments, she demanded more commitment from him and he backed away. In our office we asked them to look each other in the eye and make a complete, whole-body commitment to the relationship. Her eyes flashed as she said yes, but she

71

unconsciously scratched her left arm vigorously. He took a slight step backward. We called these bits of body language to their attention and asked them to tune in to what they might mean. She got angry and defensive, accusing us of pettiness and picking on her. She thought our observation was quite insightful about *his* body language, however, saying that it meant he wasn't committed.

Exploring whole-body responses can bring about great breakthroughs. As we worked with her pattern of getting defensive about feedback, it emerged that her father had deserted her mother, leaving behind four children, of which our client was the eldest. During her mother's grief and anger at the loss of the marriage, she had become the substitute mother for the children. She had become strong and responsible, even bemoaning her mother's wimpiness to us thirty years after the fact. As an adult, she tended to attract weak men who were not really there for her. In fact, she was deeply afraid that any fully engaged relationship would bring her the same grief and anger her mother had experienced.

As is often the case, she blamed her partner for a commitment problem that was really sourced within herself. That's not to say he didn't have problems on his end as well, but as long as he was busy defending himself from her criticism, he wasn't motivated to look his own issues squarely in the face. As she learned to take the blame off of him and deal with the issue inside herself, magic began to happen. He became more able to make a commitment to her, and they met in the middle ground of mutual responsibility. They *both* closed their own back doors, instead of being obsessed with the other's faults and flaws.

Making Unconscious Commitments

When someone sabotages a conscious commitment, it is always because they had an unconscious commitment to something else. For example, you may consciously commit to being sexually faithful to your partner, then a day later pay a visit to another lover.

It is clear from your actions that you are committed to infidelity. *The negative results you produce show you what your unconscious commitments are.* This concept is incredibly powerful—even life-changing—yet it is also one of the most difficult ones to grasp. We frequently get stiff opposition from our clients when we ask them to acknowledge their unconscious commitments. They often cling righteously to their position: "No," they say, "I'm really committed to being faithful." "No," we say, "you're really committed to being unfaithful, because that's the result you produced." Embracing the unconscious commitment and acknowledging that it's what you're really committed to opens up the possibility of change. It's similar to the power of an alcoholic declaring, "My name's John and I'm an alcoholic." Declaring his powerful commitment to drinking gives John the power to choose a more conscious commitment to being free of alcohol *this day*.

THE DEEP SOURCES OF COMMITMENT FEARS

Issues from developmental stages at the very beginning of life are brought to the surface when we commit ourselves fully to a close adult relationship. A few minutes or a few months into the relationship, you will be acting like a two-year-old if you're lucky, a baby if you're typical. These regressions are normal and natural and are a problem only if they are ignored.

No matter if you're twenty or fifty, you roll the clock back to zero the moment you make a commitment. You may meet and fall in love in middle age, but when you have a conflict, the reasons more likely lie in the first six months of your lives than in the first six months of your relationship. We have seen this basic truth emerge in hundreds of therapy sessions.

Assume, then, that when you make a relationship commitment, you start at zero, invoking issues from the moment of your own conception. Here are some of the unconscious questions that emerge from the early developmental stages.

Conception

"Am I wanted? Do I deserve to be here? Am I feeling ineffective or unable to impact this situation?"

These are the issues that surround conception. They often reemerge when you are reinventing yourselves or the relationship. A couple may think they are fighting about financial investments or whether to buy a house, for example, when the real issue is a conception-era question.

People discover that they inherit attitudes and issues, along with their physical features, that impact their adult interactions. One couple had a repeated pattern in which he backed out of agreements at the last minute and she dutifully picked up the pieces. In therapy he learned that his father had wanted to back out of his relationship and had married reluctantly when pregnancy occurred. She knew that her mother never passionately loved her husband but covered for his alcoholism because she was grateful to be married at all. At first these clients were dubious about considering whether their current issues actually started before they were born, but as they discerned their inherited attitudes, their problem resolved. As therapists, we have found that acknowledging the authentic original issue allows the present-day problem to be resolved much more quickly.

Birth and Bonding

During the vulnerable time of our birth, we take our first body-snapshot of life in the world. Here we form questions like: "Is this a safe place where I can get my needs met? Are people reliably there for me? Is this a nourishing universe, or one of struggle and scarcity?"

For almost everyone these questions arise again in the early stages of a committed relationship. Making a commitment calls forth from your body and mind the questions that are as yet unresolved from your first bonding experiences. Birth and bonding questions can also emerge at any transition time in a relationship. For example, many people surface their own unresolved birth issues when their children are born. A couple we worked with recently became quite frightened that each would leave the other, shortly after the birth of their daughter. As they asked these birth and bonding questions, they realized that they both had felt abandoned early in their own lives and had formed an unconscious pact with each other that they would never be apart. Their daughter's birth coincided with an increase in work demands for the husband, who had to go out of town more frequently. These trips had triggered the upset. After they identified and expressed their feelings, they spontaneously invented solutions to the problem of separation. They realized how much of their energy had been tied up in getting sad about upcoming separations, anticipating how difficult they would be, and the like. Both laughed ruefully when they realized they had abandoned themselves—and the present possibilities of celebrating their deep essence-connection—when they slid into this anticipation mode. They committed to fully enjoying each other when they were together and to expressing their feelings of fear and sadness so they could free their attention and return to enjoyment. They later reported that the separation issue had disappeared from their relationship.

The Exploration Stage

Developmental psychologists tell us that the second six months of life are about exploring. Crawling is the dominant mode of transportation, and we are trying to teach ourselves that it is all right to explore on our own and then come back to home base. Questions that arise during this phase: "Can I be me in this relationship? Is it all right to grow in my own special way within the bounds of the relationship?"

In adult relationships one of the struggle-points is whether it is all right to grow in separate and autonomous ways. One woman went through a huge struggle with her husband about whether to go back to junior college. She had interrupted her education for marriage and pregnancy. Now, with her children in school, she wanted to go back to finish her degree. He mounted fierce resistance, arguing in favor of preserving the roles they had occupied for the past decade. She persisted with her drive toward autonomy and enrolled for a full load of classes. At the end of her first day of classes, she came home happy and energized, only to find her husband flat on his back with a ruptured disk. She dropped her classes and took care of him for three weeks, during which time she contracted a serious respiratory infection.

As she sorted through these events in counseling, she realized that his back problem was a largely unconscious way of trying to keep their roles from changing. She also realized that she feared her own autonomy, and the possibility that they might grow in separate ways. While in the grip of these fears, she had seen no alternative but to drop out of school. Fortunately she saw the pattern in time to change it and got back into school the next semester.

As she talked over her fears with her husband, he began to realize the extent of his own anxieties. He had taken such pride in being a solid provider for his family that he didn't realize how threatened he felt by her growing independence. He had never given himself the option to explore other interests or to take time off from work. The eldest child of a working-class family, he had taken on the helper role while he was still in school, when his father's latest get-rich-quick scheme left the family on the verge of homelessness. Now he began to consider that he was still outrunning his fear of economic collapse. This resulted in his giving himself more time to explore his lifelong love of gardening. His wife was delighted to support this interest. They shifted to a deeper essence-connection by letting their relationship encompass their individual passions.

The Authority Phase

During the toilet-training stage, many of us get into a power struggle with authority that is never resolved and comes to dominate our later lives. The questions that emerge from this developmental era: "Do I have to do it their way? Who is boss? Do I keep my agreements voluntarily, or do I need policing from others?"

One of the quickest ways to put the brakes on growth in a relationship is to get into an authority interlock, in which one person plays cop and the other plays criminal. This pattern is visible in about one-third of the couples we have counseled. A common scenario is the tidy-messy conflict, where the more orderly partner polices the messier partner's habits. Many people don't initially realize that it takes two to play cops and robbers. You can't have a criminal if there's no judicial system.

We often ask couples who attend our workshops to bring pictures of themselves taken at home. Here's what we saw in one case: His photograph showed him standing in his home office, which was immaculate, airy, and primarily beige and white geometric shapes. His wife's photograph showed her in her art studio at the other end of the house. It was difficult to see her work table through the stacks of canvases and other materials that covered every possible surface and spilled over onto the floor. She was beaming; he stood with arms crossed and a severe expression. We sometimes jokingly categorize people into two types: the happy idiot and the sharp pencil. This couple certainly illustrated those labels. But it's also important to recognize that the sharp pencil and happy idiot have much to teach each other if they can separate their old anger at authority figures from the current learning opportunities. Cops and robbers was fun as kids and can be fun as adults if you play and appreciate rather than judge and control. In our relationship Kathlyn fills the sharp pencil role and Gay the happy idiot. As each of us has expanded our range, we've come to deeply appreciate our complementary skills and to relax fairly easily out of power struggles.

The Sexual Feelings Era

On the heels of the authority phase comes the time when our sexual feelings start to develop. This awakening of ourselves as male and female occurs simultaneously with the development of wonder and creativity. We begin to move in an expanded world beyond the family and to play actively with running, tricycles, forts, and other "pretend" games. Our questions during this three-to-four-year-old time include: "Is it all right to be fully sexual? Is it safe to feel all my feelings? Is it safe to communicate about them? Will my creativity be supported or stymied here?"

In adult relationships issues from this developmental stage often come to light when we feel sexual feelings for people other than the one to whom we're committed. In a healthy relationship sexual feelings are felt, acknowledged, and expressed in straightforward ways. You say, "When we were at the party tonight, I felt some sexual attraction for Jerry. I have no intention of acting on it, but I wanted to let you know I was feeling it." If your partner is committed to an authentic relationship, he or she will appreciate you for saying this.

Issues from this era also emerge when we feel our creative or sexual impulses are being stopped. People may interrupt their partner's passionate speeches to go check the wash, stop a spontaneous song with a question about a tax return, or deaden wordplay with a reminder about not being late for the dentist. In this era we become intimate and friendly with the zone of the unknown, or else we tighten down around the security of routine.

The Power of Acknowledgment

When these developmental issues arise, you can best deal with them by noticing them in your interaction patterns and in your whole-body responses. For example, at birth Kathlyn experienced some trauma as a result of her forceps delivery with anesthesia. But she eventually resolved the residual pattern: "I noticed several cues that pointed toward birth issues. Whenever we would be getting ready to go to the airport for a trip, I would get very anxious about being late and missing the plane. We have noticed how similar the experience of taking an airplane trip is to the birth process. You start in an open space and enter into smaller and smaller corridors until you're strapped into a small space where the pressure increases and there's a lot of roaring and forward momentum that you absolutely cannot control. Often chemical fumes appear as the plane is getting ready for takeoff, which invariably made me nauseous. I would start trying to hurry Gay and would get impatient if he wanted to make a last cup of coffee to take in the car. I noticed that getting mad or getting worried didn't help, but talking about my body sensations and what they reminded me of did shift my anxiety so I could participate again in the moment.

"An even stronger clue about birth issues was my response to the unexpected, especially when Gay and I were presenting a lecture or workshop together. We would make a plan, but then practically immediately—'right out of the chute' springs to mind—he would improvise something and go off in another direction. I would instantly get angry, stop being spontaneous, and feel helpless—all very familiar states."

In discussing any of these stages, we suggest you complete two sentences: "From the past, this reminds me of . . ." and "I keep this going by . . ." Then we suggest you begin to unwind your past patterns by imagining what the most beneficial, friendly outcome of the issue could be.

This worked for Kathlyn: "When I completed the first sentence out loud, I realized almost immediately that the situation reminded me of birth. I kept it going by withholding my feelings and assuming that Gay's motives were to control me and the lecture. I imagined the most beneficial outcome would be to acknowledge when I noticed the familiar pattern and to develop my initiating and improvisational skills. When I put my attention into building on whatever Gay presented, the whole pattern disappeared, and I had a lot more fun."

TRUE COMMITMENT IS THE
ULTIMATE SAFETY

We have watched hundreds of people make big commitments to each other. Within a split second after the commitment is made, waves of fear and joy sweep over each of them. Sometimes the fear wins out, sometimes the joy, but both need to be acknowledged. If a couple tries to sweep the fear under the rug, it comes back to haunt them by causing them to sabotage their commitment.

If you say to your partner, "I commit to telling you the truth in our relationship," you step into the unknown. You enter the third zone, the zone of things you don't know that you don't know about yourself. Perhaps your body and mind don't know what it's like to tell the truth in a close relationship. You may never have seen it growing up, and you have never practiced it before. Your body knows a lot about lying but little or nothing about telling the truth. Nonetheless you choose plum-blossom courage and forge into the unknown. You risk the commitment because it is something you consciously choose.

What will often happen next is that the fear will come up in your body very quickly. *Expect this, and simply acknowledge it and take a few breaths into it. Talk about your present experience of the fear, and dance around with it if your body wants to move. All it wants is your recognition.*

If you ignore your fear, it has a way of tugging on you. If you persist in turning your back on it, it will act as an undertow, pulling you under and sabotaging your conscious commitments. That's the way fear works, and it's best to know about its power as you embrace larger commitments.

The trick is to recognize and acknowledge our responses without letting them take us over. After all, we humans aren't the only animals who go into contraction under threat. Turtles pull into their shell; snakes coil; we tighten our belly muscles and hunch up. It's our wired-in way of protecting ourselves when we're venturing into the unknown. Each of the Four F's is a way of contracting. But when we surrender to fear and let it make our decisions, we give free rein to our repository of conditioned survival responses.

Commitment is very threatening to conditioned reality. A commitment says, "I'm going to try something brand new." When you make such a statement, another survival voice inside may well say, "No, you're not. You're going to keep things just the same, because even though you're not happy, at least you're still here." It's hard to argue with this sort of logic, so we don't recommend getting into an adverse relationship with your inner survivor.

Simply love it to death. Gently bring awareness to your sensations and thoughts. Be with your fear, the way you would sit next to a close friend on a porch swing. Embrace it, the same way you'd hold your frightened child. Think of someone you absolutely know you love, and give that same love to your fear. Your conditioned responses are concerned with your survival and have done a pretty good job so far. It's just that now you've upped the ante. You've decided you're no longer interested in mere survival. You want to experiment with total fulfillment. This is news your conditioned self greets with shock, derision, and spasms of incredulous fear. Its job is to keep you in the zone of the known. Your job is to thank it and honor it and love it but not be held back by it. Your home is now the zone of the unknown, the moment-by-moment invention of yourself as a completely fulfilled person.

❦

FIVE

Moving Through Seven Waves of Intimacy, Navigating with Seven Soul-Choices

For one human being to love another: that is perhaps the most difficult of all our tasks, the last test and proof, the work for which all other work is but preparation.

—RAINER MARIA RILKE

As we walk the path of conscious relationship, the challenges we encounter sometimes seem overwhelming. Perhaps the most frequently asked question at our lectures is: "Should I leave the troubled relationship I'm in, or should I stay and continue to learn in spite of the pain?" We have great respect for this question because we've asked it ourselves many times. In our early days we often wondered if the learning was worth it. Wouldn't it be easier to bail out and start afresh somewhere else?

As an answer to this question (and the other profound questions that emerge during the waves of relationship), we can offer you are a number of moves to make when the waves get treacherous. We call these moves soul-choices. A soul-choice allows you to come back into harmony with the wave so you can consciously choose to ride it out, deal with it directly, and enjoy the expanded energy of the moment.

We have developed our own confidence in soul-choices the hard way. We've used each of them in our own relationship and in over twenty years of therapy sessions. Thus, each of them has been tested hundreds of times in the most rigorous of all proving grounds: the real world of close relationships.

A soul-choice can take the form of an attitude or a skill. We will spell out those we've found most useful later in this chapter.

The reason we need soul-choices—safe ways to reconnect with who we really are—is that the conscious heart of relationship develops in waves. Developing intimacy often feels like standing on the seashore, deciding whether to jump in the water, without knowing how cold the water is or where rocks or riptides might lurk.

SEVEN WAVES OF INTIMACY

We have identified seven waves of spiritual growth and awareness that occur as relationships deepen. These waves occur in couples of all religious backgrounds—or no religious background—and cut across racial and ethnic lines. They seem to be universal, whether or not we know about them.

We think of them as waves for several reasons. Like waves, they are predictable yet extremely variable. If you go to the ocean, you can count on waves being there, but you cannot count on how close together they'll be, or how rough. You can also learn how to be with waves: You can learn to surf on them with the right equipment, or you can turn your back on them, hold your breath, and take what you get. This latter move does not affect the wave, but it greatly affects your experience of it. We recommend that you try the surf option.

The First Wave
Awakening: Essence Is Revealed

The first wave begins in that magic moment when two people experience their initial moment of attraction. Sometimes this moment is charged with a galvanic snap of sexual attraction. Sometimes it begins with a mutual recognition on the mental, emotional, or spiritual level. However it occurs, the two people awaken to new possibilities in themselves and the other. They experience their own essences—who they really are—at a deeper level. They feel more real inside, and they open the field of all possibilities in the other person.

One couple, with a four-year relationship, gave us a magnificent example of the first wave, complete with a water image. She said, "I felt as if Niagara Falls were flowing in my veins right after I met him. The energy rush was so overwhelming, I began sweating and feeling like I wanted to cry. I felt like I was releasing what I called locks—those places in my body where I had been storing a lot of grief about past relationships that hadn't worked out. Those locks let go and opened a floodgate of energy. Then I began thinking about his possibly being my life partner, and I felt very scared. Everything felt so incredibly right, though, so I knew I had to pursue the possibility no matter how scared I felt. Once I made this decision, everything became easy. Bill's very essence is gentleness and flowing easiness, so the fear dissipated in very short order."

From her partner's viewpoint: "I remember the thrill of being met so completely. Sparks of energy flew between us, and I felt myself becoming what I called disassembled. As we embraced the first time, I found myself saying, 'I don't know who you are, but I love you,' to which she replied, 'I am your beloved.' Those words penetrated to the core of my being, to that place where I longed for my true partner. I knew we had a spiritual connection, but I didn't have a clue as to whether we were compatible in the world. Over the course of the next week, we got to know each other, and it became evident that we were life partners. Everything said yes! and we followed it."

We sent out a survey to thirty couples in long-term relationships who are committed to the path of the conscious heart. The following quotes come from their responses about recognizing essence in their partners.

I love her open heart, which is quick to embrace—her openness to everybody and everything. I found that I can express all dimensions of who I am, and that her love will expand to encompass all of these dimensions. Also, she was straightforward, not gamey, and gently undermined my neurotic tendencies. Another big draw is that we have a lot of fun together; we're happy playmates.

The first time we made eye contact, the moment seemed endless. I experienced waves of fear, excitement, and an instantaneous body-felt "knowing" . . . a sense that this person was both familiar, magnetic, and oppositional. On the physical level I was drawn to his eyes, his smile, his physique . . . and somehow, all of that was less compelling than his quiet strength, his masculinity, his brilliance, his leadership, his compassion, his passion, his spirituality, sensuality, and sexuality.

The thing that seemed possible that had not seemed possible before I met my partner was to be loved in spite of my shortcomings. I feel consistently loved and supported in spite of my fears. I also feel safe in expressing my true feelings without fear of retribution. I feel consistently supported.

The thing in our relationship that brings me such joy is the experience of being truly seen, then having that which is seen cherished and celebrated. This has changed my whole life.

In *Conscious Loving* we referred to this wave as the Romance phase. It awakens the deep feelings in us that cause poets to reach for the pen and songwriters for the guitar. The first wave rearranges human beings from top to bottom. Everything from sleeping and eating to predictable emotions gets tossed by this wave of awakening. Without it, human life would be flat and dull. The trouble is, this wave passes by quickly, and most people do not know how to bring it back. Having interviewed hundreds of couples, we find that the first wave lasts about six months on the average. One couple said theirs vanished in a matter of minutes; another couple stayed in the first wave for over a year. Eventually, though, the wave passes because its energy pulls unconscious patterns to the surface—patterns that take over the relationship.

The Second Wave
Sleeping: Essence Is Obscured

Many people we've worked with compare the second wave to sleep. They felt a great awakening in the first wave, then promptly went to sleep. During the deep sleep of their conscious intentions, their shadows—those unexamined and unowned aspects of each person—emerged and obscured the real features of their loved ones. Old patterns took over, and intimacy dwindled—a fog came over the relationship.

When essence is obscured, the first symptoms are usually subtle and can be overlooked. The second wave can roll in the first time you don't say what you want and instead go along with what you assume your partner desires. You can also usher in this wave when your partner does something you find irritating and you don't tell the truth about how you feel about it.

This is the wave of power struggles: Whose version of reality will become dominant in the relationship? To the fore come our deepest fears, such as abandonment or the loss of the opportunity to fulfill our potential. During the second wave we lose touch with our own essence and the essence of the other person. In fact, we are in a trance, replaying dramas usually rooted in early childhood.

How do couples become stuck in defensive patterns? If, as a child, you were wounded but survived by contracting, you'll tend to repeat that contraction when you are threatened or under stress as an adult. For example, when Susan was young, her alcoholic father would rage at her and the other children; her response was to get very quiet and small, so as not to draw attention to herself. Now in her marriage, when her husband becomes annoyed and raises his voice, Susan cringes unconsciously and holds her breath—in other words, she freezes. Only after examining several videotaped interactions did she begin to see her behavior and separate the past from the present. The contraction was so deep and habitual that it felt natural to her. When Susan awakened from her trance and stayed present with her current experience, her husband's sails lost some wind. He spontaneously lowered his voice, noticed her expressions, and asked her what she thought about whatever issue was causing the problem. Both partners can help to bring more essence to the relationship by waking up.

One central task of the conscious heart is to awaken from the second-wave trance. Nonverbal patterns produce the trance more rapidly and more deeply than does speech; glances, grimaces, and gestures communicate contempt and criticism so directly that the reasoning, boundary-making brain is bypassed. The child, and later the entranced adult, receives a direct blow to the psychophysical being. People take those looks personally, even though the logical mind knows that the partner is being defensive.

The trance will always repeat in the same pattern. One quality of trance is amnesia: When the pattern repeats, it surprises all over again. One of our workshop participants defined neurosis as "always being surprised by the same damn thing." Many people have told us how difficult it is to see the pattern when they're in the middle of a drama. But when the drama clears for the time being, they forget the issue altogether. Until next time.

In the second wave everything we have learned from our families of origin comes to the fore. A month after his wedding, one of our clients—already in the trance—found himself initiating sexual flirtations with a number of women. He said, "It felt like I was watching myself do these insane things, like I was watching it through a screen. I loved my wife deeply and felt a deep commitment to her, but it felt like I had no control over these flirtations. I woke up when you asked me how this pattern was familiar. My father's womanizing had dominated my family growing up. Hardly a day went by without some reference to it. Here I was, married to a woman I loved for only a month, and something in me was causing me to repeat the same pattern. I was blown away by how much power this pattern had over me." This is the second wave in action. A pall falls over the relationship, in which the same trance patterns recycle. This man woke up in time, but many people don't. They think their fog is the way life has to be and continue to retreat deeper into the old pattern rather than going forward into the next wave.

Just as in going to sleep, the early stages of trance are light and easily disturbed. But as the sleep deepens, it becomes harder to wake up. During deep slumber the third wave begins.

The Third Wave
Dreaming: While Deeply Unconscious,
Primal Dramas Unfold

While you are asleep at night, your body may twitch and struggle with an imaginary opponent. In the waking dream world of a close relationship precisely the same process occurs when you are going through this most unconscious of phases. The central dramatic motivator is the struggle for control. Essence has become so obscured that the partners go on automatic; each tends to require the very behavior in the other that drives them crazy, and both entrench the relationship in an escalating drama.

In the third wave the partners' patterns tend to polarize. The fog of the second wave solidifies into masks. The forceful partner becomes the dominator; the shy one sinks into the loner role. Unacknowledged fear creates this distance, escalating it until the partners look like strangers to each other. They cannot imagine how they made such a bad choice. Since most of us don't know how to shift from fear to love, the first tendrils of fear grow into a tangled bramble through which it seems virtually impossible to see each other clearly.

In one session Martha said to Greg, "I'm afraid I don't love you anymore. I'm afraid you don't love me."

"I try really hard—I do all these things for you," said Greg.

"You just try to control me all the time, tell me what to do, criticize what I'm wearing. That's not doing things for me," she responded sharply.

As she spoke, Greg yawned and felt weary, slipping from fighting into the fainting pattern of the Four F's. His shoulders hunched and his chest collapsed as he said, "What's the use, I might as well give up." When Martha leaned forward, her brow furrowed. She was holding her breath. We asked her what she was experiencing in that moment. She discovered that when Greg collapsed, she would lose awareness of her own experience and focus exclusively on comforting him. She tended to freeze when she was afraid, then flee into his feelings to separate herself from her own fear. Rather than register her concern, he would sense her withdrawal from her own experience and assume she was abandoning him. He would get desperate, and she would feel more controlled and withdraw further. Without knowing how to recognize their dream-state personas, they had gotten more and more distant from each other, until they questioned their basic connection. In the third wave people can get colossally stuck. Dream states can be vivid and compelling; we can be sure that we can fly and that cars turn into helium balloons. While dreaming deeply in the third wave, the partners are tossed and churned by dramas they don't realize they're creating.

We often inherit feelings and impulses that our parents and grandparents have denied in their lives. Wounded parents who are unable to see the essence of their children simply pass on the wound. Essence is obscured before it has a chance to become fully rooted, and the children then see themselves in distorted ways. Many of the creatively gifted people we have worked with seem to share a common trait: Close relatives or friends belittled or ignored their talent. That early lack of acknowledgment implanted deep roots of self-doubt, which later sprouted into persistent critical voices that linger into adult life and build into relationship riptides in the third wave.

For one artist the strong and consistent belittling he received from his older brother fueled a perfectionism that drives him to exceed each previous achievement. None of his paintings quite measure up to his standards. His wife holds herself a little separate from his frenzy of perfectionism. Her intuitive skills were ridiculed in her family, where she was forced to conform to a common standard of mediocrity. Rather than criticism, she is vulnerable to approval or to withheld approval.

In their relationship they express a responsible/playful polarity. He acts responsible and vigilant, always keeping an eye on the bottom line—whether she is feeding the children adequately, whether the dog's water dishes are full. She acts flighty and free, flitting from one interest to another, lighting on projects long enough to lift them into life, then moving on before the heaviness of completion pulls her down again. Her playful persona wants him to lighten up. His responsible persona wants her to follow through and take some of the burden. As we worked together, each of them began to see how they required the very behavior they resented. He realized he couldn't continue to act superresponsibly if she took full, healthy responsibility. She realized that she required his regular disapproval to ground herself. Each of them realized that they were missing balance. Each expected the other to supply their missing parts.

As each of them began to claim and balance these unowned parts, an underlying urge to control emerged in both of them. He controlled situations by constantly redirecting their energy. With high and shallow breathing, darting eyes, and a clipped verbal tone, he made the following moves over the course of fifteen minutes:

- commenting on something wrong in the house
- noticing that the light was glaring and getting up to adjust the blinds
- noticing that the children in the other room were making too much noise
- commenting on a spot on his wife's blouse
- wondering out loud if the oven was on
- commenting that the phones were too loud
- getting up to move the furniture
- getting more water

She controlled by spacing out, so that he had to pursue her to make contact. She holds herself with an arch in her neck, as if her chin were perched on the edge of a table, her head poised delicately above her body—and lightly above it all. He speaks like an infrared sensor, honing in on what's wrong. Neither of them was aware of their verbal interplay or body language until we pointed it out to them; it was as if they were deeply asleep.

Many relationships stagnate in the eddies of the third wave. Routine replaces renewal, and diminishing expectations overtake the possibility of wonder. Our culture tends to reinforce this wave by promoting the view that people need to compromise, that romance withers, and that partners need to learn to settle for less. But in our explorations with couples, we have found that people can shift from power struggles and dream dramas to seeing and supporting essence.

The Fourth Wave
Awake and Dreaming: Essence Develops and Becomes the Backdrop of Struggle

Like the sun peeking through clouds as they break up, essence grows as the partners choose the relationship over conflict time and again. Essence becomes the field in which relationship dramas unfold. You begin to see that you are bigger than your dramas: You have dramas, but they no longer have you. You see that you are making all these dramas up, that you are the source of them. As you claim responsibility for them, you also open up your ability to create freely, to choose what you really want.

In one of our group workshops, one couple's experience taught the rest of the group the major principles of the fourth wave. We call their conflict *The Cheese Drama*, and like most conflicts it was based on a superficially trivial issue. It seems that she had fed *his* cheese to *her* cat the day before, and they were still upset when they came back to the workshop the next day.

They agreed to work with us in front of the entire group, and we invited them to stand several feet apart within the circle of participants. Our exchange was videotaped, and we so appreciated the dynamics of their conflict that we transcribed their ride on the fourth wave.

HIS PART

HE: We had a fight.

US: What was the nature of the fight, in a sentence?

HE: I was fighting about whether I could have as much cheese on my hamburger as I want. (*He gestures to his stomach.*)

US: Since that's the area of the body that's usually connected to fear, ask yourself what you are afraid of.

HE (*after a pause*): I'm afraid it'll never work out.

US: What is your unenlightened view of the situation?

HE: I was out running around getting the french fries for lunch, and she gave my cheese to her cat. It means she's selfish, and because she's that way, I'll never have the relationship I want, I'll never get my needs met.

US: Are you willing to take 100 percent responsibility for clearing up this issue?

HE: Yes.

US: Take a moment to love and accept the way you created this drama.

HE: I feel sadness welling up.

US: Love the sadness just as it is.

HE (*sighs and tears up and, after a moment, takes a deeper breath and looks up*).

US: Would you be willing to take complete responsibility for having a relationship with your wife that completely meets your needs?

HE: Yes (*smiling*).

HER PART

US: What is your unenlightened view of this situation?

SHE: I want to be in control. The cheese was for the cat. He's said he doesn't like cheese, so I just buy cheese for the cat, who loves it.

US: How is this situation familiar?

SHE: No matter what I did in my family, it wasn't appreciated.

US: So you spend the time and creative energy to design this lunch, and he walks in and complains about no cheese, not noticing the array of tasty items decoratively arranged.

SHE: Yes.

US: What persona does all that designing?

SHE: The person who arranges it so everyone gets their needs met.

US: And in return are you supposed to get appreciated?

SHE: Yes (*starting to cry*), but I never did.

This is an amazing example of a perfect persona interlock: A guy who never gets his needs met gets together with a woman whose idea of relating is to arrange it so everyone gets their needs met. So why do they both require the very behaviors that make it impossible to be satisfied? Both of them adopted those personas to mask deeper feelings and issues when their authentic selves, their essences, didn't work.

HE AND SHE TOGETHER

US: What feeling is under the attempt to control?

SHE: I'm sad and afraid that I'm worthless, broken.

HE: I'm afraid I'll be alone and isolated.

US: Come into the middle of the circle for a moment. (*They sit knee to knee.*)

US (*to her*): Can you love him for feeling alone and isolated?

SHE: Yes, easily.

US (*to him*): Can you love her for feeling worthless?

HE: Yes. (*He beams at her.*)

US: Take a moment to love each other now.

(They gaze at each other as the other participants become very still.)

US: Would you be willing to have a relationship where you see and support each other's essence, where you look for wholeness and keep choosing to express all of who you are?

BOTH: Yes. *(They're giggling now, and their radiance lights up the whole group, who are also beaming.)*

Through making the courageous choice of having relationship harmony over being right, and making this choice repeatedly until it becomes second nature, the personal experience of essence takes hold. A feeling of warmth and space, usually felt in the chest, grows in the fourth wave. It comes and goes, and sometimes it feels like it has been lost altogether. It can be a frustrating wave because the partners often feel so stuck, yet clarity feels so close at hand. The contrast feels nearly unbearable between the way it is at the moment and the way they sense it could be.

In the fourth wave you often feel the rapid flip between making assumptions and judgments and seeing the world as it is. One moment, when you are asleep to your own essence, your partner may look like the enemy. The next moment, when your own sense of essence is restored, you see your partner's essence. You remember why you chose the other person, and the floodgates of love open again.

People in successful long-term relationships tend to develop an ability to let go of attachment to their own points of view. In other words, they learn to handle the universal addiction to being right. Many couples founder in the fourth wave because they do not develop this ability. When the pressure is on, each of them chooses being right over seeing and supporting essence. A great deal of the work in the fourth wave involves the partners making graceful exits from the points of view in which they are stuck. As one couple put it, "What saved our marriage was learning that there was life beyond being right. We were both so attached to making each other wrong that it seemed like a life-and-death struggle. What a relief when we found that it was entirely unnecessary."

As couples drop their power struggle and begin to address the issues that each partner needs to resolve, they can become allies and learn from each other. One practice that allows both of them to expand their daily experience of essence is the skill we call interrupting routines. That human beings are all creatures of habit has been elaborately demonstrated by philosophers and animal trainers alike. But there is one major difference between us and our animal friends. A dolphin who fails to get the fish from the trainer's hand will eventually stop doing its crowd-pleasing leap. A rat who runs down the tunnel that has the cheese in it will choose another tunnel if it stops finding cheese at the end. But human beings are different. We will keep going down a cheeseless tunnel for years. Why? Because we believe in it. We think it's right, even though it doesn't have any cheese anymore. We'll defend it until the end, even discarding friends of many years who suggest that there's no payoff for our efforts.

The practice of interrupting routines helps you let go of your repetitive patterns that no longer work and make choices that develop essence. Sometimes it's a simple change, like unplugging the TV for a week. Other times it's a more complex practice, such as finding a way to interrupt an argument that tends to repeat itself. The point is to do something that interrupts your routine. One couple, when they felt their arguments becoming repetitive, would interrupt that routine by falling silent and shifting to non-verbal communication. In another couple a passive sexual partner learned to initiate sex at an unexpected time. A procrastinator made a short list and completed one thing each day. An organizer learned to drift in the hammock, starting with ten minutes each day. A shy partner took a public-speaking class. An adventurous couple in their fifties interrupted their television-watching habit by taking an African-dance class together one evening a week.

The Fifth Wave
Essence Becomes Permanent

In this wave you no longer take struggles as seriously as you once did, because you are identified more with your own essence than with the part of you that is addicted to struggle. Also, you can see your partner's essence clearly, even when you are struggling together. Conflict does not disappear in this wave; it simply becomes absorbed in a larger version of yourselves.

One workshop participant said that early in his relationship conflict with his partner felt like being in a small pen with an angry bull. As he became grounded in the experience of essence, however, the bull was still there, but now it had a vast pasture to roam in. His personal feeling of essence and space had developed to the extent that conflict was not overwhelming.

One buoy in this fifth wave is ease: Partners shift readily from fear to essence. They develop a real skill at surfing. They choose bigger waves to ride, and they turn fear into excitement with breath and truth. Compassion blooms. Each of them sees through the survival filters that the other has erected, and they appreciate each other's essence qualities.

In one couple the fifth wave rolled organically into the sixth, the birth of co-creation. Says Laura: "Tom would often come home from work exhausted and retreat to the den. He wouldn't be interested in what the kids had done that day or the graphics project I was working on. I used to get so frightened when he would withdraw, and I couldn't seem to get through to him at all. I'd get frantic and scurry around trying to engage him."

Tom remembers: "Laura looked like a madwoman, and I really curled up like an armadillo until she'd go away. It took several months for us to learn to let go of being right and trying to get each other to change. I realized that I had been repeating my father's role of the reluctant provider, toiling away at a job I hated because it paid well, then coming home with no energy left for me, let alone the family."

Laura recalls: "I began to see that I had inherited so many expectations from my parents' rigid roles that I hadn't really gotten to know Tom and his wants. I was afraid that if we didn't keep the picture-perfect household, we'd fall into a void. It took a while for me to realize that my parents' roles covered the void in their marriage, and that Tom and I could create our own relationship based on what *we* wanted."

Tom adds: "You know what it came down to, over and over? I'd realize I was afraid and would say so. Then Laura would look really different, softer and calmer. Or she'd say, 'Tom, I just noticed I'm doing my mother's make-nice thing again,' and *I'd* relax. That seemed to make room for love to grow. I started noticing how talented Laura is—not just in her design work, but in encouraging the kids' creativity and making our home an oasis of color and tranquility."

Says Laura: "I began to focus more on supporting Tom in expressing himself rather than on requiring him to be like my dad. I got really interested in what he wanted to do, and I listened more to his daydreams and the articles he'd bring home about building. He'd built things since he was really little but had gone into engineering because his dad told him over and over how he needed a reliable profession. Tom took several months to get his contractor's license and is now full of energy when he comes home from his latest project. We've even started to work together sometimes on the computer designing an interior. Jenny, our sixth-grader, helps out when we get stuck on the computer program."

The Sixth Wave
The Birth of Co-Creation

In this wave a true partnership forms. We become connected through our essence, not our personas. A genuine mutual creativity develops where both partners can express themselves creatively from essence. During the conflict and power struggle of the earlier waves, they could not look toward the horizon together, toward what they want to create. In the sixth wave both of them are more committed to the horizon—to realizing their mutual goals— than to the drama of conflict.

Many couples never reach the sixth wave because their unconscious commitment to drama and conflict is stronger than their commitment to mutual creativity. People who do attain it often have miniwaves within it, in which they go back and forth between making their dreams real and getting sucked back into power struggles. However, as the feeling of space and essence grows inside them and in the relationship, they feel less compelled to continue those struggles.

One couple who has been involved in our work for several years told us recently that they realized, even after four years of marriage, that they weren't as close as they wanted to be. They had been more interested in recycling a power struggle, in which each of them believed that the other held them back from really enjoying life and creative possibilities. After a recent training the husband, Tony, decided to really be transparent. He told Julie that he hadn't really been committed to their relationship. In contrast to whatever reaction you might imagine she had, his openness stimulated her to claim what she wanted. "I want to be happy *now*," she said. "I don't want to wait ten years while we suffer and struggle. I want to be committed *now*!" Each of them saw that they were frightened to step out of the familiar swamp where they both could be fairly comfortable victims. They didn't know how to be happy. But they decided to go ahead and choose happiness now, to be committed now. Almost immediately they began seeing new possibilities for remodeling their house, so that each of them could do their artwork and have some separate space.

They've also become more permeable to getting feedback from each other. They had agreed to give and receive information whenever either of them seemed stuck. At first Julie said that she bristled at someone telling her what to do (her fighting response to fear). But she didn't sink into the old swamp. Instead she sprang into appreciating and using the feedback of her "best friend" in order to be happy now. As Tony and Julie noticed, the time they spent on drama and conflict became less and less. It virtually disappears in the seventh wave.

The Seventh Wave
Living in Co-Creation

No longer addicted to conflict and drama, the partnership now rests in essence and lives on a continuous wave of rebirth. Creativity, appreciation, abundance, and rekindled romance characterize the union. The partners notice an increase in synchronous flow, in which what is needed appears and daily tasks move smoothly and easily. Paula, whose relationship is in the seventh wave, told us: "What seemed possible that hadn't previously occurred was a union of true equality. A union of mutual respect, equal energy exchange and input, equal willingness to grow, to be close, to 'meet' the other. Actually, we seem to naturally and effortlessly meet each other, and that ease was an exhilarating surprise." Time seems to expand, so that everything can happen without strain.

In our research on approximately three thousand couples, we have identified about 5 percent as being in seventh wave partnerships. At first glance, 150 couples out of three thousand may not seem like many. But take heart—we have to start somewhere, and compared with our parents' generation or our grandparents', perhaps 5 percent is not doing too badly. We hope these figures will inspire you to try to reach the seventh wave rather than depress you. After all, only about 5 percent of the citizens participated in the American Revolution, and look where we ended up just a couple of hundred years later.

We asked these couples in a survey, "What surprised you about what it takes to have a thriving relationship?" Here are some of their reflections.

- "At first I was surprised by how difficult it is. The myth of 'happily ever after if I find the right prince' was quite compelling. Now I am surprised by how simple it is . . . it is not *easy*, but it is very simple."
- "To thrive you must free each other up—empower each other, not control them or attempt to take care of them."
- "Increasingly I've learned that the deepest joy is not so much in being *loved*—though that is certainly a delight!—but in being and expressing love in relation to the 'other.'"
- "*Surprise!* . . . that I created who showed up and my experience . . . I was responsible. I was truly a frog and had to eat what bugged me, my projections."
- "That the deeper the intimacy with one's mate, the greater and wider one's capacity is to embrace others and the world. True intimacy *includes* a greater and greater sphere. It is not an excluding or separating activity."
- "Surprisingly, one of the most fulfilling aspects of our relationship has been our co-creativity. We dream of projects together that neither of us could accomplish alone. . . . We augment each other's skills and make a great team—and we have a lot of fun doing it!"

Richard and Toni Merrick, who have participated in our work for several years, journeyed through the seven waves:

TONI: In the first relationship training we attended, we realized we each carried a belief that marriage is not fun. Richard's grandfather repeatedly told his father, "Marriage is hell!" Both of us had spent a considerable amount of time in recovery from addictions and codependency and felt ready to make a new commitment. In that training we adopted a new vision that marriage could be about joy and companionship.

RICHARD: For a long time I felt stuck in a very unhappy relationship with a long list of specific complaints about Toni.

I felt constantly tense and obsessed about what to do to change things.

TONI: I began to look at how much I needed to blame Richard and how invested I was in it! Finally I saw what I really wanted and faced my terror of thinking I didn't know how or what to do and shifted into wanting the relationship more than wanting to be a victim. I still didn't *really* want to give up blaming, and I notice that I still blame occasionally.

RICHARD: I began to step back and take a fresh look at what I really wanted. I saw that I was creating what was happening and was truly 100 percent responsible for what I was experiencing. Then some obvious questions began to occur to me. For example, instead of focusing on how to win an argument, I asked myself if I liked arguing. I found that I really don't. I asked, "How can I step out of this arguing and into the state of body and mind that I really enjoy?" Boy, this took a lot of practice, but I get better at it every day. I had to acknowledge the part of me that wanted—needed—the negative intensity of the power struggles. Learning to tune in to my body sensations that told me what I was really feeling gave me essential information in my search for my own truth and my wish to be present in my body, in my relationship, and in the world. In my body sensations I began to be able to tell the difference between a victim attitude and my true creative impulses. The more I knew my own truth, the easier it was to be honest with Toni and others. I particularly appreciated the encouragement and love that Toni and I gave each other as we were learning these skills.

Early on, the six co-commitments from *Conscious Loving* gave me a wake-up call about how to approach my relationship differently. The idea of 100 percent responsibility, telling the microscopic truth, and keeping my agreements were radical at first. Yet soon so much positive energy returned and built on itself that it encouraged more excursions into telling my truth about what I really wanted and then risking creating it. Seeing that this process works raised my self-esteem and confidence that I could take charge of my world, and the upward spiral continued.

TONI: Now the most important moment for me is recognizing when I am triggered, which I notice through body sensations in my middle and a *yamma-yamma* in my head. I realize then that I'm caught in fear and in a feeling that I'm being blamed and accused of not being good enough. I've learned to let go of the need to be right, listen consciously to Richard, and breathe more fully to quiet the one inside who still wants to jump forward and defend. This is the most important shift I've learned. Love, love, love, remembering that perspective above all else, has been invaluable. I'm amazed how much I can shift when I'm love-centered.

We've been having fewer and fewer arguments. With all this freed-up energy, we've been working together more as a team. We generate synergy and create from that: relationship workshops, energizing activities in our relationship, singing together, great sex, more fun with our kids. We appreciate each other's contributions daily in actually creating our vision of joy and companionship.

THE SOUL-CHOICES

We can all obtain the pleasures and glories of the seventh wave by repeatedly making seven soul-choices. These are the navigational practices of the path, the moment-to-moment choices you make to create genuine intimacy. Think of these choices as the lifelong learning curriculum of close relationships.

We call them soul-choices because each of the seven takes you closer to your own essence and to the essence of the other person. In the early years of our own relationship, we discovered that we were presented with choice-moments repeatedly. They came fast and furious, often by the minute, and certainly by the hour. As we learned to make these choices, not only did they become much easier, but we had to make them less often.

Each time you make one of these soul-choices, you step into harmony with your soul-commitments. For example, if you are caught in a difficult choice-moment—perhaps to tell the truth about your feelings or to hide them—you honor your commitment to honesty by making the soul-choice to reveal instead of conceal. After making this move a few times, then a few hundred times, your commitment becomes real and alive.

The First Soul-Choice
Generosity

On a shopping trip to our favorite area of Denver, Gay suggested we walk around together for a while, and then split up so he could have some time alone sipping an espresso. Kathlyn readily agreed, and Gay said he appreciated how she didn't complain about his request but rather supported his need. Kathlyn replied, "Well, I love you, and I want you to have whatever increases your happiness."

In that simple exchange we recognized the foundation of the path of the conscious heart: the shift from scarcity to generosity. Instead of demanding, "What's in it for me?" we wonder, "How can I nurture the essence of both of us?" We look for and support essence in each other and in ourselves. Whatever supports essence in one supports essence in both partners. Supporting essence awakens and reawakens your deepest connection with yourself and with each other.

In our office we get to observe the physical changes that occur when people make the soul-choice of generosity. The skin glows with an unmistakable vibrant coloring, and a sparkle springs from the eyes when people deeply connect, when they go from scarcity to generosity. Another place where it shows is in listening. Thousands of times in therapy we have seen people shift from listening-to-make-the-other-wrong to listening-to-understand. This move requires a choice for generosity.

Being generous with yourself deepens your connection to the well of wholeness in and around you. Generosity with money allows the resources of the universe to flow through you. Buckminster Fuller once said that there are enough resources on the planet for everyone to be a billionaire. Generosity sows brilliant seeds into the future that draw you forward into flow. Generosity allows the future to gently tug you into your vision rather than having the past push you forward while loading your back pockets with lead.

Ultimately generosity heals by revealing essence. True generosity means giving yourself what you most want, not a temporary pacifier. In relationships people repeatedly identify their wish to be loved for who they are, to be seen and appreciated for their deepest being. We can be generous in seeing and receiving our partner's actions and words, and in allowing differences and changes.

As an experiment, here are some questions that evoke conversations about generosity and essence. Try asking your partner:

- What do you want that's really important to you?
- If anything were possible, what would you like to be doing? To learn? To explore? To create?
- What do you experience when you're deeply connected to yourself and the world around you?
- What do you most love to do that would get you out of bed in the morning without an alarm clock?
- What qualities do you have, without whose presence you wouldn't recognize yourself?

The Second Soul-Choice
Authenticity

Imagine how useless prayer would be if you lied to your God. The same authenticity is needed for intimacy: Relationship lives in truth and dies in lies. Truth is the safest place to stand in relationship. If we have learned one thing in our lives, both as lovers and as healers, it's that truth heals.

While growing up, we often heard that "truth hurts," but this is a falsehood whose purpose is to justify withholding the truth. We have seen thousands of people tell the truth about something they've been withholding, but we have yet to hear any one of them say later that they regretted it. What hurts is the pain of lying and being lied to. What hurts is when people bluntly say something that is arguable (and therefore not true) and call it the truth. In our culture truth has gotten such a dangerous name that when we talk about it on television shows, it sometimes produces outraged reactions in the audience. We were surprised until we realized sadly how many people's lives are based on carefully constructed webs of deceit.

In one of the most memorable experiences of our public lives, we appeared on a late-night talk show; shortly afterward we got a call from one of the producers of the CBS show *48 Hours*. He wanted to make sure he had heard us clearly: Were we really suggesting that people in close relationships make a practice of telling each other the truth? Absolutely, we said. If you tell the truth, you have a relationship. If you don't, you have an entanglement. It's as simple as that. "Wow," he said, "that's radical." Really?

He went further. Could he send a camera crew to follow us around the house for a couple of days? The producers were doing a show on truth and wanted to show the extreme uses to which people might put it. They would document how we told the truth in our relationship and would eavesdrop on a couple of therapy sessions with willing clients. Eager to put the issue of authenticity before thirty million people, we agreed, and soon a squadron of producers, technicians, and helpers arrived, led by a smooth, artic-ulate, and well-informed anchorman.

The first question he asked us was: Weren't we afraid that if people told each other the truth, it would trigger a national wave of "spontaneous combustion"? No, we replied, we have more to fear from the cancer of lies than from an outbreak of health. Would America be a worse place if Nixon had told the truth about Watergate? If all the smokers quit smoking, would they get sick from all that fresh air? Probably not. In both cases, we'd all just breathe a lot easier.

His second question (we're not making this up). Were we at all concerned that this practice might fall into the hands of chil-dren? As talk-show veterans, we are accustomed to answering all manner of off-the-wall questions, but this one truly stumped us. We looked at him in amazement for a few long seconds while our minds grappled with the assumptions upon which this question was based. No! we sputtered finally. As adults, most of our prob-lems come from learning, when we're kids, that we have to lie. It *should* fall into the hands of children! Our anchorman knitted his eyebrows to indicate he was skeptical, but the interview continued: Would we demonstrate an example of truth-telling in our own relationship?

Gay tells the story: "Kathlyn had been in Berlin for the previ-ous week, conducting a workshop. I'd just picked her up from the airport the night before their camera crew arrived. We really hadn't had a chance to have any intimate conversations. One of the things I'd wanted to talk to her about was some sexual fantasies I'd had during her absence, about a girlfriend of mine I'd known before I met Kathlyn. I hadn't thought about her in years, and I had no idea why she was coming so strongly into my awareness now. With the cameras rolling, I launched into relating my experi-ence. As I gave her the details about Nancy, our anchorman was virtually hyperventilating. When I finished, he asked in an out-raged tone, 'Now, Kathlyn, did you really need to hear that?' "

Kathlyn says: "I told him I was thoroughly glad Gay was

telling me the truth, although I also said that it triggered some fear in my stomach. I said that I'd much rather live in a world where people revealed themselves than in one where we concealed ourselves."

So it went. When the show aired, we saw that they had contacted another relationship expert to offer a disclaimer. He came on at the end of our segment and said, in essence, "Truth *can* be dangerous. Kids, don't try this at home." Perhaps it's our imagination, but he looked as if he were in a great deal of pain as he was saying it.

The path of the conscious heart is made real through authenticity. In other words, relationship does not live in essence unless you can reliably tell the truth without being prompted. Many of us will tell the truth when we're asked or threatened, but fewer of us have such a powerful urge for authenticity that we will initiate telling the truth.

Three areas of ourselves call most urgently for the light of transparency: facts, feelings, and fantasies. We discovered that our spiritual path deepened significantly when we could become completely authentic in these three areas. Both of us entered our relationship with a strong pull toward hiding all three of them, so it took a lot of work to achieve transparency. We both came from families where we got punished for communicating the truth. Withdrawing into ourselves became a survival strategy.

First the partners in a relationship have to learn to be authentic with themselves. To do this they have to overcome the myth of blissful ignorance, which says that it is better to ignore the truth of experience than to feel and speak it. The idea is that if you do not feel or say certain truths, they will cease to be true. Countless relationships have been destroyed because one or both partners lied to themselves about something that was real.

An accompanying myth says that awareness is painful, but actually awareness is light and blissful. It is resistance to awareness that is painful. Gay recalls such an experience: "I was taking a shower when I found myself thinking a lot of scary thoughts about a minor surgical procedure that I was scheduled to have the following week. I pictured myself having a bad reaction to the anesthetic, waking up feeling groggy, and having to be cared for in a way that inconvenienced Kathlyn. I realized that I was scared about something; I could feel the shivering 'butterfly' feeling in my belly. I let myself feel the fear, focusing my attention on it. As I did this, I first felt more fear, but as I watched my mind at work, I saw that part of me wanted to feel it and part of me was resisting it. I noted this and dismissed the resister part, thanking it for looking out for me but telling it to be quiet for a moment. With my full attention now on the fear, I realized I was afraid of dying. Without the resistance, though, the awareness of the fear felt delicious. Instead of pain, I felt waves of bliss in the same place the fear had been.

"Taking anesthesia is probably a trigger for the fear of dying, I thought, so I deliberately lingered on the fantasy of taking the drug and sliding into unconsciousness. Then I inserted a better idea into my thought-stream: a fantasy of waking up feeling hale, happy, and healed. That shift allowed me to go through the surgery with only minor discomfort and, more importantly, to let Kathlyn support me. Our essence-connection deepened through each of us sharing our fears and desires."

In speaking the truth to someone else, most of us fear the other person will have a blowup or some other unpleasant reaction. We have surveyed many audiences over the years, asking them if they can remember being punished for telling the truth about something as children. Often half an audience can remember incidents of being hit or scolded, instead of celebrated, for telling the truth. No wonder "truth hurts." In therapy, however, our experiences have been very different. We have been present on hundreds of occasions when people have said truths to each other that they had been hiding, truths such as:

- I've been having an affair for the past three years.
- I have a number of secret bank accounts.
- I have another family in another state.

- I feel angry at you for shunning your children.
- I hate your mother.

If "truth hurts," then people should get very upset on hearing these confessions. But our experience is exactly the opposite. Nearly every time the listener greets the truth with relief or wonder—relief, when it is a truth that the listener has suspected, often unconsciously, but has not articulated; wonder, when it is something the listener has not thought of. Sometimes anger comes later, but it is a secondary emotion, born of the fear of life-changes that the revealed truth might cause. But when partners can speak the truth about these fears, very little anger rattles around in their relationship.

Intentions are very important when communicating a truth in a relationship. If my intention is to make you wrong or to dump something I've felt guilty about, I'll get a troublesome reaction from you. But if my intention is to be transparent, to share everything with you, then your reaction, although sometimes intense, may well open more authenticity and respect. I'm actually letting you know that I consider you an equal and capable of hearing the truth.

Many of our clients and students have told us that their first-date policy now is to let the person know right off the bat that they are interested in developing an authentic relationship. Then they say something that is unarguably true, such as, "I'm afraid that you'll think I'm pushy," or "I'm experiencing waves of warmth up the center of my body." They notice whether their date becomes excited by this authenticity and responds with interest. Starting a relationship with authenticity establishes safety for exploration.

Longer-term relationships, of course, have more baggage, more stashes of secrets, and more layers of withholding, so making a new commitment to authenticity may be more complicated for established couples. Hundreds of couples we know have navigated their relationships to greater transparency by sharing their fears first—such as acknowledging that their pile of baggage seems overwhelming, or that they don't know who they really are under the layers of trying to please or control. We recommend starting with simple truths like body-sensations. Get familiar with noticing your flow of feelings and sharing those. Establish a shared world of authenticity, then step into those secrets that linger in your dreams or dull your aliveness. Each choice to be authentic invites more essence into your relationship.

The Third Soul-Choice
Balance

In most relationships power is skewed toward one person or the other. The conscious heart of relationship comes to full flower only when there is absolute equality. There is no relationship—only entanglement—unless it is between complete equals. Many people try to impose equality from the outside, by establishing joint checking accounts, sharing housework, and performing other external tasks equally. These things can be important, but unless they come from an inner intention toward equality, they usually do not produce happiness.

Much energy in close relationships is squandered in power struggles. From early in our lives, many of us battle to dominate others or to avoid domination by them; as one of our clients put it, "I spent my childhood trying to avoid being controlled by my mother and father, and my adulthood trying to avoid being controlled by my wife." Not until his thirties did he begin to see that this struggle over domination was not something he had chosen consciously. In childhood he found himself already engaged in the struggle, so that is the way he thought life was supposed to be. In fact, his parents were quite high on the control scale (they had him completely toilet trained by his first birthday), so getting married at all was actually a step in the right direction for him. When he and his wife were able to eliminate the control issues from their relationship, their happiness and productivity took a giant leap.

On the soul level balance comes from a genuine recognition

that there is only one reality in the universe and we are all part of it. Since we're all made of this one reality, we are all, at the most fundamental level, completely equal with each other and with everything else in the universe. It does not matter what you call that one thing, as long as you realize that we are all expressions of it. This equality puts us in balance with all of creation: No expression of creation has any more value, or any less, than any other. We are all it, and it is us. When we know this deeply in our cells, we see everyone and everything differently. Knowing we are all one and the same resolves all metaphysical issues as well as all relationship problems.

Here's why. Most relationship problems are rooted in a struggle for control: One person struggles to control the thoughts, feelings, or life-direction of another. Remember the couple who were growing in different areas: She wanted to go back to school, while he ruptured a disk to keep her from doing so? The disk-slipper was scared of the anticipated life-change and slipped the disk to control not only this fear but the behavior of the other person. His unconscious thought was: "If I can get her to continue in our old life-direction, my fear will go away." Such attempts at control never work in the long run, but in the short run such maneuvers give us temporary relief from our pain.

Notice carefully where the fear comes from: It emerges because the person has stepped out of an equal relationship with the universe. It is based on the assumption that the other person has created our fear through his or her actions, and if they would change those actions, our fear would disappear. In other words, we see ourselves as the victim of their actions. We claim inequality and defend ourselves as if we are one-down to them.

When we're scared, we project onto others that they are "the other"; in fact, we often treat fear itself as if it's "the other." We step out of our connection with the source of creation and pretend that other people are the source of our feelings. In that moment of pretended inequality, a host of miseries is born.

In close relationships the most common type of power imbalance is thinking that we're the victim of the other person. This way of thinking is a factor in nearly all relationship disputes. In fact, in our experience nearly all relationship problems involve a race to occupy the victim position. We dash for the victim position because of the seductive, addictive glee of casting the other person as the persecutor. It feels so good to feel so wronged. But if we took responsibility for our problems, if we let go of our claim on the victim position, what would we do with all our extra time? And where would all the country-western songs come from?

The soul-choice for balance gives power to your soul-commitment to full responsibility. Here are some powerful ideas that counteract the victim programming that most of us have soaked up in our lives.

- From the victim position, we wonder, "Is it safe in this relationship?" From the position of full responsibility, we know: "I am the source of safety in the world."
- From the victim position, we look to others to confirm our lovability. From full responsibility, we know that if we fail to experience beauty and love around us, it is because we're not loving ourselves. The responsible person knows: "As I grow in love toward myself, I automatically attract more love to me."
- From the victim position, we wait for an invitation to tell the truth. The responsible person knows: "It is my responsibility to initiate speaking the truth."
- From the victim position, we expect others to read our minds. When we shift into equality, we know: "It is my responsibility to know what I want and to ask for it clearly."
- The victim hopes to get what's missing from others. The responsible person knows: "What I judge in others reflects what I have not embraced in myself."
- The victim expends a great deal of effort trying to get others to change. The responsible person knows: "The

experience I'm having is the one I'm supposed to be having, given my attitudes and programming. My job is to learn from this experience."

- The victim complains; he or she is always being "done to." The fully responsible person knows that: "If I am complaining about other people or the world, it is a sign that I am not embracing my full creativity. My job is to claim ownership of my full potential and express it in the world."

These attitudes are all ways of claiming full responsibility for ourselves and the direction of our lives. They are part of the soul-choice of balance, because only on the level field of full responsibility can people meet as equals. Anything less than 100 percent responsibility results in a power struggle.

The Fourth and Fifth Soul-Choices
Wonder and Play

You might be surprised to see "wonder and play" listed as attitudes or skills essential to the conscious heart. But they are essentials of the path, present in all the people we know who are truly successful in their relationship.

Wonder and play can be lifesavers on the path, especially in the third wave of primal drama and in the fourth-wave cultivation of essence. Thinking you already know the way things are is often the problem; wonder—being genuinely, playfully curious about them—is the solution. Many times you will be stuck, and you and a panel of your closest friends are absolutely sure you know why: It's your partner's fault. Wonder will get you out of this.

People in troubled relationships essentially point their finger at their partner and say "Ha!" as in "Gotcha!", gloating in the glee of self-righteous victimhood.

But let's point the finger back at ourselves, albeit with a loving spirit of curiosity and wonder: "Hmm, I wonder how I am creating this situation?" you might ask. When you do this move in the spirit of wonder, miracles can occur. Wondering takes us out of the state of consciousness in which problems occur and puts us in the state where they can be resolved.

Play is another essential part of the conscious heart. Deep learnings do not have to be done with a heavy heart. Play uncovers essence. Anything you can't or won't play with imprisons you in a programmed version of yourself and bars you from essence. If you're imprisoned in an attitude or judgment, you can't play. Anything that is NOT FUNNY deepens the gulf between breath and essence. Around our house we have probably solved more of our problems by turning on music and dancing than through talking. In fact, getting stuck talking is a cue for us to do something playful rather than grind away at something that isn't working. By the time we come back from a bike ride or skipping stones down at the pond, we are often in a different state of consciousness and can solve the problem much more quickly.

If you are grounded in wonder and play, rather than in routine, then you can flow with change easily. It may be more familiar to seek safety in projections and routine, but these soul-choices breathe safety into the deepest experiences. They are buoys in the waves of change. When I discover, when you discover, it's a brand-new connection in the universe, no matter how many thousands of people have walked into the same river.

In therapy we have found that wonder and play are very powerful healers. One couple transformed their relationship before our eyes with a moment of play. The partners were extreme opposites in personality: He was a happy-go-lucky chap whose passions were bicycling, Rollerblading, going to hockey games, wearing wild ties, and late nights watching Jay Leno. She was a sober soul who wore thick glasses, sensible dresses, and a pinched mouth. When they came in, they had not slept together in several months. Each spent much of their first session trying to get us to agree that the other was wrong.

When we could get a word in edgewise, we pointed out something they had never considered: Partners often mate with an opposite to balance themselves out. A serious person will often mate with the class clown to learn a key life-lesson: Lighten up. The class clown will choose the sober partner to gain focus and groundedness. We asked these two: "What if your selection of each other was not some colossal mistake but a magnificently tailored learning opportunity?" They were stunned to momentary stillness, which in our opinion was a great improvement over where they had been a few minutes before.

They asked, "You mean we could be learning from each other's gifts, rather than criticizing them all the time?" "Yes," we said, "that's exactly it." So great was their state of wonder at this new notion that their eyes actually rolled back in their heads. We suggested that they try it on the spot. We asked our light-hearted fellow, "What would demonstrate to you that she was lightening up a little?" "Telling a joke she found funny," he said. To her, we asked, "What would indicate to you that he was taking life a little more seriously?" Her answer: "Having an uninterrupted, thirty-minute conversation about the pros and cons of having a baby," she replied.

It took work, but we finally got them to do both things. After considerable resistance she told a truly awful joke about the love life of Bill Clinton. Then we umpired a discussion of the baby question. By the end of the session, they both had visibly melted. She had lost her stiff disapproval, and he had chucked his tendency to use humor as a defense. Both felt that a miracle had happened, but we congratulated them on engineering their own miracle. What brought them back together was their willingness to use the power of wonder and play to heal blame and criticism. They had put into practice the master commitment—to learn from every interaction—with stunning results.

Some couples can keep discovering new qualities and stories about their partners, even after many years or decades. For others, sadly, the constriction of predictability descends quickly. The eyes of wonder allow you to see new facets of even the most familiar face. Each day, each interaction, each choice to see things as they are, to develop attention without an agenda, peels away the layers of familiarity. If you know that this moment is unique, that your partner is always changing, you're more likely to really notice the particular shade of violet in her eyelids this morning. Re-creation blooms in the hothouse of wonder.

When we look at childhood pictures, we notice a great deal of wonder on those young faces, but it is missing in those same faces in high school yearbooks. What happens? Where do the wonder and sense of play go? The answer is that it disappears under masks that help us get recognition and that protect us from pain and loss. In the same family one person becomes Class Clown, another becomes Sullen Delinquent, and yet another Mom's Helper. Even useful, positive masks become a layer that we have to shed in order to embrace our own essence.

Wonder and play are intrinsically enjoyable states of consciousness, and at the same time they are problem-solvers of the highest order.

The Sixth Soul-Choice
Gratitude

༺ঌৎ঵

Sometimes gratitude comes upon us by surprise; at other times we consciously invoke it. As we learn to speak the truth and take responsibility, spontaneous waves of gratitude sweep over us nearly every day. We will be going about our business—paying bills, riding bikes, straightening up the kitchen—and a warm glow of gratitude will come out of nowhere and suffuse our bodies. We think of these waves as winks from the universe that acknowledge that we are doing a good job with the basics of truth and equality.

Leading with gratitude, taking the initiative, is important to the health of a close relationship. Many people wait for others to do something positive before they open their own heart valves of appreciation. This strategy is akin to standing in the garden and saying, "Give me some vegetables, and then maybe I'll water them for you." For gardens and relationships to thrive, they must be watered first. Expressing appreciation is at first an act of faith, as watering seeds is an act of faith. In relationship, however, you do not have to wait so long to see the fruits of your appreciation.

Many people habitually expect their partners to earn little niblets of appreciation from them. Their relationships have the shriveled look of a parched, untended garden. When we shift from the position that gratitude is scarce and must be conserved to the position that gratitude is abundant, appreciation itself increases the opportunities to appreciate. So many couples long for a refreshing splash of appreciation without even knowing why they're vaguely dissatisfied.

Several couples have commented to us on the essence-sparkle they enjoy when their partners shift from criticism to appreciation. One woman said: "I used to cringe inside when Cameron came home, because he'd open the door complaining about the kids' leaving their toys on the lawn or my not clipping the flowers correctly. I listened for 'Now what's wrong?!' When we learned to shift to gratitude, I looked forward to greeting Cam again. We had to really practice at first because the skill was so unfamiliar. I remember, though, the first time he said, 'I love the way you always make time for me when I come home, no matter what you're doing. I really appreciate the time you take to talk over the day before we move into the evening.' I felt so seen; some icy place in me melted, and I could see again why I first fell in love with Cam. It became easier to find things to appreciate about him, like his incredible sense of humor and his patience with our exuberant eight-year-old. We're really on a roll now with appreciations—it's changed the whole nature of our lives."

As we caught on to the power of appreciation, we began to look for things to appreciate about each other on a daily, then hourly, basis. The appreciations could be simple or complex. Gay might say, "I appreciate the color and flowing beauty of the clothes you're wearing today. It's like a visual symphony." Kathlyn might say, "I'm grateful for the easy way you relate to Chris. Even when you disciplined him, you did it in such a straightforward way, it never seemed like you were putting him down." Sometimes the appreciation is on the soul level. Gay may say, "I appreciate your fundamental good nature. I grew up in a family where I was always working overtime to cheer my mother up. It's so refreshing not to have to do that with you, to have you always be willing to have a good time." Kathlyn might say, "I appreciate the way you see everyone as equals. I remember the day [a big politician] introduced himself to you. You chatted with him exactly the same way you'd just been talking to the hotel bellhop." These are magic moments in a relationship; to have our essence seen by another person is one of our deepest hungers.

Sometimes when we're stuck in a conflict, we use gratitude to break us out of the "vapor lock" of negativity. We force ourselves (and it often feels like pulling teeth) to think of something we appreciate about the other person. We think about it until we can feel the gratitude in our chest, then we say it aloud. Miraculously this act of gratitude will bring a wave of fresh energy into the relationship, popping us out of the trance of negativity.

The Seventh Soul-Choice
Creativity

❧

As we travel through our own relationship journey, and as we work with others on theirs, we encounter time and again a deep source of pain: the pain caused by untapped creative potential. So many people have settled for being so much less than they could become. To mute their expression of their potential, they have dulled themselves to the screams of their inner voice, the one that says, "Make every moment count! Express every ounce of your creativity!" Tuning this voice out leaves people open to a host of ills—both physical sickness and its psychic counterpart.

Most relationship problems are symptoms of unexpressed creativity. When creativity is not being expressed, the morass of languishing potential becomes a breeding ground for disharmony. When we are feeling limited by the other person, it is almost always because there is some aspect of our own creativity we are not expressing.

Kathlyn found this to be a problem early in our relationship: "One of the big divisions in our relationship used to be that Gay was the creative one and I was the organizer. I *am* very organized, but I felt limited by this role. Unconsciously I began to resent that Gay seemed to get all the credit and glory while I (who secretly knew who was really responsible for making the whole show come together!) would stew in silent obscurity. One day I complained that Gay had done most of the talking at a workshop and hadn't let me speak very much. I accused him of always having to be number one. Even as I said it, I realized how ridiculous and victimy it sounded. He said, 'I wondered why you weren't participating. I would pause and look over toward you now and then, but you didn't jump in.' I suddenly realized that he had no attachment whatsoever to being number one. In fact, he seemed genuinely interested in my being a full partner. In a rush I saw what it was all about. My adored older brother had been the family star and is always referred to by my mother as 'number one.' My role was to be Mom's busy beaver, the helper who could always be relied upon to do the dishes and clean up my brother's messes. I realized I was projecting that drama onto my relationship with Gay, and it was getting in the way of our being equal partners.

"I realized that what I needed to do was make a full commitment to my own creativity. I needed to take responsibility for expressing myself fully in the world, and that if I did that, the world would open up in front of me. And in fact, that's been the way it's worked. Once I woke up and stopped my projection, the issue completely disappeared as a problem for us."

Gay welcomed the change: "I was deeply impressed with the power of Kathlyn's shift in consciousness. From that moment on the quality of our interactions changed, especially when we were out in public. Kathlyn stepped forward instead of hanging back. A key shift in her daily schedule also helped: In the beginning she would always make sure her desk was tidy, her calls returned, and the house in order before she would do any creative work like writing or painting. As she embraced her commitment to creativity, she turned this schedule upside down (or right side up, as I like to think of it). She would disappear into her den first thing in the morning. Only later, when she was finished with her creative work, would she tackle the ever-present backlog of phone calls, errands, and details. Since making this shift, she has published nine books, among numerous other creative activities."

This is the power of creativity.

PART TWO

SEX, MONEY,
AND THE CONSCIOUS
HEART

Sex and Money Are Springboards to Essence

Money and sex are two of the thorniest areas in relationships. Our therapy records reveal that the top three complaints people have sought help for are communication, money, and sex, in that order. On the surface, you might not think money and sex issues have much to do with the unfolding of relationship as a spiritual path. In fact, they are both crucial to it. When we make friends with our sex and money issues, we free up the very energy that is necessary for the higher potential of our relationships.

Our work with couples has shown us a true surprise: Sex and money problems are almost never about sex and money. They are the proverbial tip of the iceberg; what is below the surface is often ancient and fundamental. When the real issue is confronted and handled, sex and money problems shift organically toward resolution.

Many of us look toward the outside when we have sex or money problems. Stuck in this old way of seeing the world, we may ask:

Why won't they value me as I deserve?

Why does he/she seem sexually interested in other people?

Why won't he/she spend less (or make love more)?

But in fact, the fundamental issue beneath both sex and money has to do with the flow of energy and who controls it. Sex is a flow of energy inside each person and back and forth between them. So is money. Once you understand this foundation principle you open up a powerful new type of question:

Where am I restricting the flow of my sexual energy and why?

What is it about me that causes me to attract scarcity?

Why am I trying to control the sexual feelings of my partner?

This sort of inquiry will prove much more fruitful.

In this section we aim for utter frankness about some of the sex and money issues that have been the biggest challenge in our relationship. We've gone into great detail not only to illustrate the principles involved, but because we want to be absolutely transparent ourselves. We are committed to "walking our talk." We have told thousands of students our position on honesty: *If there is anything in your life you wouldn't be willing to talk about over the loudspeakers in Yankee Stadium, it's got a grip on you.* We have tried our best to eliminate secrets from our own lives, to have nothing we are not willing to communicate.

There is a big difference between privacy and secrecy. Secrecy is based on fear: It is something you're defensive about. You don't reveal secrets because you fear someone's reaction to the truth. Privacy is something you treasure, a sacred part of your life that sharing would dilute. Many people confuse the two.

Sigmund Freud said it very clearly: Secrets make you sick. Privacy doesn't cause any problems at all; in fact, it's a source of joy and delight. We have found that clear communication about both sex and money involves letting go of secrets immediately.

SIX

Breakup or Breakthrough: How We Confronted a Sexual Crisis

*Love is an ocean without shores. You have to jump in, never to come
back. You have to give up your life; you can never have your life back.
This isn't a path for cautious people.*

—KIRPAL SINGH

It is useful to regard any trouble spot in a relationship as an
invitation to make a deeper commitment to creativity. In our
work we have noticed that people often create a conflict just as
they are about to make a creative breakthrough. It's as if they
administer a test or challenge to themselves to see if they have the
courage to break through to the next level of expression. Many
even contemplate ending the relationship. When we helped them
sort out what was really going on, however, the threatened break*up*
turned out to actually be a break*through* trying to happen. They
were on the verge of inventing a larger version of themselves:
building a dream house, making a baby, launching a creative proj-

ect. They were insecure about making this leap into the unknown and retreated into the zone of the familiar—the old drama that they unconsciously knew would keep them grounded.

In our own relationship we have also generated dramas just before expanding into greater creativity. Here's the most striking example so far.

We've developed a special new year's tradition in our relationship; as each year begins, we spend a week focusing on our life-goals. These can be both project-goals—such as writing books, conducting seminars, and making large purchases—and process-goals, such as enjoying ourselves, learning, and expanding into new frontiers of ourselves. Usually during the first week of January we set aside an hour each morning to brainstorm and refine our goals. Then we type them up and put them on the wall in our respective dens. Often we modify and add to them as the year goes on.

This particular year we had set some very large goals. One of our project-goals was to purchase a house near the beach in Santa Barbara. It was more than a house: Both of us love that part of the world (it's where Kathlyn grew up), and Kathlyn's parents, now in their seventies, make their home there. Moving there from Colorado represented a major life-change, as well as the uprooting of our friendship network and a number of changes in our business office. It also coincided with Gay's fiftieth birthday and his retirement from university teaching, which he had done for twenty years. Our plan was to live in Santa Barbara during the winter and spring, then spend the summer and autumn back in Colorado. Would all these changes trigger shifts in our relationship? We were about to find out. In fact, we were about to embark on a journey that would test our ability to use all the skills we teach: truth, responsibility, commitment, creativity, wonder, play, and gratitude.

Gay begins the story: "A few weeks after my fiftieth birthday, I began an adventure that is unique in my life-experience. To set the stage, I should tell you that things had been going very well in my life for a long time. My health is excellent, my children are launched, and my bank account is such that I am free to focus on what I most like to do. Kathlyn and I have had many years of happiness and creativity together, which have resulted in several co-authored popular books, a successful business, and a circle of friends around the world. Further, I should tell you that for many years I have taught a course over cable TV on developmental psychology. Many times I have lectured on the adult developmental stages. I devote an entire class to each decade, so I know all the intellectual information about the decade from fifty to sixty. According to the psychologist Erik Erikson, the developmental crisis of people in their fifties centers on 'generativity versus stagnation.' You are faced with many choices—to expand, to grow, to challenge yourself—or to slide into stagnation.

"Now I know what Erikson is talking about. In one sense I have it made. I could retire and sit on a beach if I wanted to, yet my work is compelling enough to make me want to keep doing it. So as I approached my fiftieth birthday, I could feel a real sense of satisfaction about the way I've lived my life. Yet at the same time part of me felt like I was rusting a little. I was aware of a gnawing sense of dissatisfaction, some internal danger signals that told me I was beginning to lose a creative edge. For example, Kathlyn and I would be giving a lecture to an enthusiastic audience, and though they were obviously enjoying it, I knew I was just going through the motions. I found that I could go on automatic pilot, and the audience would still respond very favorably. They didn't seem to notice—but I sure did. This feeling was anathema to me; I had always prided myself on being on a growing and learning edge. Aliveness and creativity were probably the most important sensations in my body that let me know all was well. And I was losing my ability to feel them.

"All this was happening beneath the surface and beneath my ability to articulate it. I knew something was going on down in me, but I couldn't quite grasp what it was. Then a watershed event brought it all to the surface.

"I was among a large number of friends gathered at the fortieth birthday party of a friend of mine. A superb band was playing loud roadhouse blues, my favorite type of dance music. I was dancing wildly with Kathlyn and others in a crowd of perhaps fifty people. Suddenly across the room, as if bathed in a shaft of radiance, I saw Kristin.

"I had known Kristin for a year or so, having first met her at some of the trainings (mainly for mental health professionals and transformationally oriented people) that Kathlyn and I offer. She was just beginning her doctoral work in the field of body-centered psychotherapy, the field in which I am a contributor of some of the primary books. Up until then I had looked upon her with somewhat fatherly feelings, since she was about the same age as my daughter. I had also been very impressed with her intellectual strengths, her natural healing gifts, and her sunny demeanor.

"Now, on the dance floor, I saw a different Kristin. Her long auburn curls shimmered in the soft light, her lithe body moved to the music with the grace of an earthy ballerina, and her low-cut dress revealed aspects of her to which I had previously been oblivious. Suddenly every cell in my body felt alive. I felt a wave of light and bliss cascade through my body; actually, it seemed beyond my body, surrounding me like an aura. It was as if I had been living at 50 percent when a sudden shift took me to 150 percent. I had been in love before: once at sixteen, another time at twenty-nine, and finally with Kathlyn at thirty-five. This was something different. I had no context to put it in. Being a psychologist, I was fascinated as an observer as well as a participant. It felt like some part of me was waking up at long last. It certainly had a sexual component, although it reached into areas of myself that felt spiritual as well.

"I have an agreement with myself to tell the truth about any feeling I have within ten seconds of feeling it, if it's physically possible to do so. This is based on my conviction that true relationship is possible only with complete transparency. Most of the time this agreement means I say something like, 'I was scared when you didn't come home when you said you'd be there,' or, 'I'm angry that you dinged the fender.' Reporting my feelings and body sensations keeps my body relaxed and my mind free of noise.

"So I motioned to Kristin, who was close by, to dance over my way. 'I want to talk to you about a feeling I just had. Can we talk?' She nodded over the music, and we went to the sidelines.

" 'I've had some fatherly feelings for you and an affection for you for a long time, but just now on the dance floor, I felt a strong rush of energy that feels anything but fatherly. In fact, it feels like a powerful sexual feeling. I'm scared to tell you about it, because I don't know how you'll react. I don't know much more than that, but I wanted to tell you so you didn't get any mixed signals.'

" 'Great,' Kristin said, beaming. 'I feel that for you, too. I've felt it for a long time.' "

For Kristin, that moment, though surprising, seemed to come from issues she had been exploring over the prior months: "I see that in the months before Gay first spoke to me about his sexual feelings toward me, I had been exploring in depth the relationship between my talent and creativity and my unconscious commitment to feel victimized by those same things. I had been working on manifesting a partner who would be delighted in creating a radically alive relationship with me, yet I had created relationships in the past where it looked like I was the creative one and he was the practical one. I looked carefully at my unconscious resistances to a relationship that catalyzed creativity in both of us. I then committed to clearing up anything in the way of creating a relationship of equality where we both committed to aliveness and vast creative expression.

"Three weeks later at the party, when Gay revealed his feelings toward me, I felt elated that he communicated this and also that my new commitment had produced results so quickly. However, I hadn't imagined that it would involve such a prominent psychologist. Over the years that I had been attending trainings and assisting Gay and Kathlyn, I saw them consistently live the principles they teach. I became greatly impressed with Gay's immense energy and passion for living. To me Gay was a friend, teacher, supporter, and creativity explorer. I had also felt a great mix of both daughterly and sexual feelings toward him."

Gay recalls: "Omigod. I felt a knot form deep in my belly. I waved to Kathlyn on the other side of the room and motioned her over to where Kristin and I were talking.

"She arrived, smiling and out of breath from the dancing. She knew Kristin primarily as an enthusiastic young student of our work and an assistant at our trainings.

" 'I'm very scared to tell you this,' I said, 'but I just had a very powerful feeling come up with Kristin.' I explained to her what had happened.

"I watched fear and worry cloud her face as I talked. The more I talked, the more intense it seemed to get. It scared me to see so much feeling mounting up in her.

"She said she was angry and scared and hurt. Her eyes moistened as she gestured toward Kristin's lush and trim figure. 'There's no way I can compete with that,' she said. She also said a few judgmental things, implying deficiencies of character on my part, and I felt the conversation veer sharply toward an argument. 'Hold on,' I said. 'I'd like to be appreciated for telling the truth. It would have been easy to hide all this or do something sneaky. I feel like I'm being punished for being honest.'

"I'm glad I said this, because it brought everybody up short. We suddenly had to look at whether we were more committed to telling the truth and hearing the truth or to being right. We nipped ourselves in the bud and brought the conversation back to speaking the truth and listening to it nonjudgmentally. This was the first of many dozens of times we would catch ourselves going toward criticism and then returning to generously listening to the other person's feelings.

"After a conversation that lasted about twenty minutes, we all had acknowledged our various fears, angers, hurts, and feelings of aliveness. We agreed to keep each other up to date, and I returned to the big group on the dance floor.

"Later, as we were going to bed, I raised the crucial question to Kathlyn: Would she object strongly to my having a sexual relationship with Kristin? Absolutely, she said. 'I'd be out of here in a minute.' That was the show-stopper comment of the evening, and I could think of nothing further to say. I went to sleep.

"The next morning I woke up furious. I think I had an unspoken expectation that my fifteen years of being a faithful husband and an all-around good guy had built me up some credit. I think I had expected Katie to say something like: 'Hey, why don't you two go outside and plant a big smacker on each other? Let yourself feel it to the max, and then see if you actually want to have sex.' I had wanted a 'follow your bliss' injunction and instead got a critical response. Venting my anger, I went on a passionate rant: I cited numerous instances of my saintly acceptance of her, times in which I had gone overboard to be helpful and supportive. I recalled how pleasant and reasonable I'd been when she wrecked my Saab. I mentioned the times I had insisted that talk shows take us as a package instead of just me. I proudly pointed out how I always put the toilet seat back down. I soared to great heights of outraged victimhood.

"It was a world-class self-righteous tirade, and a major run for the victim position. I hadn't figured out how stupid all this sounded, so I continued my rant: 'Why not cut me a little slack here? Gimme a break! After all I've done for you, the least you can do is give me room to have a little sexual attraction.'

"Hearing my tone of voice during this tirade finally woke me up from my trance. I realized I was projecting all my old anger at my mother onto Kathlyn. When I tuned in to what was going on in my body, I saw that what was running was perhaps the deepest issue of my life: the war between my aliveness and my mother's anger at my existence in the world. I had Kathlyn in the role of policeman. I had made her responsible for my aliveness and was projecting onto her that she was trying to squelch it. As soon as I figured this out, I felt a lot more at ease inside. My task became to take responsibility for this issue rather than project it onto Kathlyn. It was about me, opening up to my full aliveness and creative energy, not about Kathlyn trying to keep me from it. In the midst of blaming her, I shifted to taking responsibility for it."

Kathlyn recalls her response in these pages from her journal: "That night on the dance floor is studded with several visual images: of Gay standing with his arm around Kristin, who was dressed in a low-cut black lace top, of Gay with a wide grin, of the room shrinking and turning gray. I had lived in our relationship with the agreement that we shared our sexual feelings about other people and had settled into a kind of security of trusting that we had decided to be monogamous. When Gay announced his attraction and desire, I felt that ground break open and shake me to the core of so many assumptions on which I'd been standing.

"When Gay first shared his sexual feelings, I felt happy that he was telling me about them so quickly and fully, and then I began to see that this was not just like other times when we'd shared deep feelings with each other. I saw a zing in Gay and noticed that he was looking at Kristin in a way he hadn't looked at me for some time. I also noticed that as he told the truth, his feelings didn't dissipate as they had in previous communications about the periodic pulls of heart and groin.

"I felt this incredible aching in my chest and had difficulty breathing. I suddenly realized my heart was breaking. At the same time that I felt the entire structure of my life crumbling, I felt the undercurrent of the same kind of totally transformative electric energy as when Gay and I first got together. My personal internal editor was commenting, 'You're an expert on relationships—this kind of thing doesn't happen to you! Oh, man, this is going to be interesting for our trainings and presentations! Headlines reading: "Renowned Relationship Therapists Just As Messed Up As Rest of Us!"'

"I was most pulled to compare. In my mind I saw a strobelike stream of aging women comparing themselves with younger and more beautiful women, opting for comparison rather than creativity. I was partly in shock and partly electrified. The stream of yes and the stream of no were dancing wildly in my body. I was mad, and I wanted to lash out and hurt back. I felt so deeply hurt, I could hardly breathe. I could feel the layers of the hurt, the victim that would kill me if I embraced it, the warrior facing into the storm, and the clam that must be softened to be edible. I was most stunned by Gay's turning his attention away from me. One of my short poems expresses my experience at that moment:

I tore myself from your lifeforce
like a leech from the leg
of a long-distance swimmer.
Both the leech and the leg bleed.

"I heard, once he mentioned it, the tone of control covering the fury I felt, and I knew the fury at being left belonged at least back in my childhood, but further back to the men who left my grandmother's mother without nurture or support. The steely resolve of women to do it themselves is part of my genetic heritage."

Gay picks up the narrative of the day after the dance: "That afternoon, as we were driving around the California wine country and talking intently, Kathlyn turned to me and told me that I was free to have any kind of relationship I wanted with Kristin. She said she was going to let go of trying to control me and put that energy into expressing her own creativity.

"As the shift toward full responsibility happened in me, Kathlyn began to shift also. She woke up to her own end of the issue. She realized that her central creativity issues were woven into this event. She saw that she had submerged her own creativity to be the administrator of our institute and the main teacher of our trainings. She had taken on the role of the CEO so I could occupy the role of Creative Genius. She was mad about the role she'd created but hadn't said anything. Her anger had been expressed through gaining weight and pulling back from me sexually. These roles were keeping her from opening up to her own Creative Genius. She saw that she had projected onto me all the responsibility for carrying the wild and crazy creative energy in the relationship, while she played the Good Reliable Stodgy Wife. After taking a look at all this, she decided to make a major commitment to owning her own creativity again. Poetry started to pour out of her over the next few weeks. She also lost fifteen pounds in about a week.

"Over the next week or so, I kept opening up to all the different feelings I had for Kristin. I would get a burst of sexual feeling for her, and I would let myself go into it. Sometimes I would feel guilty, but then I would consciously let go of the guilt and permit myself to feel the strong energy. When I allowed myself to feel the energy cleanly, it usually shifted into more of a whole-body feeling, like a sparkle in my bloodstream. Kristin and I talked on the phone a few times, but it wasn't until two weeks later that I saw her again. Being around her for two days at that time gave me ample opportunity to open up to the sexual energy I felt, although I chose not to engage in actual physical sex with her.

"I'm glad we didn't rush into a physical relationship, because there were other types of relationships I wanted to explore with her. For one thing, she was going to be doing her doctoral work in areas related to our work, and I was considering offering her a job doing research for our institute and helping at the trainings while she was working on her doctorate. For another, she had a facilitative effect on my creativity; I found myself generating a lot of new ideas after I was around her. Third, she had a 'best friend' feel to her; I felt very comfortable in her presence and could 'think out loud' with her. I also have that kind of relationship with Kathlyn, but I had not experienced it very often in my life. I treasured it."

Kristin was also exploring her feelings: "I began to notice sensations in my body that were signaling me that I was most interested in a mutually creative and spiritual friendship rather than a sexual relationship with Gay. I noticed that I felt streaming aliveness throughout my body when we supported each other in dreaming up a new creative idea, and as I allowed myself to fully feel my sexual feelings, they were replaced by a deep celebration of Gay's being."

Gay continues: "The next two weeks were full of much processing of our feelings—all three of us—and since Kathlyn was often out on the road teaching and Kristin was in California, this often required conference telephone calls. It was one of those months the phone company dreams of."

Kristin continues: "I felt radiantly open to hearing both Gay's and Kathlyn's feelings as we continued to tell the truth about them. My intentions were to feel my feelings thoroughly, to be a space in which Kathlyn and Gay might feel their feelings completely, to continue to tell the truth about them, and to live in the question of how we might reach a resolution. I am particularly grateful that we set the intention together early on that our lessons be gentle and friendly for everyone involved."

Kathlyn's journals during this time reflect her intense inner work: "I continued to teach and work a very full schedule during this whole crisis. Teaching reminded me to ask, 'What can I learn and apply from this current transition?' We have no obligation to stay the same, and in fact relationships where people stay the same require more and more energy to fortify the structure, to prevent leakage of affection or attention. The issue seems to be to allow our phases of individuation and closeness, to find ways to recognize the waves, and to support creativity when we are exploring unknown territory. I am convinced that a way can be found to honor both within the whole of our relationships without having to break the whole to break out. . . .

"I remember Gay saying that his anger at me was the result of not knowing what to do with this new sense of internal yearning. He said he didn't want to slip into comfortable old age in a better BarcaLounger, but to find a new source of energy.

"We have been so focused on work for so long that I think it has put us out of balance. Both of us have a strong drive to contribute to the world, but it has taken the balance askew, so that now much more time needs to be given to our individual idiosyncratic impulses. Maybe this time needs to be approached as archetypal energy, with deep-breathing appreciation of its force and power, a time when intellect and reason won't confine or channel the energy. . . .

"I felt excited and stimulated to receive another wake-up call about continuing to open up to my full energy and power, both sexual and creative. There must be a place that people can't share, a place that is full of unspoken thoughts and feelings: images of things not done and things that won't be done; regrets and limitations that may be constitutional or learned; the finality of time, the looking into the future and seeing an end to time for you; the wild sperm energy of starburst dissemination. I know that Gay has issues to resolve that are separate from me or us, and yet I live in the midst of them, surrounded by the mists. The silverback has other responsibilities from the rest of the pack, carries a different burden and vision, sees the pack as whole and as his to guide safely. I wonder how big Gay's pack is. . . .

"Gay suggested that the best way to have fun with this experience would be to fully value myself and let go of whatever no longer has value, to discover the constant stream of creativity that can serve the rest of my life. My first response was anger: 'Are you really interested in me having fun or in me not getting in your way?' After many layers of exploration and nights filled with epic dreams, I realized that I was really afraid of the awesomeness of my energy. I decided to let this transition purify my body and to heal myself completely of old patterns, to make space for new creativity that I couldn't yet imagine.

"I formed my frontier on some new commitments that Gay and I created in many phone and in-person conversations. These turned out to be anchors and jumping-off places for the next several months as I tore down and rebuilt my sense of myself as an individual and in our relationship.

- *I commit to appreciating my experiences.*
  Rather than indulge my critic, who loves to devalue my feelings, I focused on appreciating my experiences as they

arose, the way I would appreciate a Noguchi sculpture or a bunch of freesias.

- *I commit to turning my experiences into artistic expression.*
This commitment saved my life. Many nights it was the only choice I could see. In the midst of so much turmoil, much of my structure just disappeared. This commitment anchored me. I had no idea that it would free my poetic voice and bring forth a stream of moving and liberating verse. But that's what happened as I used everything I was experiencing to make art. Poems erupted from me, often as I was waking. When I stopped filtering my experience through Gay, I opened a channel where the universe could speak through me directly. Here is one poem from this time:

Remains

What remains?
The spires of hope,
down.
The highway of the future,
closed.
The clear space of trust,
bombed.
Expectations,
pried out of their shells
and left to dry.
Gestures,
cut off at the shoulder.

What remains?
after the whiteout of withdrawal and
random thoughts sputtering in the night.
The mind stunned and stuttering,

streams of connection diverted or
dropping over the edge of the past.

What remains?
Some rhythm of grieving
undulates under the surface
with a keen whistle and low hum
of I am.
I am plucking sweet words from my bones
with a blunt crochet hook
to hear them sing again before soaring
into blue and black.

What remains of love?
when the web of knowing and holding
shimmers and sinks into the vast pool.
A mutation glimmers in the depths
that is still unformed
and yearning with a lidless eye.

- *I commit to speaking to myself or you free of criticism.*
  This commitment popped me loose from a vise of internal criticism that had hampered my freedom to experiment with new behavior and adventures. As a result, I began inventing new training activities, went skydiving and sea kayaking in Alaska, and deeply claimed my right to be in the world.

- *I commit to speaking to myself or you free of evaluation.*

- *I commit to speaking to myself or you free of judging.*
  I saw that most of my internal and external speaking flowed through a judge who determined the worth of my utterance or idea and usually found me wanting, especially in comparison to Gay. When I noticed these filters, I consciously turned my attention to the first two commitments, to appreciate my experiences and turn them into artistic

expression. I found this a fierce discipline at first, especially when I realized how much I evaluated and criticized.

- *I commit to listening to myself and you as an artistic work in progress.*
From the time I was a little girl, I thought I was supposed to know things without being taught. Mistakes and progress were supposed to be invisible, and only the polished result was to be evident at all times. To consider Gay and myself like Michelangelo's marble being sculpted by life released some deep tension in my body that allowed me to be spontaneous and to appreciate Gay's unfolding discoveries.

- *I commit to speaking to myself or you free of comparison.*
This commitment was the tough one. I was embarrassed and horrified to see how much of my mind and emotions were entrenched in a sticky mass of comparisons. As I looked at the act of comparing straightforwardly, it led me to a deeper understanding of my social and cultural heritage. I saw that women are socialized to compare and to see themselves as decorations in a fierce and mostly silent competition with other women to grace the arm of the available men. If my age was showing, I was terrified of slipping into the invisible realm where men no longer saw me. Until I freed myself from comparison, I couldn't access my true value and genuine curiosity about life.

- *I commit to being open to feedback when I slip into criticism, control, evaluation, or comparison and to letting go efficiently and to returning to healthy communication quickly.*
This commitment was so helpful. Prior to choosing feedback I had defended against any sign that I wasn't perfect, since I was already supposed to know everything. I began to learn more quickly and more deeply than I had since I was a young child, and to get excited about the possibilities of this adventure. For the most part, of course. The battle

between my conditioning and freedom often paralyzed me for *hours* before I popped into choice again.

"Time after time over the next few months, I relearned a fundamental lesson: I have absolutely no control over any aspect of Gay. Not what he feels, who he talks to, his sexuality, his creativity, his actions, any part of him. This led me to a central discovery. The unconscious commitments and personality tasks we set at the beginning of our relationship were complete. I saw that I have my life and can accomplish the kind of magic that I had always thought Gay owned. I realized that for about a year I had been full of power and not owning it, not fully stepping into sourcing responsibility. I had been referencing to Gay out of a profound confusion between genuine love and my devoted persona. I think my devoted persona and Gay's critic interlocked and that this crisis was the final jolt I needed to destroy the grip of the devoted persona. I felt waves of gratitude and appreciation for Gay's assistance in helping me find my expression.

"When I got angry and asserted myself, and also didn't eat very much, I felt free in my body in some way that I don't usually, some new energy and liveliness. I've used food to deaden those moments of sharp shaking up of my system. I think I have believed that Gay has held me as an improvement project all these years. I've been afraid that he didn't really love me just as I am but was always making some improvement in me. At some point I began to resent his criticisms. I responded to them and tried to improve in the desired direction while simultaneously resenting his lack of acceptance. As I get hold of that idea, I feel less diffuse and spacey, feel some more vibrance and focus in my body. That must be accurate. . . . I can sense the freedom of not being his improvement project now and having the opportunity to stretch out into my wants and hear the subtle urgings more clearly without the strong channel of Gay's being. . . .

"I know that I carry the history of the devaluation of women in my cells, and I feel very sad about that. I know I am modeling a strong and soft woman for others in the trainings and in presentations, but I sometimes get totally discouraged that I can make a real difference, that equality will really change and relationships be balanced, truly honoring the rhythms and flows of women as well as men. Fear, we need to get to the root fear that holds men in such a stance of opposition to letting women in. Maybe men are also afraid of losing familiar roles. If men don't do the providing role and the dominant role, maybe they're afraid they don't matter? . . .

"Who am I without Gay? I told him the other day that who I am is totally interwoven with our relationship, and I don't know who I am otherwise. I realized yesterday that part of this time is for me to discover what it is to be alone, that I've always been with someone and defined by someone. . . .

"I need to become unshakable in my experience of my own worth and contribution and simply do that, which I have, and let the rest go because I really have no control over it anyway, I can't control how Gay feels or what he decides to do. . . .

"In the dream I was sitting on the carpeted floor and either cleaning my right toenails or just looking at them when a dozen or so worms of various kinds spilled out of the space between the flesh and the toenail, like emptying out. The dream was so vivid that I woke up, with a feeling of relief and almost awe that those had been in there all this time and I didn't know it, grateful that they were out. They were all different kinds and varieties and black and yellow and fat and tiny; totally gross like stomach turning and also new energy and the feeling that I'm not going to be sick now. Something too about my right toe, my right side, probably masculine, something rotting and decaying about my masculine or relationship to my masculine that has emptied out. Contempt comes to mind. . . .

"I'm reminded of the Hindu spiritual stages of building, sustaining, and destroying. We had been in a period of both building and sustaining for many years, and now it looks as if we are in a period of destroying the old structures and assumptions. I know I experience each day as a gift and an opportunity to expand my capacity to love and encompass more aspects of being truly human. The wave is just building, but I can feel it underneath the surface a little way off, the excitement of opening to new cycles of growth that can come from unexpected sources. Routine is ended, and each day brings choices and events from the universe that give me the expansion of essence and opportunity to choose truth and deeper levels of taking responsibility for each moment of life, to be awake. The task of training my mind to move out of its old ruts into some new paths is splitting my body into jagged raw fragments where some light emerges in gasps. . . .

"What is different about this from the typical midlife crisis? Seeing it as a gift and wake-up call is one choice that has made a big difference. Before I went to bed last night, I was thinking about the possibility of an unconscious cooperation on my part, with a deep holding on to his grandmother on Gay's part. I wondered if somehow I have continued to be like her for Gay so she isn't really dead. Gay has often said that my love reminds him of his grandmother's, that it's the only truly unconditional love he's experienced since her death. I wondered if I was becoming more like her or shaping my body to be somewhat like the way Gay remembers his grandmother and the vital love connection he felt with her. His grandmother had a soft and large body. She totally approved of Gay but expressed lots of anger and disapproval to almost everyone else. I had tried to lose weight for years and just couldn't seem to change a fundamental doughiness. I had meditated about being released from that deep holding so I could continue to unfold my own journey. Then I had the dream about the worms coming out of my toe. . . .

"I'm afraid we will fall into some old patterns; I still feel tender in the places that got twanged, and I feel a little roily sensation in my stomach that must be fear. I am excited to see Gay—he is very important to me—and I am assuming nothing right now about the next day or the next interaction. I know that I love Gay. I tap a deep clarity for me when I realize that I love Gay. I know that Gay loves me, and beyond that, I don't know. . . .

"I think this new emphasis on harmony in closeness and

harmony in individuation is a key, and I hear that Gay wants this evolution to happen in ways that are friendly to everyone and particularly that don't drain his bank account and cause him to live in a van down by the river. As I live on this edge, I seem to make close friends with fear every day, going deeper with each breath and discovering what to do each day as if I have no history. . . .

"I'm just having another set of waves of fear that I'll be alone and unloved, that deep alone and loneliness that I experienced as a child. I am still not totally friendly with being alone, I guess. Gay was saying that he has stepped into a new relationship, closer in some way to me, of absolute love, that he has absolute love for me. Any pulling back from loving me is just ego, that there is no question. And he said he can understand my feelings about being in my forties and fearing being no longer desirable, although he sees me as beautiful and more beautiful every day, that he can understand from the culture how I might feel and some of why I was so upset. And that that is not his problem, it's really my issue. He can't deal with my getting older; only I can do that. And I can't deal with his getting older; only he can do that. And we can honor each other in this journey. . . .

"So what about sex and sexuality? This issue seems to be about life-energy and the expression of life-energy. Whatever Gay decides—or I decide—at any point to do about our sexual feelings is something that we can honor in each other and just have to see what seems best to do. I can't control that, nor do I want to, although I do feel scared when I think of the possibility of Gay having a sexual relationship with another woman. Some base, some home base disappeared this spring in which I could rest and have deep space. Maybe that time is just over for now and evolving into something else. I feel some profound dumbness rolling through, where I can only say, 'I don't know.' The edge that not knowing provides is a daily lesson in the impermanence of life, that Gay could get hit by a bus, that I could drop out of the sky. . . .

"We started having sex, and it became really clear that the charge builds to a certain point, then my breathing goes on backward and the muscles in my belly tighten almost spasmodically. It reminds me of not being able to participate with pushing with my son Chris because of the caudal and because the doctor and nurses were saying, 'Don't push,' when I couldn't feel whether I was pushing or not. I had lots of tears and some new sensations began to open up in my pelvis, and I really appreciated being attended to and paid attention to so closely. . . .

"To declare our love complete in each moment is a new concept. To have love be the vehicle for going all the way in individual evolution is the new path. The usual temptation is to have love be a security blanket, a place to also go to sleep against the vast insecurities of life, a buffer against chaos. Most people get their mate and ignore or sidestep affairs or flirtations with others in order not to disrupt the buffer. To face into the attractions and use them to evolve consciousness, to learn from them, is my current challenge. . . .

"I want all my life-energy to be expressed, and I want all of Gay's life-energy to be expressed, to really celebrate who he is and the moment-to-moment unfolding of his essence. I can only tell the truth and continue to take responsibility. I can't separate my life from my being with Gay; that is my life, and what life gives me, I bless and use and dance with as far as I can. I want to fully honor my own intelligence—which is, if I don't move, I don't get it—and I want to come back home to fully honor the way my intelligence works and offer that to the world because that's what I love. I am a work in progress with legions of projects and pages and questions to share. If partners lived each day into a question, or questions, that could open a new breeze through the routine and things that need to be done. What question could best serve me today? How can I experience and express love and full responsibility in each moment today?

"I want total passion in my life again. I want Gay to look at me with passion, to grab me and want to ravish me. I don't want to be the perfect wife who has no sexual energy, whom Gay doesn't desire. I want him to tell me what he's feeling and wanting, and want to touch me and be close to me. I want to be fully celebrated for my magnificence and to have my continuing magnificence supported. I take a stand for expressing and supporting my full magnificence.

"After being in the grip of fear on and off during the day and falling into the void several times during the evening, I popped through into a new sense of peace and excitement about ten-thirty or so. I realized at a new body level that I am responsible for all my life, my interactions, and my energy level and interests and responses and creativity and feelings. In the morning Gay had asked me to focus on letting go of trying to control any aspect of his life. I think that started the refocusing of my energy and thoughts. I feel in charge of my own life and ready to take on the task of creating my future. . . .

"I wonder what new rhythms and container will be created out of this new wave of growth? I feel happy to have these projects, to have my close friends and allies that I've developed over the years, and to have the opportunity to step into this new space. Some of these experiences are fleeting, and I want to have the permanent, unshakable ongoing experience of joyful responsibility that weaves and cycles up my body with each breath and allows me to create magic with people when I work, by myself or in Gay's presence. I can blend so well and want to discover the firmness and definition of self, individual, resolution. Not will, or efforting, but flowing like a river of light that is so inviting that people just dive into their radiance and discover how to swim.

"The cellular program that drives me to compare is fused down in my cells, and it takes big medicine to bust it free. Ms. Disgusted Miserable Victim and Passionate Poet. I shifted into PP late last night in a conversation with Gay. To take total responsibility for my permanent embrace of PP, I need to take over the shift to flow rather than make Gay responsible and me reactive; to spot the places in life where I (and students) are reactive, where the world is doing something to me, or them. The feel of victim in the body for me is: limp, drained, tunnel vision, sadness that is not genuine but rather totally about self and being wronged and comparing in my mind while wringing out my chest. I had been stubbornly clinging to reacting to Gay, which cannot happen anymore. Well, I could try, but I would just bark the skin of my soul against his enormity, and I wouldn't stop him. . . .

"The pure excitement of consciousness and going all the way in this lifetime is the true impulse. I knew that by being with Gay I could have the best opportunity to go all the way in my evolution and possibilities. And I am truly grateful and feel blessed to have made that choice and have had this time. Whether it continues or not, I made the only choice that my soul could, given my longing to be fully human.

"There is some big rewiring to do in my pelvis, and Gay suggested looking at it as a one-year or ten-year project. Gay said yesterday that he realized, when he let himself feel sexual feelings for another woman, that he really didn't want to have actual genital sex with her. It was more like a whole-body energy experience that he wanted, and he felt that allowing himself to experience this feeling had already opened up his creativity. He said he didn't know whether that would always be true, but today that is so.

"We have the basis of deep friendship and caring, laughter and knowing each other's history and preferences. A deeper door can be opened by becoming whole in this deepest realm that I had really given up on years ago, as Gay gave up in his way. I had thought that sexual ecstasy was not possible and had rationalized that by focusing on what was possible and channeling my life-energy into our relationship and the work. I said what I want is to re-create our relationship from both of us being whole, and that my quest over the next period of time is to follow the impulses that will allow me to regain my wholeness. . . .

"I still feel regular waves of territoriality and anger at this disruption of my life, and I'm grateful for the impact and the aliveness I'm already experiencing. I imagine that part of the shock is having my base of reference so abruptly removed. When I look at Gay now, I see almost no sparks; I can't read the looks, which are so different. I can see that Gay's forehead is bunched, or that he looks turgid, but I don't know what that means. I really like not being labeled and judged and interpreted; I think the future lies in our new set of commitments. . . .

"I have huge blank spots where meaning used to live. A whiteout of meaning and association, and still I can be happy. I love doing what I do and don't know where that will take me. I discovered again yesterday that a withheld angry thought produces misery. I realized last night at the theater that I have been resisting the way things are. I had been hoping that if I just grit through this, that Kristin will disappear. When we were at the theater before the play started, Gay whispered something to her, and she whispered something back. My stomach dropped again, and I went crazy inside, got white-hot angry and wanted to get up and walk over them as I left. It must have reminded me of all the secrets in my family that never got communicated, how messages were indirectly delivered and delivered for someone else. And I didn't say anything in the theater, got to accepting the situation inside before acknowledging the anger out loud. When I finally got the anger out in the morning, I returned to feeling fine. . . .

Gay, meanwhile, was coming to his own realizations: "As I gave myself permission to feel all my feelings toward Kristin, I became clear that I did not really want a sexual relationship with her. Rather, part of me did, but most of me wanted to keep our relationship on a spiritual and friendship level. I got to this awareness by letting myself feel my sexual feelings for her without acting on them. After feeling them thoroughly over several weeks, they completely dissolved, replaced by an enthusiasm for her potential and a warm feeling of being a friend and supporter. I love her in some way that is unfamiliar to me. Now I can no longer imagine actually having physical sex with her, though I continue to find her radiantly beautiful and full of loving kindness.

"As I have gone deeper into all my feelings, I have discovered that this adventure was really about my relationship with my creativity. Kristin was a living representative of a young, wild, and free version of myself. Unconsciously, I felt this part of me was dying, replaced by the prosperous, worldly-wise father-figure who knew everything there was to know. In fact, during the peak of my sexual feelings for Kristin, I kept having a fantasy of driving off to California with her beside me in a VW bus, the same kind of bus I had sold shortly after I met Kathlyn. In the fantasy, loud music was throbbing through the speakers, and Kristin's curls were streaming in the wind. We would be happy and free and out of range of the fax machine. Apparently the latter device had become my metaphor for all the pressures of prosperity and fame.

"My Kristin adventure was a wake-up call, an opportunity to claim that wild creative energy that I was in danger of submerging. The questions became: 'Would I make a complete, turn-myself-inside-out commitment to the expression of my creativity? Or would I settle for the ease and comfort of resting on my laurels?' As I settled into these questions, I realized I had little choice. Of course I had to open up to the full expression of my creativity. Anything less would mean stultification and slow rust.

"Sitting at home in my study late one night, I made a pact with myself and the universe. From now on creativity would be my highest priority. I decided to turn myself over to its full expression through me. If my relationship with Kathlyn was humming with love and good energy, I would assume that my relationship with my creativity was good. If my relationship with her was feeling disharmonious, I would regard it as a symptom that I was out of harmony with my creativity. Everything began to shift in my body and spirit. I could feel an actual different set of sensations emerging. A fresh new field of energy began to pulsate in me, a new and vaster spaciousness than I had felt before. It was something I could feel and see at the same time. I felt a benign breeze coursing through my body, and it felt like it was outside me at the same time. Along with the breeze I could see more radiance and light inside me. Wherever I scanned, in my mind or body, I could see a backdrop of light. All the usual phenomena of my consciousness— my breathing, the beating of my heart, my thoughts—all took place against the screen of light and the sweet feeling of the breeze."

Kathlyn's journal reflects this growing sense of resolution: "What a day yesterday, wonderful play and making love with Gay for the first time in a couple of weeks, with feeling and contact and communication. 'It's so easy,' I said, to which he replied, 'Yes, when we're not in a trance.' That's 10 percent—let's go for 100 over the next five years or so. I can see the bass note that has been missing, why Gay would be so sexually frustrated and pulled to look elsewhere to open up to the sexuality that is a part of being human, that I had gotten jammed up and cross-wired. . . .

"At dinner last night Gay asked, 'Do you think that you can maintain your creativity by yourself now that you have access to it, without the underlying anxiety, if I should choose not to have a sexual relationship outside ours?' I said yes, that the anxiety had dropped off about two days ago. And I'm glad to have the opportunity, the timing, of going off to Europe for two weeks or so now to stabilize my own responsibility for my creativity.

"Actually turning my attention to supporting my life-energy stream has been like blowing up a marvelous new balloon that has pockets and turns I hadn't seen until I blew energy into them. I'm being carried along under the iridescent puffs of a cosmic clown, bouncing lightly over the possible gulleys in my old psyche and gathering momentum for flight. To find my family has been a sigh of gratitude. To recognize that I have always seen the world as a poet, playing with the images and possible meanings, the sliding proportions of absurdity and clear abundance from source. I am full of the delight of the panorama, the continual play of humanity.

"I spoke with Gay last night (from Amsterdam), who said that he is getting clearer and deeper into both his creativity and his commitment to me. I am very glad for this time by myself to deeply think and consider who I am and how to maintain and nurture my own creativity and still be with Gay. I don't know yet if the dying process has completed. I haven't burst into tears in about a week now. When I think of Gay, I'm aware of supporting and caring for him, and also supporting and caring for me. I am not pulled to let go of whatever I'm focused on when he comes through the room, and that is what I want to make unshakable during this period of time apart.

"I declare the end of focusing on dying. I want to focus on the beginning of things, the possibilities, listening for the creative urges as they occur to me and through me. I am now open for new business. I think I have drained the old anger and have no more that I can find now. I am available to know and express my anger as I feel it—to say, when I feel a blip, 'Tell the truth about it.' And I realize, as I become more and more grounded in telling the truth—catching the blip, and taking responsibility—that creativity is the natural result. Now there is the opportunity to create a new dance of absolute equality. What has replaced my devoted and chameleon personas is happiness and creativity. I appreciate Gay and what happens when we talk together and are together. The rest is waiting to be created over time."

The happy outcome of this major event in our lives has surprised even us. Both of us feel a deeper commitment to each other than we have ever felt. Both of us also feel an enhanced connection to our source of creativity. We were creatively productive before, but what has poured out of us since it occurred has been truly astonishing to us. Kristin remains in our lives as a friend, coworker, and confidante.

Says Kristin: "I am grateful to have learned that when I consistently speak the unarguable truth, I release an abundance of creative energy. My creativity grows exponentially. In communicating the truth in the moment, I let go of agendas, assumptions, and the illusion of control. That lets me allow the perfection of the universe to unfold. I also saw where I resist my own uprising energy, and that I had been requiring others to express less of their creative energy so that I could stay comfortable. I have now committed to being a space in which creativity blossoms in me and those around me."

Gay concludes: "What I see now is that Kristin was a huge reminder to me to keep my deep creative connection alive. It wasn't about sex or having a beautiful twenty-five-year-old attracted to me; it was about whether I was going to do whatever it took to keep the juicy, wild energy flowing through me. It was about whether I was going to be truly alive, or to cash in my chips and turn the rest of my life into a greatest hits album. I feel magnificently alive now, and I see Kathlyn surfing on the edge of that same wave of aliveness. To see the light of creativity and love flowing through her at a higher level, and to feel it in myself: That is the best of all possible outcomes."

SEVEN

Consciously Creating Abundance: Dealing with Money Issues

Clay is molded to make a pot,
but it is in the space where there is nothing
that the usefulness of the clay pot lies.

—*TAO TE CHING* (trans. VICTOR H. MAIR)

In our own relationship few things have created a bigger challenge than money. Neither of us comes from a wealthy family, and we were poor when we met. In the early days of our relationship, we struggled about money long and hard. Then we discovered a more enlightening way of approaching it, and our lives were changed for the better in a very short time. With some major shifts in our attitudes, plus some old-fashioned creativity and hard work, we went from poverty to financial independence in a fairly short time, by our standards.

When we first met, Kathlyn had about three thousand dollars in savings, most of which she used to move to Colorado. Gay was close to the bone, the most broke he had ever been. He says: "I was changing my life from top to bottom, from getting out of the relationship I was in, to changing the nature of my income-stream. I was relying more on writing and speaking and giving seminars and less on university-professoring for my income. As a result, I was in debt. Although I had a good feeling about what I was doing, I definitely hadn't begun to show any evidence that the new path worked. In fact, American Express had just repossessed my card because I had not paid them in two months."

From this beginning, as you can see, we had to do a lot of work on creating financial abundance. Now, after years of working on this area of our relationship, we almost never have any disharmony about money. That is not because we have more of it, either. To our surprise, we found that creating harmony about money had to come first. Then, with the freed-up energy we had been wasting in conflict, we were able to generate financial independence in a remarkably short period of time. We got to that point by making several crucial discoveries and taking some even more crucial actions. Resolving our money struggles was nothing like we thought it was going to be.

We discovered the hard way, through much trial and error, that having a healthy money supply is as much about metaphysics as it is about financial savvy. There are learnings in the spiritual arena that will do as much to generate financial well-being as any technical information. We would like to tell how we transformed our money issues, in hopes that it will be helpful to you in transforming yours.

Gay tells the story: "I had never considered the subject of creating financial harmony in my life until the winter of 1978, when I was in my early thirties. Until then I was simply making a living, trying to pay my bills, sometimes having a little left over. As often as not, I fell short at the end of the month and had to do some creative shuffling to make it all come out. It had certainly never occurred to me that I might design my own life in regard to financial abundance. One day a friend of mine, another psychologist, called to my attention that I had made a disparaging comment about wealthy people—I'd made a remark about how rich people were never happy. He pointed out that he had never heard me make such a comment before about any other category of people. It sounded odd to him, as if I were repeating some old family chestnut. I was definitely coming from a limiting point of view. He said that it might be keeping me poor, as well as limiting my effectiveness with my clients.

"I reflected on this feedback and concluded that I had a poverty mentality based on my past conditioning. I realized that I had never consciously chosen my own relationship with money. I had simply accepted the point of view of my family and their friends and was busily running my own life from a set of assumptions colored by the Roaring Twenties, the Crash of '29, the Great Depression, and other cataclysms that I had never experienced. For me, this realization was like the cartoon moment when a lightbulb flashes on above the hero's head as he smacks himself on the forehead. I was on my exercise bike when this flash of enlightenment occurred, and my pulse rate and pedal speed probably doubled in the grip of my enthusiasm. I saw that I was free to choose my own money-consciousness, and that this choice might affect the outer circumstances of my life! I made a choice in that moment, to mount a deep inquiry into my money-attitudes and to select new ones that reflected my own values.

"The first thing I did was to confront my conditioning. What were my limiting beliefs about money and wealth? Where had they come from? There were several obvious sources. I was raised primarily by my grandmother, who placed great value on being poor but proud. It seemed likely that I had absorbed some of this attitude just from being around her. She came from an aristocratic southern family who had gotten on the wrong side of the Civil War. After the war they were penniless. My grandmother put a high value on security. My favorite story and hers, which she probably told me a hundred times as a child, was 'The Three Little Pigs.' 'Build your house on solid ground' was her great motto.

Looking back, I feel deep gratitude for this advice, which has kept me focused on the essentials in my career and personal relationships.

"Then there was my mother. My grandmother and my mother were so different that I wondered how they managed to be from the same family. My grandmother hated smoking; my mother was a chain-smoker. My grandmother was soft and warm and a great cook; my mother was tough as nails and used the kitchen primarily as a place to put her papers and typewriter. Their common point of contact, though, was in the deep grief that both of them harbored about their various losses. My mother, in particular, had a great deal of bitterness about being left destitute by my father's death. But in addition to the real-life financial obstacles she faced, she had attitudinal barriers that were at least as important.

"My mother was a dynamic, brilliant woman who had a number of maddening personal characteristics. She took great pride in being a bastion of poor, hardworking decency in a world of 'fat cats' and 'spongers.' She had a great many opportunities to prosper from her talents as a writer, yet she seemed to go out of her way to keep them from materializing. On one occasion she wrote a book-sized history of central Florida, only to refuse the offered payment for it. My brother and I were dumbfounded that she would do a year of work for nothing, on the principle that 'it wouldn't look right' to take the money. On another occasion, she refused to take money from the government's soil bank program for a fallow watermelon field she owned. My brother and I fervently wished she had taken the money, for over the next ten years we had to endure several hundred variations of the story of how the 'fat cats' in Washington had wanted to pay her for not growing watermelons. Even though I rebelled against her attitudes at the time, I now realize that I was soaking them up as well.

"When I went back further into my history, I uncovered an even bigger piece of the puzzle. The only wealthy person in the history of my family was my grandmother's uncle Jimmy, who had owned a furniture factory before the Civil War. A patriotic southerner, he turned his furniture factory into a munitions factory for the rebel side. When the smoke cleared, practically everything was wiped out. The equation: Wealth equals loss plus defeat. To complicate this equation, my grandparents fought about a related issue on and off for the sixty-plus years of their marriage. My grandfather had been a hardworking but penniless man when he married my grandmother. Uncle Jimmy had stepped in with the money to build a house for them, the house they lived in for the next sixty years. The house became something of a monument to my grandfather's ineptness at earning money, and all it took to start a skirmish between them was a sneer on my grandmother's part about 'who this house really belongs to.'

"As I evaluated all of this, I realized that I came from a long history of completely impoverished attitudes about money. The underlying ethic was healthy: Work hard. But it was weighted down with enough negative baggage to make it come out more like: Work hard, and you'll just barely keep the wolf from the door; be proud, be poor, and above all don't be like those filthy rich people. When I examined each of these attitudes, I saw that I could stand some improvement in most of them. I liked being proud and working hard, but I was definitely no longer interested in being poor or harboring grudges against rich people. So one night I sat down on the floor of my (small and sparsely furnished) apartment and asked myself how I would like my life to be in regard to money.

"After an hour of mulling it over, I formed several conscious choices. I decided that I wanted my overall wealth-attitude to be: *I always have plenty of money to do everything I want to do.* When I really reflected on it, wealth meant one key thing to me: freedom. If I had plenty of money, I could go wherever I wanted, send my daughter to any school she chose, live where I wanted. Other than freedom, I could think of no other compelling reason to have plenty of money. I didn't really care about owning a fine house or a fancy car or a portfolio of stocks (although I have acquired such things over the years), but freedom was and still is crucial. Even though I live in much better circumstances now than I did back then, Kathlyn and I have miraculously managed to increase our wealth and responsibilities without any sacrifice of freedom. In fact, I feel much freer now than I did over a decade ago, when I began the process.

"From this foundation I added several other details. First, I wanted my money life to be simple and easy. I didn't want to spend much time looking after it. Then I developed a specific goal: that I would have enough money to go without working for at least a year if I so desired. With this shift in attitude, I began the process of transforming my life so that material abundance was part of it.

"When I met Kathlyn, I'd been living with these goals for a few years, but I had not tried them out in partnership. It was one thing to be completely responsible for my own money, quite another to combine finances and money-beliefs with another person. I wanted to bring her into the game, so I explained to her how my attitudes had shifted and asked if she would be willing to join me in a mutual goal toward complete financial abundance and the enjoyment of it. This request provoked a big yes! followed shortly by a bundle of big fears. It turned out that Kathlyn had to confront as many limiting programs from the past as I did, although they were of a different nature. She had been more of a sixties activist and hippie than I had, so she had to confront ideological issues such as 'How can I be rich in a world where so many are going without?' She had personal ghosts from the past to clear up too. Her parents, though now very comfortable financially, were children of the Great Depression. These attitudes had instilled a contraction in Kathlyn around the subject of money. She and I shared the script of 'always living on the edge' of poverty, and sure enough, each month we played it out.

"In several conversations we came to an agreement that we would mutually confront our limiting money-programs as allies, not as enemies. We made a conscious commitment not to fight any more about money. We agreed to channel the energy that we had wasted in money arguments into deep inquiries into our personal issues that held us back. This decision was important, because the energy that is eaten up by money conflicts in relationships is awesome. That same energy can be redirected in the service of mutually determined goals, if both people are willing to take responsibility for creating abundance and to put their personal money-programs up for scrutiny. That's a big if, though. As I know from years of counseling couples, many people would rather be right than happy and prosperous. Looking back, I feel a deep heart-tug of appreciation for Kathlyn and her willingness to put everything on the line. She was always willing to examine her beliefs about herself and the world, and to trade those beliefs in for new ones that seemed like better ideas.

"The key to beginning was: 'Take charge of designing your own money script. Think it up the way you want it, and consciously choose it.' As soon as Kathlyn and I made the commitment, the means began to suggest themselves. I have often found that commitment starts the creativity flowing. If your goal is big, you won't know how to get there at first. But if you pay attention, the path will start to reveal itself. Among the goals we chose was a specific one, which seemed outrageously high at the time: We wanted to have ten thousand dollars in cash savings. To give you an idea how fast the principles in this chapter worked for us, the next time we sat down to choose specific goals, about two years later, we set a hundred thousand as our stretch-goal for our savings account. A few years later we had attained this and had upped our stretch-goal to $1.2 million.

"Shortly after Kathlyn and I made the commitment to our financial abundance, certain thoughts popped into my mind. The thoughts were of a man I'll call James who had loaned me money many years before. At first I didn't know why my memories of him were surfacing. Then one day I saw clearly why, and this insight had life-changing consequences for my material well-being.

"I realized I was having these thoughts because they represented broken agreements on my part. James, who was my boss, had loaned me money at a time when I really needed it. In 1970 I had borrowed $240 from him to cover tuition to finish my master's degree. Shortly after I took my degree, James and I got into a conflict. I wanted to move to a different job, but he wanted me to continue working for him. I had my usual self-righteous attitude about his wrongness, and I used my anger at him to justify not paying him back. This event had lain completely buried in my mind for fifteen years! Through some detective work I located him in New England. He had fallen on hard times and was living in a small room at a YMCA. I wrote him of my transformation and sent him a check. His grateful response was deeply moving. It allowed me to see a part of him I'd never touched before.

"I also surfaced memories of another man, John, a kind soul with a lot of money who had approached me after seeing a therapy demonstration I did in the mid-seventies. He asked me if there was any way he could support my work, and I blurted out that he could loan me $750 to help me fix up a building, which would become the first Hendricks Institute. He did, we opened, and in the busyness of the next couple of years, I only saw him a few times. Then he moved out of town and disappeared from view. Since I was not able to find him to pay him back, I decided on an alternative: I sent donations to charitable organizations I thought he might support.

"Very shortly I came across a book called *Seed Money in Action* by Jon Speller. This remarkable little book describes a completely new type of tithing, one that fit our 'lead with gratitude' philosophy. The old idea of tithing is to take a tenth of what you earn and give it away. The book's one main point is that each of us can begin the flow of abundance by becoming a philanthropist. The instructions are very simple: Set aside a specific amount of money each week or month, and donate it consciously to a charity, church, or cause you support. Send your money out into the world with the idea that the more you give away, the more you get back. Then you will have more to give away. The book recommends that you send the money with the thought that you will receive tenfold in return. You are 'leading with gratitude,' making the first move, instead of waiting to get before you give. It is a subtle shift, but one that engages a new physics, or metaphysics, in your life. You are saying, 'I'm now going to participate in the world as a source of philanthropy.' You become an initiator of abundance rather than a consumer, proactive rather than reactive.

"The amazing thing is: It works! I've taught this now to many people, and nobody who's tried it out has ever argued with it or reported less than great success. The only people who argue with it are people who haven't tried it. I did my first experiment with fifty dollars, which I sent to an organization that plants trees in areas where desert is encroaching. Interestingly, I totally forgot about the project until a month later, when I received five hundred dollars from an unexpected source. When I told Kathlyn, she said, 'Looks like the project is working.'

" 'What project?' I asked. She laughed, and pointed to the copy of the little book sitting on the edge of my desk. I stared dumbfoundedly at the book and the check for five hundred dollars, then I got it, and we both laughed.

"As we practiced this concept on an ongoing basis, the numbers grew larger until we were 'leading with gratitude' to the tune of thousands rather than fifty dollars each month when we would sit down for our philanthropy meeting. As of this writing, our most recent month saw us with over sixteen thousand dollars for dispersal. I had lunch on the West Coast recently with a former student who had learned this process well and had used it to manifest several million dollars. He was now giving away a third of his income every year, yet he was seeing his net worth grow at the same time.

"The key, which Kathlyn and I use every month of our lives, is: 'Make a conscious commitment to philanthropy, act on it, and open up to having a backdraft of abundance come your way.'

"In summary, I can see three main transformations which have generated financial abundance in my life:

1. *Realizing that I could choose consciously my own relationship to money.* This step involved confronting my programming and replacing it with ideas more congenial to my own

values. When Kathlyn and I chose to quit fighting about money and rechannel that energy into productivity, our prosperity began to increase rapidly.

2. *Clearing up incompletions from the past.* This step involved much soul-searching and looking for places where we had broken agreements or had left something unsaid. The action steps—completing whatever needed to be completed—always brought a fresh burst of life-energy and a new wave of abundance.

3. *Becoming a conscious philanthropist.* This step is an ongoing practice of sending money out into the world with the intention of creating harmony while prospering all concerned, including ourselves."

We have managed to create a life of abundance and satisfaction without ever making a budget or doing many of the usual things that people do to become financially independent. Instead, we have relied on consciousness-shifts and key spiritual principles to generate money-harmony. May these ideas work as well for you!

CLEARING MONEY ENTANGLEMENTS FROM PAST RELATIONSHIPS

Many people use an attachment to a past relationship in order to avoid intimacy in the present. During our first year together, we confronted this issue in ourselves, and found that a combination of psychospiritual and material-world shifts needed to be made in order to move through this pattern.

From Gay's perspective: "I was very surprised to find out how much the material attachments played a role in my difficulty letting go of the past relationship. Being a psychologist, I tend to deal with relationship problems by using psychological techniques like getting in touch with my feelings, expressing them clearly, inquiring into my childhood programming, and so forth. It often doesn't occur to me to look at more obvious areas like real estate. I found, though, that it is often a combination of inner and outer attachments that keeps us hooked to the past.

"During my first year with Kathlyn, I would find myself thinking about my previous lover during our times of intimacy. Sometimes these were sexual thoughts and feelings; other times I would feel anger or sadness come up. I began to notice, though, that they would frequently come up when I was moving closer to Kathlyn. I realized that I was using the unfinished business from the previous relationship as a distancing mechanism with Kathlyn. I began to ask myself an important healing question: 'What do I need to do to complete that relationship so I can be fully available to Kathlyn?' After I began living with that question, a flood of insights came.

"One big insight was that I had a number of withheld feelings and secrets that I had never shared with my previous lover. The idea came to me that I could be free of her only when I became willing to tell the full truth to her. So I swallowed hard, picked up the phone, and called her. First, I told her about my insight, then I asked her if she would be willing to meet with me for the purpose of completing our relationship so both of us could be free to move on. She said she would, so we got together over three different meetings and poured out all the stuff, trivial and significant, that we had withheld from each other. This included sexual flirtations, money secrets, and everything else we could dredge up from five years of a stormy relationship.

"I found these meetings helpful in reducing the number of thoughts and feelings about her, but after a couple of months, I still found them running through my mind and body from time to time. I called a friend of mine and asked his advice. Since he is a fellow psychologist, I expected him to perform some mental move on me that made me feel better. Instead, he asked: 'Do you own any real estate together?' I burst out laughing, because I had completely overlooked the obvious place we were still entangled. She and I owned a house together, and as soon as he asked about real estate, I could see that this was a source of a lot of strain. I had never liked the house in the first place and did not like owning it now. She didn't like my owning a part of it either. It was a security thing for her; she liked the idea of owning the house outright. But we were both attached to it for all the wrong reasons. I didn't want to let go of the equity (my share being about $25,000), and she didn't have money enough to buy me out. In fact, she had lamented that she only had $3,000 of the needed money to buy me out, so we had dropped the subject long ago. I had resigned myself to owning a house I didn't want with someone I didn't want to be in partnership with. She felt the same way, so it was a setup for misery all the way around.

"I asked my friend for his advice. 'Walk away,' he said. 'Take the $3,000 or whatever she's comfortable with, give her the house, and move on. You'll make a contribution to her happiness and well-being, and you'll collect at least $22,000 worth of psychic energy out of the deal.' I found myself holding my breath when he said all this. One part of me thought it was the most ridiculous idea I'd ever heard. I had about four hundred dollars to my name, and it was hard to conceive of giving away what seemed like a fortune. Another part of me knew he was absolutely right. After I hung up, I went downstairs and tried the idea out on Kathlyn. I was afraid she would go into contraction with the idea of giving away what constituted my only tangible asset. Instead, she lit up and immediately agreed that it was the best thing to do. I called my previous lover and told her I would be willing to give her the house free and clear for $3,000. She was dumbfounded: 'What's the catch?' 'No catch,' I said, and explained the shifts that had led up to the decision. There was a long pause, during which I could almost hear the implications sinking in, then she agreed.

"Kathlyn and I both see this decision as a crucial turning point in our becoming close. With this energy-drain out of the way, we had much more energy to focus on building what we wanted to create. The principles I drew on were authenticity, generosity, and gratitude. I used authenticity to clear out the debris from my closet of unexpressed withholds, then expressed my gratitude to my previous partner by giving her much more than she asked for. In practical reality, this move created an enormous 'backdraft' of abundance. Within a year I had bounced back financially from the schism with my previous partner and was well on my way to an expanding life of material well-being with Kathlyn."

Kathlyn had her own money entanglements to clear up. At the beginning of our relationship, one of the big struggles on a monthly basis was whether or not her ex-husband was going to send the $125 a month he was supposed to send in support of Chris, age twelve. He came through less than half the time, and often it required many phone calls, broken agreements, and promises to do better next time. It was an enormous inconvenience, because we really relied on that extra bit of money each month to make ends meet.

Kathlyn tells the story: "I grew up during the fifties and sixties in the Betty Crocker era, where clean sheets and sparkling dinnerware signaled the apex of feminine achievement. Although I had read *The Feminine Mystique* and *The Second Sex,* the forces of the surrounding culture loomed like the skyscrapers of true womanly identity.

"I mention this as a prelude to the situation I faced in 1981, when my son was twelve. I had been divorced from his father for eleven years and had run through the child-support maze, finally getting an award of $100 a month. To secure this sum (which I felt lucky to negotiate in 1969), I often had to make several calls to my ex-husband each month, cajoling and threatening. At one point I triumphed in a court appearance and had the monthly amount raised to $125. In spite of my efforts, he actually made the payments on an average of three months out of twelve.

"During the Battle for Child Support, I had completed my bachelor's, master's, and Ph.D. degrees, while practicing many years of work as a movement therapist. I had designed in-service presentations for hospitals and conferences, conducted workshops and trainings, and taught on the faculty of my graduate school. Those accomplishments seemed to exist in another, more benign world from the Battle, which had a separate set of beliefs and ground rules. Although I was very successful in the rest of my life, I seemed completely disempowered in the area of getting child support, and it became a chronic irritating feature of my life.

"I discovered this parallel world one day when Gay suggested that I fire Chris's father from his apparently reluctant role as provider. When I considered not asking for or expecting child support from him, I immediately became rather light-headed and started coughing. In my professional work and in my own commitment to growth, I had discovered that deeply honoring my experience was the most effective path to change and problem solving. But it was often much easier to see where clients were stuck than to hold up the mirror to my own life. In this moment I surrendered my mind to let my body speak directly. I breathed consciously, moved freely, and let the awarenesses pour forth. Rather than defending my point of view, I actively inquired into what my body was telling me.

"As I let my awareness rest on these symptoms and started wondering what they might mean, I uncovered a moth-eaten but entrenched set of beliefs. Here's a sample of the motley assortment that spilled out of the recesses of my mind:

- Women aren't supposed to provide; men are.
- I'm supposed to support the relationship between my son and his father, even if neither of them does.
- He means well—give him another chance.
- He's the only father Chris has.
- If you can't say something nice . . .
- On the other hand, life is hard work, and you should be grateful for any money that he provides out of his goodwill for his son.
- If I provide for Chris, it means that I'm outdoing his father,

which then means that I am shaming him and setting a bad example for the next generation of providers—that is, Chris.

"As I actually looked at my beliefs and feelings, I realized that I had been angry for years: not only at having to grovel for a below-subsistence level of financial support, but at the system of beliefs and blinders that had shaped my dependence. As I scythed through the ancient thicket of these vines, I uncovered a very painful truth. Years before, I had confused my anger at Chris's father with my seeing and supporting of Chris. I had accumulated a stack of grievances that had slowly clouded my ability to see Chris clearly and separately from his father, whose mannerisms he echoed with precision even though they had been separate for eleven years. When I saw his father's gait and expressions in Chris's body, I felt more respect for genetics in the nature-versus-nurture debate.

"I also reluctantly saw that I maintained a stance of victim in relationship to the whole battle. My view that his father didn't really care for Chis seemed verified at several points over the years. For example, on the one occasion that I had sent Chris to visit for a week, he returned with a broken wrist, a souvenir of a fall while hiking. I entered another notch on my victim chart.

"It was very difficult to look at the payoffs for continuing to expect that monthly check. I did not want to let go of the anger tickets I would regularly cash in by yelling at Chris about some shiftless and irresponsible behavior. I did not want to admit that I got additional martyr status on the occasions that I would let my women friends know that I was only receiving $125 a month and never more than a few times a year. 'You're a wonder and a saint,' they would exclaim, while referring to him as 'that bastard,' as I tucked my head humbly. And most difficult, I didn't want to see that I had limited Chris's possibilities by confining him in my belief box. Given my anger, he really couldn't have a relationship with his father. He had to be loyal to his father as long as I held the position that he was a jerk (never verbally, of course). And he couldn't form a bond with his stepfather, Gay, without resolving his relationship with his father. Above all, I got to be in *control* of my dismal little fiefdom, holding Chris's affections hostage with my anger and righteousness.

"To make matters juicier, I had my own stack of financial myths. Our family, like many, had Great Depression stories that I had heard many times while growing up and that had shaped my views about abundance and resources. The specter of scarcity, although never physically present in my childhood, continued to haunt my psyche. My brain immediately translated any fluctuation in my therapy practice as a straight slide to the gutter and starvation. I would be foolish to let go of my one stable source of income. (Oh, how the mind works!) Only with days of conscious facing and accepting could I begin to see that I was hanging Chris's and my future on this slender thread.

"After wading and hacking through these emotional brambles for several days, I decided to take a leap into the unknown. I took a deep breath and sat down to write a letter in which I fired Chris's father from any further financial responsibility, including monthly checks, medical insurance, and educational support. I edited the letter carefully to be sure that I did not speak from blame or burden and to actually release his father from any unwilling obligation he might hold toward Chris. I added that I was stepping out of the role of mediator and controller in their relationship. Any contact and relationship was up to them.

"When I mailed the letter, I felt both exhilarated and blank. What would take the place of the large swamp I had just emptied? Could I really take full responsibility for our financial well-being (and still be feminine)? I realized that I had continued the struggle rather than step into the unknown. The familiarity of feeling like a victim was comfortable. The possibility of creating abundance was not, and I was surprised by my inner roiling sensations. I spent many days breathing and opening up to a new version of myself where responsibility could engender flow and joy rather than burden and worry. I think now that the key was dreaming up a larger version of myself than I had thought either possible or realistic. To do that, I needed to jettison the anchor of the past. There's an old saying that in order to become who you really are, you need to let go of the old version.

"Over the next several weeks, I became aware of a sense of ownership that I hadn't experienced in my adult life up until then, a spacious peacefulness that may have been the beginning of self-respect. One vibrant memory stands out from the first few months. When I had enough money to get health insurance for Chris and me, I called my best friend with great excitement. I could begin to understand the satisfaction of the provider, and the balance that owning my resourcefulness was accessing.

"During a walk one day, I realized that I had attached my abundance hose to a small outlet and then spent years complaining about the amount of flow. When I let go of that small version of possibility, I began to open to the magical resources of the universe and the rivers and oceans of flow that could carry me toward my deepest dreams.

"The next year my income doubled; the year after it tripled. Ever since I made the decision to take responsibility for Chris's and my financial well-being, I have had the means to do exactly what I want and need to do and to provide for Chris to explore his martial arts passion and his university education without going into debt.

"The renewal of Chris's relationship with his biological father would have been a great happy ending. What actually occurred over ten years was both painful and freeing. To the best of my knowledge, Chris has never received as much as a phone call or a postcard from his father since 1981. Finally, after years of reaching out, Chris finally closed the door and went on with life.

"A much sweeter result was the flowering of Chris's relationship with Gay. Chris and he became best buddies, and Gay formally adopted him a few years later. Freed from my unconscious requirement that he continue to echo his father's beliefs and lifestyle, he began to reach out to Gay in touching ways. He could finally see that Gay was available for him and deeply interested in his life and what he wanted. Many times I would come home and find them deep in discussion about some philosophical point, or making fart jokes while playing croquet. This filled me with enormous gratitude. People meeting them for the first time now say, 'Chris, you look so much like your father.' "

PART THREE

THE CONSCIOUS HEART IN ACTION

Twenty-one Lessons on the Path

As we open the conscious heart of relationship, we encounter new potentials every day. Once we made the master commitment to allow our relationship itself to be our primary teacher, we have never had a dull moment together. We have had moments charged with the full range of feeling, from grief and anger to ecstasy, but these experiences have always carried learnings that were just what we needed to know at the time. In Part Three we would like to present some of the most important lessons we have learned as we've ridden these waves in our relationship and seen others take off on their own magnificent surf-journeys.

We have organized this material around common problems and issues that come up in close relationships. We often ask couples who are in relationship struggles, "What would you be doing with your energy if you weren't involved in this conflict?" Here we report on what we've learned.

1/Finding Balance

The Cirque du Soleil is a fantastic surreal circus whose performers have so mastered the art of balance that they take it into another dimension. In a recent performance one man walked backward up a pole with his body straight out horizontally. We admire and enjoy the strength and balance that makes such optical treats possible. But we don't spend a lot of time thinking about the hours of practice necessary to achieve a single moment of perfect balance.

People often don't appreciate or tolerate the hours of practice that make a balanced relationship possible. What is balance in a relationship? Is it simply dividing up the tasks, qualities, and roles?

Most of us pick partners who are not just like us but complement us. Then we spend the next years and decades trying to change them into ourselves. What would it look like to support balance, both in ourselves and in our partners?

Balance can be cultivated by deliberately going off-balance and then recovering, falling into your relating with trust that truth or love will catch you. Commentators for the 1996 Olympic gymnastics events in Atlanta often mentioned that a performer lost balance because he or she was too cautious. Contrary to what you might expect, the gymnast who held back from hurtling into the unknown was often the one who wobbled or fell. Balance does not mean clinging to your position until death pries your fingers away. When you let go of a conviction, especially being right, the load lightens. You dump ballast to ride higher on the waves of relating. Most of us have too much ballast, not too little.

Attaining balance means opening to opposites, eating and digesting opposites in yourself so you don't expect your partner or the world to take on that function for you. For example, someone who doesn't know what she wants might squander her creative skills by imagining what her partner wants or what *he* thinks she wants. She could tie up her creative energies further by evaluating whether he is meeting her vague and unformed expectations. Even if she focuses on a virtue, like giving, and consciously gives her time and skills and attention to those who need them—but doesn't look at giving to herself or receiving from others—that imbalance puts a strain on the relationship. It's like being on a seesaw with one end heavily weighted. No flow between opposites can occur. Couples can create a continuum by appreciating their opposites, by owning the fluctuation between opposites of yes and no, powerful and powerless, do and don't.

Anytime you feel stuck, your experiential seesaw may be weighted. You may not realize that you have options to rebalance it. You can ask, "What is the opposite quality from this experience?" It's probably something you see in your partner that you either resent or envy. If your complaint is about your partner's messiness, for example, you may not be giving yourself enough free unstructured time or play time. If you envy your partner's articulateness or grasp of ideas, try using the energy you are putting into that envy to develop those skills in yourself.

When you actually see life through your partner's eyes and take a few steps on his or her path, you begin to re-own the polarities of separation. List in your mind the qualities of your partner that differ from yours, both positive and gratingly negative. Here's a sample list:

- My partner is much smarter than me.
- My partner is the messiest person I've ever met.
- My partner is never on time.
- I'm the disciplinarian. My partner is just mush around the children.
- My partner lets me do all the talking and never speaks up, especially in social gatherings.
- My partner couldn't balance a checkbook if death were the consequence for failure.
- My partner is the creative one in this family.
- I'm the feeler, and my partner is the thinker.
- I'm the provider, and my partner is the homemaker.

Now take a moment and breathe. Flex your body to actually try each of your partner's qualities on yourself, as if you were putting on a new outfit. Take on the body posture of messiness or being the provider. Spend five minutes doing a daily task from your partner's perspective. What does life look like from that viewpoint?

All polarities are invitations to balance, invitations to step out onto the tightrope and find your way to the other side. Liz Barrow, a single parent, gave us an example of how ten-year-old Asa helped her regain balance:

"In our family some of our best conversations happen while we are riding in our van. Asa and I were recently discussing anger as we headed downtown to do an errand. A couple of days earlier, I had accused him of trying to control me with his anger, the way his dad used to do. Asa said that he had been thinking about my comment and believed I was mistaken. He didn't personally feel he was trying to control me. He was just angry and expressing himself appropriately. Asa thought that perhaps I was responding to his anger by imagining he was trying to control me, then behaving defensively. He suggested that I was responsible for my reaction. He then wondered if I had taken a similar approach to his dad's anger. All this from a ten-year-old! I could feel in my body the truth of his words, and I thanked him. I could see how I had been casting myself in the role of martyred anger recipient, and I stopped. I now give him the space he needs to be angry and don't feel the need to take a position about it."

2 / Cultivating Curiosity

❧

The moment we invoke curiosity and wonder, our perception
changes. We stop thinking we already know or should know
and begin wondering about the issue at hand. The need for perfection dissolves, and we suddenly have free movement, meeting each
moment as an open-eyed, full-breathing being. A question asked
from genuine curiosity has no sharpness; wonder takes the edge
away.

In curiosity there are more verbs than objects. I wonder what
something is about—I am curious about it. Curiosity is a set of
actions, not a static thing: I explore, I turn things over, I turn
myself over to look differently, to breathe into the ribs of my
"curiousing."

If I'm curious, I don't automatically label things and their functions. I haven't already decided what this thing can be used for, how it might benefit me, who this person really is, or how it all fits together. I give myself time to look at it from different angles, to toss the question up in the air and not even know if it will come down again. Keeping the ball in the air keeps the game in play. The famous children's character Curious George got into some predicaments out of his curiosity, but they were also exhilarating adventures.

Everyone has senses, but each of us registers, processes, and communicates them through a unique nervous system. Everyone has the same feelings, but not all of us cooperate with them, listen carefully to them, or do our best to express the sounds that match their momentary vibration. That's what poets do, or any artist in her medium. Everyone can be an artist expressing life as it flows through their mind, heart, and gut. We can be touched by life and want to touch back.

It may be that people are taught to rein in their curiosity to preserve social decorum. Little ones forage in the world to discover the names of things, many of which automatically go into the mouth. As adults, we still need to take data in and surround it with some sense to continue feeding our curiosity.

In a relationship interpretation dampens curiosity. When we assume and don't clarify, meanings get stuck together over time. For example, a certain look from your partner may get stuck to the thought, "Oh, she's mad again. I'll withdraw to the garage and work on the car." Being genuinely curious about your partner means letting him or her get right up under your defenses to look, smell, and taste, just to be there, just to keep the moment fresh.

When I'm not curious, I make myself all-knowing. I assemble a box labeled "you," and I keep dumping items into it. I organize you, I assemble a coherent inventory of you that I can reproduce in my mind: "You like these colors, you sleep on the right side of the bed, you don't like your sauces to touch the rest of the food on the plate, you have your coffee black, you don't like action movies." I assume that I know what your gestures mean and where your sentences are going. I have already heard everything you have to say. "Now I am safe," I think—"I cannot be surprised by you." At that fateful point where I complete my assembly, I assume that that's all you are. I close the lid and sit on the box so that none of my collection gets loose. How can I move into curiosity from already knowing everything? Genuine curiosity opens the box.

In a recent workshop Gay said that he doesn't like tomatoes, except fried green ones. A participant asked, from a place of genuine curiosity, where Gay learned to love fried green tomatoes. As Gay told the story of his southern grandmother's special green-tomato preparation, his loving relationship with her came alive to everyone listening. We could almost smell the cornmeal and frying tomatoes and see her bustling about in her apron. The curiosity of one workshop participant brought forth this rich moment.

Comparison kills curiosity. Most people compare what they are looking at to a preexisting concept and keep what already makes sense and throw out what doesn't. But as a relationship deepens, the partners need to set aside comparison—and its companions, judgment, criticism, and evaluation—and cultivate an attitude of curiosity toward each other. There is a difference between "I know" and "I know that already." "I know" is a full-body experience, the experience of vibrating in alignment with what your partner is feeling or how perfectly still the air is. But "I know that already" is a mental construct—one that may have little to do with the current reality.

Curiosity can also heal. Recently, a woman in therapy with us was struggling with her perceptions of men. As a result of childhood sexual abuse, she had come to view men as either "nice" or "sexual." The "nice" men were those who didn't want anything from her. The "sexual" men wanted something, but they often disguised themselves as "nice" and *then* aggressed. She consumed a lot of mental energy trying to determine if a given man was genuinely "nice" or was simply being nice to her so he could get something sexual from her. During one of our first sessions, she saw a twinkle in Gay's eye. Her mental filter immediately kicked in: "I know that look already; he looks nice, but he's really sexual and wants something from me." Between sessions she ruminated about Gay's intentions, which soon gave her a headache.

This woman's courage taught us to be curious. In the next session, rather than withhold her questions and concerns, she asked Gay whether he was sexually attracted to her. He thought for a moment and then gave her a full account of his feelings: "When I tune in to my body, I notice some sexual feelings for you, although I don't have any desire to act on them or do anything about them. You're not exactly my type, so even if we were two single people meeting for the first time, I probably wouldn't pursue a sexual relationship with you."

We suggested that she be curious about her sexual feelings, not just for Gay but all the time. As she shifted from defensiveness to curiosity, she began to lighten up, move more, breathe more deeply. She really hadn't seen the possibility that a man could be both "nice"—not want anything sexually from her—and "sexual," that is, have sexual feelings coursing through his blood along with oxygen and iron. Her curiosity allowed her to begin to unravel her early experience. Her relationship with Gay shifted so that she could trust him and use his feedback to help create a new map about men.

When we're curious, we can reinvent our world. Old wounds don't have to continue to poison the present. The real safety is seeing the world as it is; then we can let go of assumptions and mental constructs that no longer fit. Curiosity opens the door to playfulness and spontaneous joy.

3 / When a Troublesome Pattern Repeats

꧁꧂

When patterns repeat, they tend to become automatic, and we stop wondering about how essence can be expressed right now. We box ourselves and our partners in by already knowing the next gesture or sentence. A while back Dan, a client, said that he would feel so much better if Sylvia wouldn't always walk twenty steps ahead of him. For years they had repeated an interaction that looked like this:

- They leave a restaurant or movie, and Sylvia starts walking fast.
- Dan feels hurt and has critical thoughts about her, which he withholds.

- Sylvia feels that something is wrong but can't pinpoint it.
- Dan criticizes her later about something else.
- Sylvia gets angry.
- Their closeness decreases.
- They each feel separate and lonely.

Usually if a troublesome pattern repeats more than twice, we recommend that both partners take a look at their role in it. It does little good to ask your partner to change something if you do not look carefully at how you might be inviting or contributing to the pattern.

Sylvia added some history. At first she'd say, "Come on, let's walk together," she told us. But after several exchanges in which Dan accused her of trying to control him and criticized her speedy pace, she stopped inviting him and just walked at the speed she wanted to walk. She realized she'd given up and had closed the doors on any possibility of change in this area: "That's just the way we are, I guess."

In this session Dan was visibly upset, so we focused on his process. What meaning had he attached to her walking speed? we asked. After a moment he said that he felt rejected and angry when she didn't walk with him. As we explored what he was actually experiencing in his body, he discovered that his anger almost always covered fear. He fueled himself with anger (as did Sylvia) rather than be present with his deep fear. But focusing on what was unarguably true about his experience of the walking interaction showed him that he was deeply afraid that Sylvia didn't care about him.

We asked, "If Sylvia doesn't care about you . . ."

He replied, "I'll die."

Underlying a seemingly trivial incident of different walking paces was the fear of death. We must get in the habit of mining the richness of troublesome patterns rather than engage in cycles of criticism and retreat.

Using a technique we call "Separating the Boxes," we asked

Dan to designate one hand his "I'm afraid I'm going to die" hand. He picked his right. His left hand was designated "Sylvia's walking speed." First we asked him to grasp them together, the way he experienced confusion and anger when Sylvia walked fast. Heaviness, tension, and shoulder pain came with gluing those two experiences together; he took a moment to be present with them. Then we asked him to separate his hands and to unglue his fear of death from Sylvia's walking speed. By separating the two experiences, he realized that "I'm afraid of dying no matter how fast or slow Sylvia walks. She doesn't cause my fear of dying."

He looked at one hand and then the other, saying "I'm afraid of dying" several times. Then we asked if he'd like to make a request of Sylvia. Requests can be very effective, but often they do not get met until after you've presenced and communicated your true feelings. He asked Sylvia if she would walk with him for a little while when they came out of restaurants and movies. She said, "Sure."

They noticed that other solutions to the walking-speed problem had never occurred to him. For example, he never took the option of walking faster himself, or of making walking a "follow the leader" exchange. She never slowed down. That was one clue that both of them were contributing to the pattern that was occurring. When creative solutions to couple differences don't spontaneously occur, finding the underlying pattern can help.

4/When You Don't
Feel Loved

ᶜ🙰🙰ᶦ

One of the most powerful learnings of our first few years to-gether was that we each tended to demand from the other what we were unwilling to give ourselves. We would demand love from the other person when we were not feeling loving toward ourselves. We would demand good treatment from the other when we were not offering such treatment to ourselves or to the other person. As a result of seeing this truth, we changed our under-standing of the physics of relationship. We came to see that if we were not getting what we wanted, it was because we were not creating a space within ourselves for it to occur.

Once we understood how it worked, our satisfaction level

took a remarkable jump in the positive direction. When we didn't feel loved, we would open up to loving ourselves and all our feelings. As if by magic, everything would shift.

In one interaction, for example, Gay was making dinner in the kitchen and Kathlyn added something to the bowl. Gay stiffened and asked sharply if she wanted to make the salad. We each paused and took a breath, realizing that one of our familiar unlovable places had been poked. Gay quickly saw that he had interpreted Kathlyn's gesture as a signal that his contribution wasn't valued—an old feeling that was first triggered in his mother's kitchen. Kathlyn saw that she was trying to be helpful, an old pattern from her deep feelings of unworthiness. Each of us took a moment to love that aspect of ourself. The whole interaction took a couple of minutes, then we were back to creating dinner together and having fun.

Often the shift would occur spontaneously, without any behavior change on our part. At other times asking for something we wanted changed the other person.

Looking at our relationship this new way allowed us to take more charge of ourselves. By asking "How am I contributing to this situation?" and "What needs to be loved here?" we took ourselves out of the victim position.

Sometimes the problem is deeper. Many of us feel fundamentally bad about ourselves, so we consume our energy with overdoing to prove our worthiness. But the more you do, the worse the problem becomes. The truth is: You will never be adequately loved for doing. See if any of these phrases are familiar:

- I am only doing this for the relationship.
- If it were up to me, I wouldn't be doing this at all, but I am doing it for us.
- What are you doing, just lying there?
- I do and do, and still there's more to be done.
- Do you have any idea how much I do for you? You have no idea what I do for you every day.

- I have so much to get done, I just don't know how I'll do it all.
- What have you done today?
- It's never done—doing rises with the sun.

"I do." The vow of marriage is not "I be," "I become," "I commit." It's "I do." I vow to do and do and do—usually over and over, doing the role and the task at hand.

Then "don't" slithers up. I don't know. I don't get it. I didn't do it. I don't do windows. I don't do late dinners, early walks, prints, stripes, or polka dots. Don't. Just don't. Don't speak to me that way, don't hit your sister, don't touch the brownies, don't scuff your shoes, don't walk on the grass.

Do you have the time for a walk? Doing turns to doodling with a little more time. Doing is right. Doing is the only right. It's my right to do what I want with my body. Do whatever you want, I don't care.

Doers of the world weave the tight underwear that rides up the crack of humanity. What a doing nation we are! We get 20 percent less sleep than our ancestors a hundred years ago. We work longer hours, have fewer children, and don't see the ones we have very much. We are a huge ant farm of workers, moving piles of things and papers from one place to another. A dying person never says, "I didn't do enough." She says, "I didn't love enough, sigh at the stars enough, rest in the bathtub with music enough."

The point is this: Take time to love. Find out what it is you are afraid to be with, then love it. Many problems disappear in a moment of being present: being with a fear, being loving toward yourself, being open to your creativity.

The whole point of taking responsibility and telling the truth to yourself and your partner is to allow more love to flow. Kathlyn describes a recent experience: "Gay and I were talking about some vague upset feelings I'd been experiencing, and he said, 'It sounds as if you were waiting for the answer to surface to report on it rather than using the tools you know.' I immediately responded,

'But I *have* used the tools this week.' We both realized that I had responded defensively. I took a moment just to rest my awareness on that response, the immediate defensive retort, and on how familiar it is. And as I let myself be with it, I felt the whole middle part of my body shift. I had been having roily sensations in my belly; they now relaxed. In a few seconds I started noticing waves of excitement and warm streamers of internal giggles. I realized I was feeling more love. Intellectually I knew that Gay's feedback was loving, but this was a different, sensory experience. Defensiveness shifted to wonder, and right on its heels came more openness to receiving love. I could let Gay's love in more, which circulated in me like fine champagne bubbles."

5/Creating Space
for Essence

⟨∾⟩

Many relationship problems dissolve when you take space. Space is different from distance. Distance is space between you that is filled with fear and unspoken communications. Space is creative openness, a clearing in which you can bring yourself to full flower.

Most people long for a balance between chaos and numbing sameness in their relationships. As one of our therapy clients put it, "My husband and I seem to feel one of two extremes, either overwhelmed or bored. Why can't we find a middle ground where we feel stimulated yet serene?" This question is a good one for all of us to ponder. How can we renew and refresh our relationships every day so that we surf on waves of creative change rather than drown—or fear getting our feet wet?

Do you make enough space, in your relationship, for each of you to be completely real and completely happy? Do you have the physical space, space for your own needs and interests, for thoughts to develop, for growth to mature and flower? Taking space and owning your own space are essential to spiritual growth and to integrating new learning and more love. Taking space feeds the basic relationship pulsation of individuation and unity. We can go higher and deeper when we honor our individual needs for space. Taking space cultivates internal space, the place where we can rest and renew.

Each of us has space signals, triggers that let us know we need space. Kathlyn gets a cranky and irritable sensation under her skin. Gay's sentences get crisper and slightly critical. The space signal can also be projected, as in this example Kathlyn gives:

"I noticed that I was following Gay around and reaching across him for something in the kitchen just as he was heading in the other direction. We would bump into each other. Or I would interrupt a sentence, trying to anticipate what he was going to say. At first I thought the hovering sense of crowding meant that he needed space and was unconsciously pushing me away. Then I realized that it was my personal beeper signaling me that *I* needed space."

Many couples believe that love means being together or wanting to be together every moment. So they push against each other's expansion and prevent the growth of space in their relationship. One therapy couple had never spent any time apart in their whole marriage except when she went to the store. Even when he was at work, he'd call her every hour on the hour to make sure he knew where she was. Our first assignment for them was to take fifteen minutes apart to do something they both enjoyed. It took them a week to complete the assignment by taking separate walks in the same park.

You can consciously decide that your relationship includes

space as well as closeness. Making that decision will create spaciousness in your listening as well as in your activities. The very core of creativity comes from space, so taking space nurtures creative impulses. In space we have no agenda, no demands, no focus. It is lax time, where mind and body just float free. Gay often takes space this way by lying down and staring at the ceiling. Kathlyn likes to walk on the beach or watch the waves. One of our friends describes a sensation of letting go of weight, as if she were dropping a suitcase of thoughts and plans. Meditation is another reliable way of taking space. We have often been asked how we can accomplish so much and still have fun. Taking space and resting in space regularly increase efficiency and ease.

Taking space from routines or patterns can also produce spontaneous insight and growth. For example, in the early fall, when we were taking a retreat to write this book, we played hooky one morning and changed the schedule. We decided to take a bike ride before writing together. As we were cruising through the park, we were enjoying each other, the crisp air, and the breezy sense of space. We have always had fun together, even when we didn't have much money.

Kathlyn spontaneously asked, "Why do people settle for less?" Gay, pedaling, thought for a moment, then said, "I think most people don't want to open up to the transformation necessary to realize their essence-desires. So many people buried their true desires so long ago that they've forgotten they have them." Kathlyn then mentioned the Buddhist belief that desire is a cause of suffering. Most of us struggle with the idea that wanting is bad or selfish. But essence wants to express excitement and has desires that come from who we really are. What a tragedy that we lose touch with the flow of essence-expression!

Gay continues: "It reminds me of that interaction I had many years ago with my landlord, who was over at the house doing some repairs. I was making some coffee (I am a coffee connoisseur), and Ralph noticed the tantalizing aroma coming from the kitchen. He'd apparently never had drip coffee from freshly ground beans, and he commented on how wonderful it smelled. I offered him a cup, genuinely excited by the possibility of turning someone on to what coffee could taste like. He shook his head sadly. 'Oh, no,' he said. 'I couldn't. If I had a cup of that, I couldn't go back to what I drink every day.' I was stunned by this way of thinking. It would be just as easy to drink the cup and have it inspire you to make a commitment to a higher level of existence. He owned dozens of rental properties and was a member of a locally prominent family, so I knew money was not an issue. It was simply his self-imposed limitation of what life could be. In other words, the space he was coming from was impoverished, so he couldn't give himself room to have a more pleasurable experience."

Giving your relationships some full breath creates space. The inbreath of full experiencing and the outbreath of full expression form a spaciousness-glider where you can both rest and soar. In our relationship and in our workshops and seminars, we breathe together without words. You can breathe together with eye contact or while touching each other's ribs to feel the waves of breath. Appreciate the rhythm of your partner's breath as it interweaves with your rhythm. Match your breathing paces to experience the harmony of breathing in the same space. Perhaps such resonance happens naturally in the hammock on a summer night or just after lovemaking. You can also choose the deep space of being together that is created by breathing. We find it's a great way to shift from conflict to cooperation. Specific problems tend to disappear, and remembrance springs up in their place. We remember the sparkle of each other's laughter and the safety of closeness.

Kathlyn recalls a time where taking space changed the course of our son's life: "Chris had gone to live with his father for a year when he was thirteen. We butted against my desire for an equal relationship and Chris's choice to withhold and not keep agreements. He was getting the opportunity to take space by living with his other parent, whom he had not really known since we separated, when Chris was one.

"I went to visit Chris over the Christmas holidays and

discovered that he was scraping his ego off the floor each morning. He was the most depressed I had ever seen him. My first impulse was to fix him, to offer him suggestions about school and getting along with his father and classmates. But some deeper impulse led me to just hang out on the couch with him, watching TV and breathing together. We had little conversation over five days, but many moments where I would rub his shoulders or stroke his forehead. He allowed me to just be with him and his waves of feeling.

"About a month after that visit, Chris decided that he wanted to return to live with Gay and me. A wellspring of maturity seemed to flow from the formerly sullen and passive person who had left in the fall. He began to seek out our company and to ask questions about fine points of philosophy and how to make his life work. This, of course, thrilled us. The turnaround seemed to have come from the deep space we shared over those days."

6/The Essence of Play

❧

Some friends came back from Hawaii with a package of presents for us, including a very realistic-looking bird-of-paradise flower made of plastic. It rested on the kitchen table for a day or two. One evening Kathlyn came home from editing some videos and found it sitting in a vase on the kitchen floor. Delighted by this gesture, the next day before leaving she stuck the flower in the top of the washing machine. When she returned, it was peeking out the back door. This play went on for several days. The next morning Kathlyn heard steps coming up to the bedroom, then saw the bird-of-paradise bobbing around the corner, followed by Gay's head and the question "Would you like a hot beverage?"

197

Play is motion, keeping the spark of invention moving in new ways. Changing routines is a great way to play. One of our favorite forms is what we call persona play. Gay or Kathlyn will take one of our familiar personas—the Chameleon or the Ramblin' Guy—and exaggerate it to ridiculous proportions. Kathlyn may take her Supercompetence persona, then purse her lips, raise her eyebrows, and race around the house exclaiming, "We've got to get organized!" Gay will counter with an improvised Country Boy persona. Several exchanges occur before we move on.

Play stops in a relationship when the partners start thinking they know all there is to know about each other. What enables people in a relationship to enhance essence, a deepening sense of spiritual presence and fullness? What if your relating allowed you to dream yourselves in brand-new combinations that weren't serious? Play doesn't have to mean anything. Could you allow the golden ball of play to spin over and over, to find new glimmers of yourself laughing?

Many couples create breakthroughs by learning to play with their most deeply hidden feelings. During one relationship training we had the participants identify the emotion they had the most trouble experiencing and expressing. They chose from the core emotions: fear, anger, sadness, sexuality, joy. Working in small groups, they explored their history, their rules, and their comfort level with each of these core feelings. One man was surprised to discover that joy was the feeling that was most prohibited in his family. Many people felt acutely uncomfortable when anyone was angry. Several people identified the numb tingling they experienced as fear.

They spent some time identifying the body-sensations they were aware of with each feeling, then sharing their explorations with their group. Then we had each participant express their troublesome feeling in a simple statement: "I'm scared. I'm sad. I'm angry. I feel sexual. I'm joyful." Next, each of them picked a partner to work with and stood facing them. For the next several minutes each partner took turns saying their feeling-sentence with as many different inflections, tones, and emphases as they could. We asked them to think of the feeling as a piano or symphony and to play along its entire range with whole-body communication. From the sound and motion in the room, you might assume bed-lam had let loose. When the entire group reconvened, people were glowing and laughing. One woman exclaimed how her life had been totally controlled by her fear of anger and her attempts to siderail anyone's rising anger, much less her own. She felt exhila-rated to own anger in a new way.

The next day one couple shared with us an experiment they had carried out that morning. She had been angry, and so had he. Instead of fighting about who did what, they took a few minutes to play with saying "I'm angry" in different tones and with funny faces. They both felt enlivened and came in holding hands. When we asked them what they had been angry about, they couldn't remember.

7/Expressing Gratitude

❦

One day Kathlyn wrote in her journal: "Appreciating opens like a rose in my chest, layer upon layer of soft caresses. It wells up when I look through eyes of wonder, not the hooded eyes of getting or marking my territory. Two recent incidents reminded me how valuable appreciating is in cultivating joy. Before we taped a training video, Gay said, 'I want to tell you how proud I am of you and how much I value you.' After he said this he held my shoulders lightly and looked at me for several minutes. I felt as if a balloon had risen in my chest and elevated my whole body, clearing any fog from my insides. This was a direct expression of gratitude, and as I reflected on it, I realized how rare—nonexistent?— this had been before I met him.

"Later that day I felt gratitude for him for something entirely different. Gay asked me if I had a moment to talk. I said yes, and he said he wanted to come back to a conversation hours before, when we'd been talking about one of our children. I had been explaining some of my recent thoughts and wondering about the relationship and where it was heading. Gay said he realized he had jumped in with his point of view and wanted to know if I had more I wanted to say. He said it looked as if I felt sad, and that it felt like he had interrupted my feeling by jumping in with his point. I realized that my sadness was incomplete, like an open phone line. As I acknowledged the sadness and told him about it, I also experienced waves of love and appreciation for Gay's awareness of the incomplete communication and his willingness to give this interaction his time and attention. I immediately felt more alive, vital, and valued, not even having sensed that there had been a cord dangling."

Appreciation can be expressed verbally, as Gay did, or non-verbally in actions, touch, or gestures. One of our colleagues called home to tell her partner, Jan, how much she loved and appreciated her special attention, just as an unexpected delivery of flowers from Jan arrived at the door. Gay appreciates that Kathlyn washes his jeans with fabric softener so they feel soft and friendly against his skin.

Verbal appreciations have more power if they're specific. "I appreciate you a lot" is a start. "I appreciate the way you look at me when I'm talking" is sensory-specific and grounded in an experience that the listener can locate in time and space.

What blocks appreciation? Many people have never experienced a clear model of appreciating. Many people are looking through eyeglasses that let in only what's wrong, what's missing, or what could be improved, rather than what's possible or what they're grateful for. Jane Hamilton's novel *A Map of the World* describes a family leaving the farm they had worked for years. When the wife comes back to say good-bye to the land several months later, she sees the farmhouse without the filter of their commitment to love and steward the land. As if a veil had been lifted, she sees the shutters falling off, the broken linoleum, and the bare windows. When they had lived there, she had stopped seeing what was missing because her focus was making the home warm and full of love for her husband and children.

A full heart feeds the eyes. If your heart has been wounded, it can be hard to let it overflow with gratitude for someone else. And leaky hearts don't make good reservoirs for flowing joy. The attitude "What about me?" dampens appreciation and creates a perception of the world and of partners as stingy bankers with all the funds.

Another block to appreciation is ambition. The drive to get ahead, get to work, get a promotion, or get the kids through school often outruns appreciation of what is possible now. Some of our clients use the following question as a meditation: "How much is enough?" It helps them shift into appreciating now rather than leaning into the future.

To appreciate another, you have to see them clear of your judgments and opinions. Otherwise your own experiences shroud the polished glass that could allow their essence to shine directly. You can choose to learn to appreciate by choosing to look for what's right. What is unique about this day, this event, this person? What is the potential for acknowledging their vision, their desires, their special way of making coffee? For example, Gay doesn't think he can cook, but because he hasn't been burdened by following recipes, he combines unusual ingredients with surprising and delightful results. He doesn't know that something isn't done, so he'll put orange peel into the vegetables, or make a dessert from leftover rice, plums, and saffron. Kathlyn appreciates this creativity in him. Coming to your relating as a beginner, ever new, feeds appreciation.

As we mentioned, John Gottman has found that thriving couples have at least a five-to-one ratio of appreciations to criticisms. Two friends of ours, Susan Snowe and Darshan Mayginnes, have invented a game based on that ratio. Every time they catch themselves making a criticism, they call out, "Five appreciations." On the spot they generate five appreciations to open a wave of appreciation rather than the downward spiral of criticism. They have been enjoying this practice greatly and notice how much it increases their essence-connection. On a recent trip they had stopped at a diner out in the hinterland somewhere when Susan said, "This food is terrible." Darsh called out, "Okay, five appreciations." "There was food when I was hungry," "I had money to pay for it," and so on. They have now started to begin the day with appreciations—for each other, themselves, the day. Whenever we see them, they are wellsprings of appreciation because they choose to focus on the positive aspects of life.

8/Blending a Family

Practicing the path of the conscious heart requires plum-blossom courage in even the most adventurous of couples. We need models of couples who can celebrate their essence-connection in the midst of childrearing. Our friends Sandy and Rod Wells have supported the essence of their family for several years. Sandy describes their experience:

"My experience of our blended family brings to mind a fine vinaigrette. Vinaigrette, left unattended, always settles. The oil and herbs gravitate toward the bottom, while the colloidal vinegar floats on top. Without just the right amount of agitation, vinaigrette is piquant and caustic. Cap it up and torque a few wrist gyrations, and the blend is superb—the taste is beyond compare. So it is with our family. Left unattended, we can settle out into primordial ingredients. Six children, two parents, two phantom 'noncustodial' parents, two other stepparents, two half-siblings, ten (at last count) living grandparents, and numerous aunts, uncles, and cousins. I have two children of 'my own'; my husband has four of 'his own'; and together we've raised the five that have been in our 'custody.' We call them ours, and they call us Mom and Dad. By attending to the mix, our own style of gyration, diverse elements commingle, and the flavor is outstanding.

"Family blending is an art with metaphysical underpinnings. The wicked stepparent is not just a fairy-tale character. I've been there! I've had days when I've thought, 'Why do I have to raise someone else's kids? I didn't sign on for this!' Parenting our own children is a precarious balancing act to begin with; the complexities of blended parenting make the circus guy who balances Ming dynasty vases on the bridge of his nose look like an amateur. Blended parents palm stacks of mismatched chairs—one atop the next—while waiting for the three-hundred-pound midget to be catapulted by springboard, execute two midair flips, and land neatly in the top chair.

"In blended families issues of fairness and equality run rampant, often distorted by what the 'noncustodial' parent provides or fails to provide. Blended parents tend to view each other as parenting improvement projects. Brandishing spackle knives, sanding machines, and wallpaper paste, they saunter through the household with hip-hugging tool belts, lavishing counsel: 'If I had been you in that interaction about allowance, I would have . . .' And parental amnesia abounds: 'Before we got together, my kids never did stuff like this—they weren't like this at all!'

"Statistics poignantly suggest that blended families have a limited survival rate. The stress fractures and fault lines of multiple gene pools colliding head-on result in a finicky fragility. Even a relatively tame conflict can spike the Richter scale, and the omnipresent solution, spoken or not, is usually: 'I'm outta here!' 'Time to evacuate!' Conjugal bliss, the second, third, or fourth time around, corrodes in the face of stepsibling rivalry, unaccustomed discipline styles, and below-the-belt criticism. What's the fastest way to piss off a blended-parent partner? Just tell them how concerned you are about the behavior patterns of their oldest child, who happens to do life the same way they do. Ironically, most blended families assume that their difficulties come from the fact that they are blending together disparate elements. This, indeed, heightens the challenge of parenting and family cohesiveness. And while riding out one of our quaking aftershocks, I realized that the parenting conflicts I've had with my new husband are an eerie reflection of the parenting conflicts I had with my daughters' father—which are, of course, an eerie reflection of the dynamics of my family of origin. So the questions arise: 'What works?' 'How do we go about practicing this metaphysical artistry?' 'How can we increase the odds for survival and actually go a step further—how can blended families flourish?'

"The single, most powerful agent of longevity, joy, and effervescence in a blended family originates in the quality of commitment and intention between the partners. My husband and I have learned over the years that whenever something appears to be amiss with our children, the first place to focus in on is our relationship. Conversely, when something is amiss in our relationship, we tend to take it out on our children—more accurately, on each other's children. Like most parents in our situation, we came into our marriage as stalwart single parents, lone commanders of troops accustomed to having our attention exclusively. I was habituated to fixing my full focus on my daughters' wants and needs, just by virtue of the fact that there were no other adults in my life on a regular basis. It has been tempting, sometimes unconsciously compelling, to have my relationship with them be the primary relationship in my life while striving to control the quality and style of my husband's relationship with them. When they were younger, I used to do a lot of explaining, 'constructive' criticism, and nascent nagging. I was a self-certified parenting expert who had read all the books and gone to the workshops. Of course, as their mother, I knew best what their needs were, where they might be tender or wounded, and how to keep them from getting upset. My operative objective, as I vigilantly scanned the environment with my feeling radar, was to avoid conflict and the expression of feelings at all cost. Truthfully, I was afraid that the day might come when my loyalties would be tested: 'Okay, Mom, is it going to be *him* or *us?*' or 'Okay, dear, is it going to be *them* or *me?*' I was afraid that anger would demolish our new family, that it would tarnish and oxidize the mirror polish of our loving. This potential can exist only in the face of a fragile, ephemeral marital (or relationship) commitment where the escape hatch is ajar, the emergency exit door is off its hinges, or the windows are wide open.

"Any commitment that follows the demise of 'happily ever after' is bound to be edgy. The riptide of divorce leaves us wary of the cross-currents and the undertow. After three years of single parenting, I was easily swept off my feet. Finally, I had met the real prince! I felt much more prepared to make the initial commitment to marriage and much less tolerant of anything that looked like unworkability thereafter. Especially since leaving a relationship was no longer an unknown. I knew that I could make it on my own; I had a proven track record. Sure, single parenting got a little lonely. I had a lot more time to myself, though, and life was very simple. So on bleak days when the inevitable conflict surfaced, my commitment wobbled. I rattled the window sash and contemplated the possibilities. Leaving the relationship was always my first and predominant thought. When I actually confronted that reality, I stayed.

"Children are sensitive barometers of crumbling commitment. They know what they know without verbal communication or confirmation. They provide shockingly accurate feedback on the condition of our relationship, and they parade our unexpressed feelings without ceremony. They often participate unconsciously in our commitment spasms. Many of them live with the thinking error that they caused the demise of the relationship that spawned them. The potential thinking error that follows is: 'Hm—if I did that with Dad, I can probably do it again with this guy, who I don't really like—at least, not today. Then I'll have Mom's full attention, and until then I'll have the full attention of everyone while I'm acting out. Maybe if this guy is gone, Mom will go back to Dad.' Deep down, they yearn for the appropriate family hierarchy. They would like to live with two adults who love each other and meet each other's needs for intimacy and closeness.

"Children want to be honored in their resiliency and in their ability to forge new relationships. They want to be loved from fulfillment rather than emptiness. The more we demonstrate steadfast commitment, the more they flower. When we lower the escape hatch, bolt the exit door to its hinges, and tighten the window sash, they no longer concern themselves with whether or not Blended Mom and Dad are staying together. At that moment, family life can shift from focusing on survival to participating in conscious growth and evolution.

"What does clarity of commitment and intention look like? How does it feel? What is the experience? Although I've been clear about keeping my body in this relationship since the very beginning, my spirit has frequently fled. I recognize the pain when my heart is numb or absent and how it distorts all of my relationships and my creative expression. Likewise, I delight in the ecstasy of bringing my essence fully into the moment. Truly the only thing that has been standing in the way of my bliss is my fear of losing myself in complete union. The intentions and actions that support the deepest experience of intimacy and family harmony are simple—not necessarily easy, but simple. I express essence vibrantly when I open to full participation with all of my feelings and tell the truth in a nonblaming way. I tingle with essence-awareness when my attention is on the present moment, and I embrace and accept reality as it presents itself. When my intention is to grow and evolve in the context of blending a family, then, as Deepak Chopra says, 'the universe will handle the details.' How does this intention and awareness influence and nurture our blended family? The equations are elementary.

- Happy, fulfilled, creative parents = Happy, fulfilled, creative children.
- Parents who are friendly with their own feelings – Parents who can open to and appreciate their children's feelings.
- Parents living in the transparency of truth = Children living in the transparency of truth.
- Parents modeling growth and choiceful evolution = Children relaxing their predisposition to survive emotionally through defending and withholding their feelings.

"Blended families offer an incredibly rich opportunity for transformation and opening the conscious heart. Witness a recent quote from one of 'my' daughters: 'It's a good thing I've got older brothers now, otherwise I'd be a wimp!' Every aspect of combining the splinters of preexisting families lends itself to growth. Decisions about money, housing, rules, diet, possessions, pets—all areas provide potent learning opportunities. Inherent in the intricacies of shared holidays and visitation schedules is the potential for creating unique family traditions and a broader experience of community. If you are a blended parent, take a moment right now to appreciate yourself. Pat yourself on the back for having a great sense of humor and amazing flexibility. Appreciate your children for enduring the quirks of your growth waves and commitment spasms. Set an intention for an experience of family that goes beyond any of your wildest imaginings, and enjoy!"

9/Deepening Your Connection with Essence and Creativity

❧

We come to know ourselves mainly through the mirror of relationship. Since we can never see our faces directly or watch ourselves from the back as we move, there are some aspects of ourselves that we can see only by reflection in others. Developmental research and somatic psychology are exploring the function of the witness in the evolution of a mature human being. Stanley Keleman, one of the pioneers in this area, says, "In the beginning children need someone to be there *for* them and this is the meaning of the caring *for* and caring *about* stages." We come to view ourselves as we are viewed, to value ourselves to the degree that we are valued.

In our adult relationships we have a unique opportunity to be *for* our partners, to lovingly witness their growth, daily rhythms, and discoveries. In order to see from the conscious heart, we need to remove the veils that keep us from transparency. The daily interactions of a close relationship provide endless opportunities to lift the veil and polish the mirror, or to tie down the veil even more firmly. Each of us brings powerfully encoded self-image scripts to current relationships. These scripts tend to distort and cloud the mirror. Control and approval scripts are especially common and may underlie all other scripts, since each of us needs love to survive and autonomy to choose. For example, Kathlyn's self-image was based largely on being useful, which she developed into an Organizer, a Supercompetence persona: "In the first years of our relationship, I would tend to see and hear Gay through the supercompetent filter. When he would voice a feeling, I would rush in to fix it, to adjust something in the house or my behavior so I could feel valued."

A major task of the conscious heart is to polish the mirror of our listening and perception so that we can truly reflect our partner's essence. The most powerful path to essence that we know of is claiming our own creativity. This means owning the qualities and behaviors that we have hooked on to other people. Kathlyn continues: "I grew up seeking the approval of others; this pattern dominated my life. In my thirties I made a conscious choice to source my own value, my own approval. Over the next months and years, I began to see more quickly the times when I responded to Gay from neediness, and when I responded from being at home in my own worth. I needed to take real-life action steps to source my own value, from completing my Ph.D. to learning to speak clearly about my feelings. Most difficult was identifying and requesting what I wanted. As I began to expand to claim the worthiness I had been seeking from Gay, I could see and appreciate his essence more and more easily. The quality of our connection deepened with each step I took to become whole."

One of the most profound joys that deepens our own relationship is sharing discoveries with each other. These discoveries balance the tendency, especially in long-term relationships or during childrearing years, to communicate primarily about the business of running the household and the relationship enterprise itself. In our own relationship we save anecdotes, questions we're pondering, and amusing incidents to share with each other. In the space of soul-commitment, you can plumb the well of each other's becoming. We have found that there are no limits to deepening in ourselves and in our knowing of each other. As long as we stay true to our commitments to transparency, equality, and appreciation, we can relax into constant renewal, weathering periods of transition to new aspects and strengths, as well as the lax times of seeming stagnation.

To know one person deeply and to have the privilege of hearing their reception of the world and seeing through their eyes over time is a thrilling and sometimes frightening honor. There is great comfort in the particular fit of your partner's body, in the resonance of their voice and laughter. One danger of deepening, though, is sinking into stagnation. Many long-term couples use familiarity as an excuse to sleep through their relationships. They can predict each other's reactions and gestures, repeat their stories, finish their sentences from time to time. Familiarity is not the same as deepening. You can transform familiarity into growth by diving into the subtle and great waves of your partner's changes and your own. What a sophisticated dance: to know your partner's steps and how they blend with yours, in order to be able to improvise.

Kathlyn says: "I've begun taking piano lessons again after learning the mechanics of playing as a child. I quit playing in my teens in rebellion against the rote learning of it. Now I've come back to it with a different perspective. Now I practice the same scales, learning them by heart, because I see that familiarity creates the springboard for improvisation. Only when I absolutely know the triads and the structure of scales can I make my own music. Mastery in any discipline follows years of practice. Glenn Gould, a great pianist, practiced his scales more slowly than most students could tolerate. Going deeply into each note, feeling the relationship of each note to the whole—that joy comes after years of carefully polishing, listening, being with yourself and those close to you."

Instead of thinking, "Oh, I heard that already," you sense, "Oh, I've opened a new aspect of that story and found a larger meaning." The poet Marianne Moore said, "The world's an orphan's home." All of us are looking for a place to come home to. You and your essence partner can make a new home together by engaging in daily gestures of trust.

10 / Respect

❦

Respect sounds like an abstract concept, but it is really made up of tiny moments, of many actions we take. For example, we demonstrate respect by focusing on what our partner is saying and waiting until the communication is complete before we interject our response. This action only takes a moment, but it communicates a world of respect. Respect extends beyond courtesy, beyond knowing that your partner is a good and worthwhile person. Respect involves right action. You both expect actions that demonstrate responsibility and integrity.

Respect begins with meeting your own standards. Kathlyn was attracted to this kind of self-respect in Gay when she first met him:

"I saw immediately that he was using himself fully. His talents and qualities were blooming, not hidden or shriveled. I saw that he thought well of himself, not from delusion or arrogance, but because he had expanded to the edges of himself and met his own high criteria for being human." Years later she added this passage to her journal: "Gay continues to be consistent. He does what he says he is going to do. If he forgets something he's agreed to, he tells the truth about it and clears up whatever needs to be done. That is another cornerstone of my respect for him."

If you respect yourself and others, someone probably saw your essence and told you you were worthwhile. They might have said or subtly communicated that you have a contribution to make to life and to the community. You began to believe that assessment and to set your standards to match their regard. Respect begins in those moments of recognition, and it grows as you personally experience that you can make good on your values and agreements. Each time you choose responsibility, you grow in self-respect and in respect for your relationships.

Respect has a powerful healing value. As therapists, we have the great privilege of seeing people develop respect for themselves and their partners right before our eyes. We would like to share an example where we witnessed the power of respect: a person's choice to face her shadows and to heal despite what happened in the past. Elaine told us how angry she still was about her sexual abuse and how obsessed with revenge she still could get. She sobbed as she said she really saw how ultimately unsatisfying anger is. She spat out that she'd really "like to beat the shit out of someone," but when she physically beat up a pillow or fantasized beating up someone, she found that she just stayed angry. The anger never transformed, nor did her frustration.

We asked her what was the hardest thing to accept about all the past abuse, and she said with passion, "No one listened to me!" Clearly in Elaine's past her essence had not been celebrated but rather had been abused. We asked her to pause a moment to love and accept that no one had listened to her. After just a moment of loving herself, she took a deep breath and saw that she often complains now that her husband doesn't listen. With a little more exploration, she recognized that she was choosing to rehash the past rather than have the relationship she wanted right now.

She also realized that she was requiring her husband to turn deaf from time to time. If he didn't listen, she could continue to be angry, to feel like a victim, and then to treat him with contempt. Respect is based on considering your partner as your equal. You give as much consideration to your partner as you do to yourself. Contempt is based on considering someone as less than equal, treating them with scorn. You can heal your own contempt by feeling your feelings, telling the truth, and reclaiming your support for your partner's essence.

Deep anger often doesn't clear up until the underlying fear is identified. Elaine discovered that under her drama of retribution, she was afraid of emptiness. She was afraid that she wouldn't find her authentic self. As she continued to express and be with her fear, she realized that to find her authentic self, she would first need to listen closely to herself. And she made an agreement with herself to write about her thoughts and feelings for five minutes every morning.

As if by magic, when she began to respect herself enough to listen to herself carefully, others, particularly her husband, began to show her more respect by listening to her.

11 / When Roles and Rhythms Change

❧

A thriving relationship straddles paradox. Each day is new choice and yet is based on assumptions and shared history. As Kathlyn puts it: "I re-create my commitment each day, depending on how I see and receive my mate. I love my mate and may also simultaneously dislike his habit of leaving his cups wherever he's finished using them. If we use our relationships to reveal more about who we really are, being and doing blend to extend the rich mix between us. When I go out into the world to teach workshops, I make notes of events, people, and articles to share with Gay when I see or talk to him. I cut out ads for music I know he likes. We both bought the same book for each other not long ago when I was out of town. Gay recently said how surprised he has been by the recent role reversal in our relationship. If someone is traveling now, it is usually me. He was marveling at the paradox of a former 'ramblin' guy' loving to be home. When we first got together, I was the nest-maker and he was utterly indifferent to his domestic surroundings. He was constantly on the road doing lectures and workshops.

"One day about five years into our relationship, he blurted out that he liked sitting in our living room. It made him comfortable, he said. I was deeply touched, because I'd never heard anything like that come out of his mouth. This moment began a role shift in him. Now he takes great care to look for objects for our home and to arrange them 'just so' for their aesthetic effect. At the same time I have grown in the opposite direction. I've found that I really enjoy speaking in public, being on television, and meeting new people, activities that would have been unthinkable for me in the early days of our relationship. I definitely saw Gay as the 'doer' and me as the 'be-er.' It has shifted completely now. I have become the 'roving ambassador' for our work and have logged over a million air miles teaching for our institute in the past ten years."

Relationships may have life-spans that are similar to developmental phases. In each relationship there is the exhilarating first head of foam, the first sip, the first rose. Then you come to a plateau of challenge, when the shadows that hid in the first bright flash seem to grow with separate strength and force.

The shadows of the middle of a relationship are like the shadows at midlife. The things we've outgrown or not turned to see nip at our heels. Relationships may flow through natural cycles of death and rebirth over and over. What can hold a relationship through the changes of aging, illness, differing interests, and limitations? If we don't face and accept the little deaths, we cannot choose a new direction. I can become frozen in trying to hold on to an image of myself or my partner that is falling through the hourglass.

To die and yet remain alive happens over and over in relating.

What stays when appearance changes? What remains when a severe illness deeply marks one partner? What is renewed when children leave home, when the family moves, when your parents die? How do we keep revealing essence?

If we don't grow beyond what we were taught to be, the future can look isolated and desperate. Kathlyn's mother learned to keep house, to clean thoroughly. She learned to dress with coordinated colors, to wear formal or informal clothing on the proper occasions, to use the proper utensils and serving dishes when entertaining, to play bridge, have a luncheon, sew, decorate, and paint. She had to look under that corseted role to find out what additional purpose life might have, to read books and contribute time to organizations. Any role is both a shelter and a straitjacket.

Standing together in the larger vision of what you both want—your commitments—creates a gyroscope for the fluctuations and shifts of job, children's needs, separate interests, sexual desires, spiritual values, friends, and the whole complicated constellation that surrounds any couple. In relating there are definite cycles of ebb and flow, of intense joining and more quiet gathering, of stillness and exuberance. Each individual and each couple has preferred rhythms of close contact and separate breath that often express themselves in different role preferences.

What are your cycles? Do you recognize them in yourself and your partner? And do you honor the pulse of unity and the pulse of your individual dance?

Most difficulties in relating have to do with not seeing the rising impulse or not following it in a satisfying and friendly way. The impulse to closeness can feel like being drawn into the exhilaration of mingling and sliding with another's skin, scent, and breath. The impulse to separateness has a more focused, happy-in-my-own-skin-don't-add-any-stimuli feel for many people.

Keeping love fresh and alive acknowledges a central paradox, our human need for sameness *and* variety. I can commit to the relationship and to continued growth. Sometimes the different rates of growth between partners create stress and conflict. Often one partner will really jump into a new interest, while the other feels threatened or mystified by their mate's exuberance. Commitment can hold the ground of relating when rhythms don't match—and they rarely do between partners. The dance of relationship is inherently arrhythmic. If you have chosen down in your heart and bones to be with your partner, you breathe ease and elasticity into the structure of your relating.

We often ask couples in our intensive trainings whether they can conceive of their relationship as big enough for both partners to express their essential potentials, desires, and feelings. Is their relationship big enough for them to move at different rhythms and to be interested in different things, which they then compost back into their union? Role reversals of various kinds increase both balance and renewal in long-term relationships.

12 / Dealing with a Life Transition: Menopause

꧁꧂

Many of our women friends now speak in shorthand about menopause: "I never notice it when the temperature dips anymore." "I have my own little furnace—just can't get the thermostat set right." "I'm not blushing, I'm flushing." Kathlyn shares some recent experiences about this still-mysterious transition:

"Until I became premenopausal, I never really sweated. I could do a full hour of aerobics and not break into a sweat. In my forties, though, my body began to go through various heat changes. One day as I was moving around the kitchen in my red kimono, I smelled this strange musky odor and suddenly realized it was coming from me. I smelled like our son did after karate practice when he was fifteen, as if a layer of sticky molecules had settled over him like a mantle. I told Gay about this new smell, and he nodded as if to say, 'Yes, I already know,' then commented, 'Who is this musked woman?'

"We both burst out laughing, and I found myself appreciating Gay's relaxed acceptance of my hormonal fluctuations. We talked a little about the clash of his mother's menopause against his adolescent rising sexuality, and how we could envision this current life transition as a friendly time. Gay's mother was volatile as long as he knew her. When she entered menopause, he never knew when she would rage at him or career around the house yelling, 'I don't know what I'm going to do!'

"When a friend of Gay's brought some porno pictures over to share with him, Gay's mother caught them in the backyard and exploded in rage. Then she collapsed, sobbing, saying that she'd failed as a parent. He learned to stay away from her and to avoid mentioning anything about sex, which seemed to further enrage her. From that moment he realized she was 'a dangerous customer' and didn't really tell her the truth about anything.

"As we talked, Gay realized that he had generalized his circumspection around 'female issues.' He had held back from asking me about how my sexual feelings might be changing and what my body was actually experiencing when I had a hot flash or a mood swing. He actually knew my body in ways that I didn't, which was very helpful. For example, he could tell from my skin tone when my period was due, often before I registered any symptoms. We saw that there was a whole important area of life that we hadn't explored.

"Later Gay said, 'I love you in all your forms.' I felt such space to grow, change, and reinvent myself in his words and touch. I experienced a wash of relief that I didn't have to try to maintain an image that was fleeting at best and certainly hard to hold on to against the awesome forces of time. Suddenly the expanding waistline and falling chin receded in importance, and the possibilities of loving this new evolution of my form appeared.

"I've been able to return the favor when Gay has worried about thinning hair or liver spots. Each of these changes in appearance and functions has given us a chance to appreciate essence more and to make room for essence to find a new expression."

13 / Sexual Energy as an Evolutionary Force

◦❧◦

In conscious relationships sexual energy must be treated as an evolutionary force all its own. Sexual energy concerns a great deal more than physical lovemaking: It holds a key to the sustained regeneration of relationships over long periods of time.

As most people have probably noticed, the physical aspects of sexual attraction are often prominent in the early stages of a close relationship and tend to recede in prominence as time goes on. Many long-term couples complain about this aspect of sex. They want sexuality to have the same hot and electric qualities that it had when they first felt the attraction to each other. When the heat diminishes, they panic and try to find ways to turn it up again.

This effort is missing both the point and the potential. Here is our advice, which many couples have said changed their lives: When the physical aspect of sex begins to fade, don't try to keep things the way they are. There is a natural progression in sex from physical to emotional to spiritual—and back again to the physical—but this progression must be accepted fully if it is to flow smoothly. If you let the changes happen rather than resist them, you will find that the physical comes back stronger than before. This progression does not have to take months or years—usually it is a matter of days—but if it is resisted, denied, or overridden it can stay stuck in place for decades.

The physical part of sex was originally designed to produce a physical result: children. Then we humans adapted it to meet our emotional and spiritual needs. But if we go back to the very beginning, before there were complicated physical structures like bodies, we could also say that sex was originally a spiritual activity. If you look at one-celled organisms like amoebas, for example, you will see that they engage in what seems like vibratory sex. They cruise up near each other, vibrate rapidly, then move off. This activity does not produce a physical result, such as offspring. It is more complex organisms whose sexual unions produce physical results. Still further along in evolution, organisms turned their attention to having an emotional and an essence-connection through their unions. So up and down the evolutionary scale, all manner of transitions are going on, from the tangible to the ethereal and back again. If we resist the movement away from the physical toward the ethereal—or back again—we are resisting an evolutionary trend that is very powerful.

One couple in our acquaintance makes love every morning, and they have for years, even though they are both in their seventies. For our own benefit, as well as for the couples we counsel, we asked them how they accomplished this. Their answer speaks to the heart of the matter. They do not resist the transformations that go on in their sexual relationship every hour of every day:

"We make love all day, in a thousand different ways. Sexual

energy is flowing through us all the time—that's the way life is and the way people are put together. We are big conductors of sexual energy. We found that out when we stopped being interested in each other's genitals—it just meant that it was time to channel our sexual energy in a different way. Our bodies had had enough stimulation, maybe, and it was time to make love with our words. Then we would make love with our words, by speaking in a loving and tender way. Or maybe it was time to make love with a touch as we were passing by the other in the kitchen. But it's all sexual energy. You can make a salad with the same energy that you have actual physical sex with. Sometimes it's time to be quiet, and then we sit together. Did you know you can sit quietly next to someone with the same tender feelings that you would touch them with? That you can actually make love to the person without touching?"

We got the message. When you allow sexual expression to shift from the physical to other dimensions, you allow the physical to recharge its batteries, so to speak. The recharge doesn't take long at all. What is required is to shift into another state of consciousness, to transcend the physical for a while. If we celebrate this process rather than resist it, we come back to the physical very quickly, refreshed by our contact with a deeper and more subtle dimension of sexuality.

14 / Stretching Your Relationship

❧

The problem of "going to sleep" is endemic to long-term relationships. Couples have to put a lot of attention into keeping things fresh and alive. One way we do it is through varying our routines. We do not have set times for getting up, going to bed, eating, or exercising. We eat when we're hungry, and we go to bed when we're tired. Once when we were on vacation in the Yucatan Peninsula, we found ourselves seated at dinner next to a couple who seemed to be so bored with each other that they were virtually sleepwalking. The man mentioned that he was eating dinner a lot later than he liked. (It was about seven-thirty.) He said, with a kind of homesick satisfaction, that they always ate dinner at five-thirty. Then he turned to Gay and asked what time we ate dinner. Gay looked blankly at Kathlyn and said, "I don't know. What time do we eat?" The man blurted out, "What? You don't know when you eat dinner?!" Later, we had a laughing fit back in our room, because the fellow had reacted with the kind of surprise that would have been appropriate had we said we kept a pet rhino or were members of a transvestite church choir.

Stretching in the relationship stimulates the variety gland, which is the fuel and spice of long-term relating. You have to have room to stretch your potentials, your fears, your limitations, your preferences. The paradox of stretching is that you must stretch against something stable in order to create more length. In aerobics bouncing can produce injury; steady stretching from a stable joint gives the best result. In close relationships stretching works in a similar way. Those people who bounce all over from one new hobby to another, from one career choice to another, create more stress in the partnership. But you can actually stretch, becoming longer and fuller than your present self, by facing and accepting reality as it is now and choosing what you really want. Then action steps, often baby steps at first, gently lengthen the possibilities. Many people open new careers by going to school part-time over several years. They learn to paint, to ski, to write, to build, by taking small, steady steps, bolstered by the stability of their relationships.

In your partnership what strengths would you like to develop? What new potentials would give you more joy when you get up each morning? With what limitations would you like to experience peace and resolution? What experiences would you like to cultivate and share with your partner? These are some of the potentials of stretching. The Japanese work ethic is to improve a little each day. That is a useful description of stretching in the work sphere. We want to acknowledge the human tendency to hibernate, to repeat survival and other learned patterns, simply because those patterns worked in the past.

Kathlyn says: "When I was about nine and visiting my aunt

and uncle at their lake cottage, I sat in like an invisible ear listening to many adult conversations when groups of grownups would get together. During one particular conversation I remember this friend tossing her head back and saying, 'I don't think too much about my appearance anymore. I've already got my man.' " The hook-your-mate model of relationship has been very popular but has some frightening potentials. In many couples one partner suddenly bolts after many years of benign neglect and numbing sameness. The other extreme was brilliantly illustrated by the movie *A Thousand Clowns*. The creative and potently unpredictable hero confronts the shadow side of his Peter Pan persona when the woman he comes to love demands more consistency and when he has to choose whether to get a steady job or lose custody of his nephew.

Fortunately, humans have another urge, however dormant, to "push the envelope." That urge to become more can be a great asset to the ongoing growth and excitement of your relating. Instead of trading in your partner for a seemingly newer model, you can each re-create yourselves and the quality of your being together by looking for ways to stretch. The rewards of consciously stretching are enormous. Spark and sparkle appear at unexpected times. Hitherto unknown facets of yourself and your partner emerge from the closet and begin to shine.

Our best stretching move is to let go of being right and to step into wonder, curiosity, and not knowing. Kathlyn says: "I remember the many times that I let go of being right; it felt like stepping off a cliff. Will I fly? Will the parachute open? Where will I land? Will I survive? I can appreciate how frightening and absurd that step seems the first time, when everything in your history and everything you've learned and seen around you says, 'Hold on to survival, hold on to your beliefs about relationships!' Our experience and the experience that thousands of people have reported is, 'Wow, this is much more fun than I ever imagined! I like re-creating myself and renewing myself.' "

Down inside we have come to appreciate that this sacred

moment is all we really have. The ultimate stretch is to realize, "This is it!" Sometimes we feel sad at realizing how much of life went by while we were waiting for something better to happen. As time passes, we come more and more to savor the immediacy of this moment and to put our attention into sourcing the kind of love we want. As the Beatles told us, "In the end, the love you take is equal to the love you make." These words ring truer now than when we first heard them half a lifetime ago. We always get exactly what we give, and we have only this moment to experience it. Immediacy renews relating. This truly is the only opportunity to celebrate, to fully express our potential and support our partner's. Savoring this precious moment causes us to make choices that are very different from those we made when we thought we had time to waste.

15 / Dealing with a Betrayal

A friend of ours, whom we first met when she took one of our professional training programs, told us a powerful story of betrayal and personal redemption. It stands as a documentary example of the power of integrity and consciousness to heal wounds. "As I began my personal journey of awakening," Bev told us, "and especially after reading *Conscious Loving*, I began to want integrity in my marriage. I sensed that my husband and I did not tell the truth to each other, and certainly the joy had been gone from the relationship for years, but I didn't know exactly what the problem was. One day I clearly stated my intention to the universe, that I wanted to live in integrity and be in a relationship whose basis was integrity. Almost immediately after I expressed this intention, my husband 'out of the blue' told me that he had been having sex with my best friend for seventeen years.

"I don't know how I could have saved my sanity without the body-centered skills I'd learned: conscious breathing, feeling my feelings deeply in my body, telling the truth, moving freely to evocative music as I expressed my rage and sadness. When he told me we'd been living a lie, I felt as if someone had kicked me in the stomach. I could barely breathe and felt nauseous. I was afraid and sad and then numb. My thoughts were: 'How could I have not known this? What were they thinking of? How could this have gone on for so long?' Suddenly everything fell into place, showing me at least one reason I'd felt so unhappy and off-center for so long. My astonishment was total: I couldn't believe how I could be married to a person and be the friend of another person and not know something was going on between them.

"In the days after the revelation, I decided to apply to the mastership program [one of our advanced programs], which involved writing the answers to a number of deep questions like 'What do you most want in your life?' I found that my creativity was pouring out of me as never before. Even though I had every right to be depressed or numb or blocked, as I participated with all my feelings, tremendous creativity gushed forth from me. I am grateful also to my therapist and several friends who kept me out of claiming the victim position (which I often felt I had exclusive right to) and instead invited me to feel my authentic feelings of anger and sadness and fear. They kept me focused on what I wanted to create in my life instead of regretting what I didn't have.

"The biggest challenge I faced was to feel all my rage and sadness. In the beginning members of my family treated me as a victim. When I talked to them about my anger or sadness, they would quickly shift to blaming my husband. I found this unhelpful and asked them instead to focus on their feelings and let me have mine. I have a strong belief that 'nice girls don't get angry,' and I ran up against this constantly during the first few weeks. I would be feeling guilty about my anger and would be hearing a little voice saying, 'Anger is bad—just forgive and forget and everything will be okay.' I knew, though, that my healing depended on letting myself feel everything. As a result I learned things about myself I don't think I could have learned any other way.

"As I took responsibility—asking 'What is it about me that required this event in my life?'—I realized I carried a belief that I was not worth being treasured or valued. I felt deeply that I was fundamentally wrong and bad and therefore did not deserve to be here on this earth. This old belief had driven me to settle for less in all areas of my life. I realized that I was my own real betrayer—I betrayed myself constantly by devaluing myself, not asking for what I want, brewing and stewing over old hurt feelings.

"Now I am genuinely grateful for the gift of this experience. I am not sure I could have learned what I needed to know any other way. I have learned that I deserve to have authenticity and love in my life. I have a full-body knowing of what it means to be in a loveless marriage, and I know I'll never settle for less again. The story is still unfolding, so I don't know where it will all lead. But with a new ground for our relationship—truth, responsibility, a shared commitment to our creativity—who knows what my husband and I will be able to create?"

This woman is a living example of plum-blossom courage: the ability to open and flourish even in the midst of a deep contraction. She and her husband are still learning and remodeling a continually evolving relationship. In her latest update she said they were no longer living together but were better friends than ever and were united around parenting their two children.

16 / Finding Stillness in the Midst of Busy-ness

❧

Kathlyn recently had the opportunity to do some sea kayaking in Alaska. "I was most struck by the vast stillness of the bay," she says, "so still that we could hear each animal breathing. The distinct breathing patterns of the whales, sea lions, and porpoises defined the space and direction of each animal. As I sat paddling in the glassy waters, I became aware of the larger purpose of stillness. By participating directly with the rhythms of the water, my internal sense of stillness and space expanded. Even after being home for several days, I could close my eyes and feel the rocking and gentle lapping, punctuated at intervals with the memory of a furry head silently emerging.

"When a tugboat chugged by, I realized that the noise of civilization has no space. There is no stillness in technology, especially in engines. Most of us have grown up against the constant background of motors. I could feel how I have taken the constant drive of technology into my nervous system, and into my relationships. As I lay in my tent hearing only the drops from the spruce trees bouncing off the rain flap and the occasional *schoosh-schoosh* of bird wings, I breathed into a deeper appreciation of stillness and the gifts that conscious stillness can provide. I realized how much I value stillness, how rare it is, and how committed I am to create it in the center of the often-chaotic world of work and close relationships."

Relationship partners often glaze over the opportunities for stillness by driving an agenda in their daily interactions. This is equivalent to always taking an inbreath and never exhaling. Stillness provides a deep organization for experience, a chance to take in and integrate moments of intense intimacy and the many shifts and fluctuations of daily living. Despite the relationship mantra, "There's always something," we can renew our ability to fully participate by embracing stillness. The ebb of relationship, the receding tide, rests in the pregnant pause.

While working with a vibrant and talented client recently, we noticed that she busies herself from the moment she awakens until she collapses at night. Her mother died from cancer in her early sixties, and all her life she gave and did for others, never cultivating an inner stillness or harmony with herself. Now Ariel, in her mid-forties, has been heading down the same path. She complains about her husband's requests for midday sex when they're both home: "I just have so much to do. We're making love, and I'm making lists of the next projects I need to complete."

In our own relationship we actually structure stillness to fuel our creativity. In the mornings we have a sacred quiet time, where phone calls are not accepted and discussions of business or household items are postponed. During this inviolate time creative ideas and projects take priority. We meditate, write, draw, paint, play the piano, or co-create trainings or workshops. Sometimes we lie on the floor or sit on the deck and "just be." It may not look like something is happening, but the internal fuel cells and neurons are purring with electrical potential, waiting for the breeze of possibility to spark a new connection.

Kathlyn was amazed at how long and how tenaciously she resisted making still-time a priority. Her background and training had laid down deep tracks of busy-ness and organizational hubris. Now, she says, "committing to this time each morning was the single most important factor in changing my life and my perception of myself from a support system to a creative generator and innovator." Most of the people we know and work with long for the ongoing flow of creativity in their lives, the direct experience of inventing something new that adds to the beauty of life. The simple practice of enjoying stillness can open undreamed-of vistas.

In close relationships some of the sweetest moments are communing without words, the times of walking in the woods or sitting on a swing looking at the twilight. These moments emerge from the commitment to value simplicity and quality rather than quantity. We have come to notice the times when we interfere with a natural still point by rushing, making a list, or focusing on what's wrong. A conscious stillness is transparently different from the silence of withholding feelings or truth. In conscious silence a flowering of essence is possible. Each partner can breathe in the fragrance of simple being, and simply being together.

Since becoming grandparents, we have reentered, at least periodically, the sounds and rhythms that come with having young children in the household. Chris and his wife, Helen, reminded us recently how precious moments of stillness become when the day is structured around responding to an infant. Even in the midst of sharing child care and juggling two jobs, they recognize the renewing power of stillness and do their best to give themselves regular doses. One of them takes Elsie for a walk or plays with her while the other gardens or just sits in the rocker for ten minutes. When leaving the house isn't feasible, they use their music earphones to create a womb of stillness for shorter periods of time.

Stillness is different from withholding. Kathlyn says: "As I write this, I am looking out a hotel window at several fourteen-thousand-foot peaks in Breckenridge, Colorado. Until a dog barked briefly this morning, I hadn't realized that that daily sound in my normal urban life was missing. I hear an occasional car winding along the mountain, the tinkling hum of the refrigerator, particularly ardent grasshoppers, and that is all. Stillness of vibration in the ears, stillness of visual distractions, stillness of a quiet mind, of fullness in your relating to yourself and your partner. Withholding creates static, not stillness, something there between you that the antennae of the heart register and fuse with. Withholding interferes with the clear surface of the pond you both share, like someone dangling their toe in the water and jiggling, jiggling.

"Gay and I have spent many evenings swinging in a rope hammock on the porch. Swaying, I feel like a feather settling on a vast field of poppies, or a dandelion blown across a field of wheat."

Part of being still involves being in a state of completion, where there is no unfinished emotional business between you and your partner. The mind and heart can breathe in the cool space of completion. To achieve this stillness, we do our best to stay current with each other. When Kathlyn goes away to teach or Gay leaves on a trip, we know we've said everything that we've thought and felt. Since we're complete, we can be still inside at parting. Our times of being together have no chatter, just fundamental rhythms like swaying and turning, breathing in and out, feeling the ocean of stillness rock us.

Kathlyn continues: "When I have withheld something, usually something I'm irritated about, my mind starts buzzing, and a shield goes up around my skin that short-circuits my connection to stillness. I become a live electric wire snapping and popping randomly, or a loose cannon, as Gay says, if the withhold grows in silence. In many couples the crackling leaves of withholds between partners is so loud that they can't recognize the stillness, that rich loam underneath."

Here is a "homework" assignment to cultivate stillness: Spend five minutes with each other not doing anything. No errands, no planning, no criticism or judgment; just being. Recognize the tunes that you play in your head about yourself and your partner, and wonder what would allow them to be silent. Connection and creation spring out of stillness.

17 / Dealing with Illness and Aging

❧

Two of our most inspirational friends have given us a new model for aging. We first met Mary Kent and Jerry when they were both in their seventies, and they get more vital each year. Since taking one of our workshops five years ago, they have attended both our body-centered and our relationship transformation trainings. Most recently they have turned their children on to our books, and now a second generation of their family has started to explore the work.

A dashing couple, Jerry and Mary Kent radiate health and love. They have become mentors for us and a number of people who have had the chance to experience Mary Kent's graceful gumption and Jerry's beaming curiosity. Kathlyn interviewed them to discover more about their perspectives on this time in their lives and relationship—they've been married more than fifty years.

KATHLYN: We're interested in a couple of areas that you know intimately. First, how have you used aging as a spiritual journey in your relationship? What have you learned from aging? And second, how have the illnesses and accidents you've lived through impacted your relationship?

JERRY: When I left the navy after thirty-five years and the federal government after fifteen years, I felt that I was just starting to live, to move ahead in my life. Your trainings made a container that is very permissive, and I started to see another model for relationships than the one I had to operate in while I was in the military and the government. I also got to see just how we'd been running ourselves around all these years.

MARY KENT: The most important tool I discovered from the work was the clarity that truth-telling provides, first to myself, then with Jerry, friends, and family. Allowing and knowing what's really going on—what a revelation! I felt so accepted and acceptable in the trainings that it opened the possibility that I could be that way. The moment when you had us looking at each other and asking, "Would you be willing to let go of each other as your personal improvement project and celebrate your essences?"—that was a turning point for me.

JERRY: Boy, the hardest thing for me was this whole commitment business. It was hard for me to live up to it at first—it was such a new and different way of living my life. The most important thing I learned was to recognize and feel my feelings when they came up. When Mary Kent had her accident [a serious car accident about a year after Gay and I met them] and I got the news on the phone, I just cried. And I let that happen, which was great! For about a week, when friends and the kids would do something for Mary Kent or me, I just cried. That's when I *really* started to appreciate Mary Kent and our relationship. I really got my priorities straight there.

MARY KENT: Yes, when I came out of the hospital and Jerry was there—he could have been dead from the heart attack he'd had a couple of years before—I just had this huge, heart-opening gratitude. It was powerful! I'm so grateful to have Jerry as a partner.

JERRY: I'd had this near-death experience and knew it wasn't painful at all. And somehow I can enjoy what we have right now in the present. I really feel I have all the time in the world. Fifty percent of my Naval Academy classmates are dead, and the rest are still talking about the battles they fought in World War II. I have time now to be here, like talking to you right now.

MARY KENT: When Jerry had his heart attack, I had just graduated from Barbara Brennan's school [healing through the human energy field]. Boy, I just used everything—heartwise, energetically, spiritually—to help Jerry get better. And the response from the family and friends was *enormous*! It really gave me a sense of my value and the contribution I can make.

JERRY: When we came to this work, I had been looking for a long time. Something was missing for me. We'd been together forever, but we were still operating out of personas. I was looking for a better way of life when we first met you and Gay. Now I have a different relationship with time. The kids are out on their own, and I can look at taking 100 percent responsibility for what I want, for what we want.

MARY KENT: The longing, really. We were longing to find a way to connect that wasn't tinged with right and wrong. We had been exploring and searching. We went to Shalom Mountain, a place of process and love and community. We learned there to combine the sacred and sexual, that they're the same.

JERRY: And right after that, we came to the workshop, where we met you. I have to admit I was resistant to the idea, and I was saying, "Okay, I'll do it to please you."

MARY KENT: Yeah, I almost gave in to the badgering, then finally I just wouldn't give in. I said, "If this is something you don't like and you lay it on me, I'll kill you."

KATHLYN: It sounds like that got your attention, Jerry.

JERRY: Yes, well, we've often been the catalyst for each other moving ahead, sometimes one of us, sometimes the other. And often, I'll have to say, Mary Kent was the first one interested in the way-out things. But now I'll be just as likely to suggest something we learn or do—and you know how tight I can be with money. But I've never regretted spending it on our relationship. Boy, this is the happiest time of our lives.

MARY KENT: Oh, yes, the feeling of aliveness is so much more now than when I was fifty. I'm much less frantic. I meditate more, and I'm walking more clearly now. This accident really smashed up my body, but I didn't acknowledge that at first. I just thought, well, I'll do this rehab stuff and be fine in a couple of weeks. I wasn't fine for a long time. It was really hard to accept the ways things are. I did that with aging too. I've wanted to deny getting older—I *feel* young—I look in the mirror and I know differently. Just getting the way it really is lets me know that, yes, my time is valuable. I can ask the big questions now, like, "How can I be an aging woman who inspires others in the most delightful and fun way?"

KATHLYN: It sounds as if you're putting your attention on creativity and generativity—enjoying and passing on what you know.

MARY KENT: We taught a class on creating conscious relationships last year and had a great time. Now we're doing the work for us, especially learning how to take space, which I always used to think was selfish.

JERRY: Now I really appreciate Mary Kent and our relationship, each day.

Jerry, nearing eighty when he made that last statement, beamed at Mary Kent with his piercing blue eyes and looked like a schoolkid at his birthday party. Mary Kent accepted his love with serenity and returned gratitude. The interview over, we looked at each other with tears in our eyes. Both Gay and I feel that we've been touched by grace, that we've been given the opportunity to be in the presence of a holy relationship.

18 / Removing Projections

❦

On the path of the conscious heart, flexibility is both a gift and a tool. Most couples who come to work with us have foundered on the issue of control, which stifles flexibility. In many partnerships the power struggle of who gets to be right—who's the boss, whose agenda gets priority—consumes the creative energy. Faced with decisions that seem to imply compromise, many partners wonder, "How can I get what I want here?" rather than, "How can we both have what we want?" What are they afraid will happen if they let go a little? Why do they hold to their positions with such life-or-death rigidity? The answer is that most couples are projecting onto each other in those moments: They *are* in the grip of a life-or-death issue, but it is one from long ago that has nothing to do with the present.

A key element of our work with couples is to remove such projections. We do this in a radical manner: We listen carefully to the central complaints of both partners, then ask each one to take responsibility for having created the specific things they are complaining about. An uproar usually follows. He may say: "But wait! That's the way she actually *is!* She *is* lazy (or crabby or sexually stingy)." She may say: "But wait! That's the way he actually *is!* He *is* uncommunicative (or lazy or critical)." We sometimes call this issue the "is-ing" problem. "Is-ing" kills flexibility. "This *is* a clothespin." "This *is* a chair." "This *is* my husband. He *is* stubborn. He *is* the person who only eats eggs over easy, with two, not one, dollops of ketchup." When we stop "is-ing" the other person, we are faced with the unknown. The floppy, flabby, spineless monster oozes out to terrify us—the nothing-definite, nothing-to-plan-on-or-count-on, no-structure monster. But from this void springs the possibility of the creative reinvention of the relationship. Many people would rather sacrifice their relationships than bend and stretch, consider another perspective, or confront their fear of loss of control.

We say in reply to these outcries: "The other person may be that way or may not be, but one thing's for sure. You have a role in it—at the very least you picked this person. So your goal now is to drop your end of it. The point is this: *The very same energy that has gone into complaining or making the other person wrong is the energy that is required to make a personal change within ourselves.*

From an essence perspective, making this move is crucial. Only by opening up to complete responsibility in ourselves can we reconnect with the universe at large. When we are withdrawing into victimhood, we are breaking our connection with the universe. From this position of cosmic aloneness, everything looks bleak. Only when we connect ourselves again with the source of creation do we make a seamless union with the universe again.

That is why when we find ourselves blaming the other person, we must (often reluctantly) point the finger back at ourselves—in a wondering and not in a blameful way, if possible—and ask ourselves, "What is my contribution to this situation?"

Usually these power struggles spring from fear, especially fear of change, of the form dissolving. We're afraid a changed relationship won't re-form into anything we'll like. We're especially afraid of our partner's changes. If you married a button-down suited partner and he begins to change, part of your brain immediately equates his changes with Uncle Ed's transformation from a bank president into a Bermuda-shorts-and-striped-shirt bird watcher. But by resisting change we actually argue with the way life moves. The universe is always forming, dissolving, and re-forming in new patterns. If you consciously embrace change in your relationship, you can surf the waves of change more easily. And you might even have fun.

19 / Synchronicity: Making Friends with the Universe

ᴄ᷈ᴠᴡ᷈

You may have experienced days where everything seems to go your way. You want something, and it appears; you think of a person, and they call; the picture you've been searching for for months turns up in a book you pick up off the shelf. These seemingly magical times appear and disappear without reason, as you know if you've ever tried to think your way into grace.

This smooth blend of right place and right time, which we sometimes call synchronicity, sweetens a relationship. Kathlyn says, "I was in Germany teaching a seminar and picked up the phone to call Gay just as he was picking up the phone nine thousand miles away to dial me. The timing was so close, the phone didn't even ring on either end." In our lectures one of us will sometimes think of an example or experience a split second before the other one says it. We'll both start humming the same song at the same time. We'll call each other from a trip and say, "I just had the idea that it would be great to . . ." and the other one will laugh and say, "I just had the same idea."

A friend of ours, Steve, shares his experiences of synchronicity from one twenty-four-hour period: "I formed a new intention one evening and spent time saying it as a whole-body communication, letting my muscles, organs, and bones express the intention as well as my mind. The intention was, 'I am content in knowing that I have and will continue to have all that I need—easily and flowing.' I voiced this intention at the beginning of a session with a bodyworker who was about to give me a deep massage.

"The next day after meditation it was nine-thirty, and I wanted to talk with my accountant. His office opens at nine-thirty. As I was thinking that, the phone rang; it was his assistant saying my accountant wanted to talk to me. Fantastic! I didn't even have to dial! Then I thought about my new video being reproduced and remembered something I needed to remind the director about. Seconds later he called to tell me my videos were ready to be picked up. Similar events happened all day. I wanted to share a new CD with my son Jesse, and he called, as if having read my mind. I faxed Gay about something, and he called to say he was thinking the same thought when the fax came through. I wondered whether an important business client had left for a trip yet, and he called. Gay and Kathlyn's office director called me to ask for a phone number to order a new water filter that I have. I wasn't sure where it was, but I was thinking about it as I went out to check the mail. Among the letters was a card from the filter company with their number reminding me to reorder.

"I wanted and couldn't find oranges today. When I went to a restaurant with a friend for lunch, we didn't like the menu. We walked three blocks to a great Thai restaurant and on the way saw the farmers' market, with ten-pound bags of oranges on every table. That evening as Katie and I were walking into a movie, I was telling her a new presentation story I had invented and tried out on my assistant. We walked into the theater, and there was my assistant, getting ready to see another movie in the same theater. Later that evening, as a finale, Katie and I were silently sitting side by side on the couch working on our PowerBooks. She looked up and said, 'I'm working on the synchronicity section and would love to get your notes about today as an example,' just as I was printing them out!"

File all that in the category called "having a good day." What had happened to produce such a stream of easy connections? That number of incidents seems too high to be coincidental. We think that one key to synchronicity in daily life is whole-body participation. When life itself is your dance partner, such events are not surprising. Steve didn't just think about what he wanted; he took his intention into a bodywork session and got the support of another person for his desire. Then he faced, breathed, and moved with his whole body's response. Sometimes with a big positive intention we flush up big resistance or barriers—what we call the Upper Limits Problem. Essentially Steve let his body get big enough to hold a new direction.

Steve also let go of trying or worrying. He set his intention and then went into his day. We've found countless times that the universe is ready to support our expression. But if we don't catch the wave, we can't experience support. The more we cultivate an inner experience of space, the more synchronous events occur. Synchronicity seems to come from space, so the more time we spend in the space of meditation, nondoing, or being, the more events flow harmoniously.

Another key seems to be full participation with life as it's actually happening. When you argue with life, you fall off the wave into the push-pull of a power struggle. It's a struggle you're not going to win. As Frank Zappa once said, "In the war between you and the world, back the world." Our good friend Alex shares an experience that illustrates the relationship between accepting the way things are and synchronicity.

"Recently," she told us, "I have been exploring the activity of letting go of worrying and trying to make things happen. My interest was piqued when I noticed that amazing results occurred in my life directly after letting go.

"My partner and I had a conversation one afternoon about meaningful, intimate relationships from our past. I told him about Tom, a passionate, long-distance romance that ended abruptly years ago. One day we just stopped writing and calling, neither of us willing to relocate or to state the obvious. I wondered about him from time to time. He had moved, and the hours I invested in directory research had failed to turn up his current address.

"My bewildered current partner asked if I was still carrying a torch for Tom. Of course, the answer was yes. This fellow was occupying a big space in my heart. I agreed to come to resolution with this old relationship as soon as possible.

"I pondered for quite a while how this resolution was going to happen. I live on the West Coast, but the last connection I'd had with Tom was in New York. Was it back to directories, endless hours of operator assistance, or hiring a detective? I felt frustrated and realized that I was getting paltry results for the amount of time and energy I was investing. Then I decided to let go and be willing to have resolution happen easily, even if I didn't know how.

"Two days later my partner and I were checking in at the airport. As we left the ticket agent and headed for our departure gate, there was Tom standing just a few feet away. We simultaneously caught sight of each other. Even though twelve years had passed, we chatted easily and briefly. He was just in the airport to change planes. He had moved to the West Coast, married, and was thoroughly enjoying raising his two daughters. I left our encounter with a full sense of resolution and a freed heart."

20 / Healing Old Traumas

We were all born into a party that was going on before we arrived. The rules, language, and power structure were already established and in many cases had been running on automatic pilot for decades, if not centuries. Our survival depended on our being able to learn the rules without being told what they were. We're all very skilled at fitting in and following the thousands of nonverbal cues that allow us to continue getting fed. The problem is that we think there's only one party available. We don't realize we can create a better one.

A big mistake in adult relationships is to insist on getting from our partners what we didn't get as children. In close relationships partners will unconsciously repeat their old family patterns and continue to be surprised and hurt that they still get the same result. Even when people have dumped the partner they thought was the source of the problem and gone to great lengths to find someone totally different, lo and behold, the same pattern emerges. Most people don't realize that part of their brain is still two or three years old, whenever a fundamental need was thwarted and denied. Our effusive life-force dwindles each time our essence isn't appreciated and supported, and our snapshot of life includes all those crimps and stagnant pools. Based on this snapshot, we think that's the way life is. We may forget the moment we took the snapshot, but our bodies and our unconscious minds don't forget.

Many people simply do not see their partners clearly. They see the overlay of old hurts, which they unconsciously expect their partners to fix. There are many examples: You might expect your partner to be the opposite of your parents' shortcoming—strong if they were weak, a good listener if they were aloof, tender and compassionate if they were distant and abusive. The amazing irony of these surface desires is that we tend to re-create the original wound in order to get a chance to finally complete it, to finally get the love and recognition we long for. Since the unconscious mind doesn't have a linear sense of time, it's always two years old or four and a half, depending on how old you were when your flow got interrupted. Many of us don't realize that our adult relationships are being run by very angry, hurt children.

The solution is not only psychological but spiritual. What heals old traumas is a willingness to feel the old pain and breathe through it, and to take responsibility now for issues and experiences that couldn't be resolved in the past. Many well-intentioned spiritual people make a crucial error: They pray or meditate to transcend or avoid feeling. If you use prayer or meditation in this way, you deny and suppress body experience that needs to be felt, celebrated, and welcomed into the wholeness of yourself. When you can love your whole-body experience and accept what happened in the past, then you can consciously decide how to design a life the way you want it now. When you develop a set of goals that stands in the present rather than in the past, you are pulled toward them rather than being pushed by the past.

21 / Moving from Persona-Sex to Essence-Sex

❧

Sex is the place where many relationship problems come to light, but we have found that the problem is seldom with the technical aspects of sex. Sexual union is an exquisite connection-point between people. The intimacy of the sexual embrace is at once spiritual and physical; for this reason, it reflects any distortion in communication and balance that is occurring in the rest of the relationship.

One of our friends, Rod Wells, experienced a powerful awakening in his marriage through focusing on the lesson that a sexual issue was bringing to his attention. We asked him to write the story of his relationship miracle.

"A marriage has transformative potential," he wrote, "only when the energy it produces is brought to bear on the evolution of the partners. I found that I was wasting my energy, using past relationships as escape routes. I call these incomplete prior relationships ghosts, which I define as illusions generated by selecting out the pleasurable past experiences with the person to produce a romanticized fantasy of them. I found that to access the exquisite transformations possible in my marriage, I had to sever the umbilical cord of the past loves I was using as escape routes. I discovered that when I stood with all my attention on the present, some real magic began to happen with Sandy, my wife.

"Before I got married, I dated several different women at the same time. Since I was committed to none of them, I used them all as escape routes from each other. I was always able to escape any unpleasant feeling with one of them by running to another. The problem was that I also escaped any personal growth, which resulted in a feeling of entropy or stagnation. I never stayed put long enough to get to the other side of an issue. I began to wonder, 'Is this all there is?' My circle of friends spotted my game before I did and began referring to me as a snake. When I first heard this characterization, I couldn't understand what they were talking about. However, my own 'snake,' in the Freudian sense, soon communicated with me by failing to rear its head on several occasions.

"I began to fail in my attempts to make love to Sandy because ghosts of other women would be haunting my consciousness even though I was monogamous with Sandy. I became afraid that I would say 'Sally!' or 'Jane!' instead of 'Sandy!' In the past the equipment had always worked, no matter what self-deceptions I was engaged in. But now, probably because of the increased level of commitment with Sandy, it let me down. 'Is anything wrong, Rod?' was a difficult question to answer, because my very integrity, or lack thereof, was the answer to the question. I found it difficult to say the simple truth, like 'I was thinking of making love to someone else and my body got confused.' Reluctantly, though, I forced myself to be honest with both Sandy and myself. I consciously let go of using the fantasies and focused all my attention on the present. As a result, an immediate shift occurred.

"Suddenly I shifted into a deeper purpose for our relationship. A tender sensual quality and essence-connection became present. Through the gate of integrity, I had stumbled on a spiritual sexual intimacy. It felt as holy as those exalted mountaintop moments when I felt connected to the whole universe. I was making the same spiritual connection through a whole-being commitment to another person, and it felt great. No wonder I had been confused. Once I tasted true intimacy, I saw that it was the ultimate evolutionary capability I had been endowed with. I had been arguing with it, and that argument affected my body because I was arguing with the greatest force there was. When I started letting go into it, it took me places I had only dreamed of before. Now I'm afraid and excited, and I know what 'high' fidelity means."

PART FOUR

THE ESSENTIAL PRACTICES

❦

Six Exercises in Transformation

In this section we will describe several essential practices that produce the most rapid transformation in our relationship workshops. They were developed first in our own relationship as we focused on it as a spiritual path. Leading hundreds of couples and thousands of workshop participants through these practices has helped us to refine them and to continue uncovering the essential attitudes and skills we all need. We invite you to experiment with each one and to personalize them to reflect your life and your close relationships.

There are six practices we recommend you do to bring the spiritual path of conscious relationship into practical reality. In our (humble) opinion, any human being could benefit from doing these practices at least once in their lives. But you may do them repeatedly, with increasing value with each repetition. They are designed in such a way that they never go stale. The six are:

Conscious Listening
Making Soul-Commitments
The Essence-Meditations
Balancing Power
Ending Control Struggles
Developing Appreciation

1/Conscious Listening

❧

Listening is incredibly important to any relationship but especially to our love lives. The first practice, conscious listening, has three levels. People grow on the spiritual path of relationships when they practice conscious listening, and they transform their relationships as well. Fortunately for all of us, listening is something that can be learned and mastered through practice. To listen carefully and deeply in the heat of a relationship conflict is a lifeskill of the highest order. It has taken us years of practice to become skilled listeners, but it is possibly the most rewarding thing we've ever learned, because it has made life richer at home, at work, and in the myriad interactions in between.

Given the importance of conscious listening, it borders on criminal that it is not taught every day in every educational institution. Most of us must learn in adulthood a skill that should have been well in place by the time we moved up from elementary school. But we all have to start somewhere. In our own relationship we began by making a conscious commitment to listening. Once we both made this commitment, we mapped out the skills we needed and began the tough work of applying them in the heat of action. They worked miracle after miracle in our lives, even when we did not practice them surefootedly. As our confidence in them grew, we began to teach them to people in therapy, in workshops, and in corporate settings. The miracles flowed in even greater abundance. Nowadays we value this practice so much that if we have a situation where we can only teach one skill—such as a three-hour seminar with busy executives—this is what we often choose.

Here are the specific commitments that we made to begin our explorations of conscious listening:

THE LISTENING COMMITMENTS

- *I commit to listening carefully enough that I can restate the content of what you have said without adding my point of view to it.*
- *I commit to listening to the feelings embedded in your communication.*
- *I commit to listening in such a way that our mutual creativity is facilitated.*
- *I commit to speaking and listening to myself and you free of criticism. (Criticism is defined as "finding fault, censuring, disapproving.")*
- *I commit to speaking and listening to myself and you free of evaluating either of us. (Evaluating is defined as "appraising, determining the worth of.")*

- I commit to speaking and listening to myself and you free of judging either of us as right or wrong, good or bad, smart or stupid.
- I commit to speaking and listening to myself and you free of comparing us to each other or to anyone else. (*Comparing is defined as "bringing things together to ascertain their differences and similarities."*)
- I commit to speaking and listening to myself and you free from controlling the feelings, energies, or actions of either of us. (*Controlling is defined as "curbing, restraining, holding back, having authority over, directing, or commanding."*)
- I commit to speaking and listening to myself and you with appreciation. (*Appreciation is defined in two senses: "sensitive awareness" and "focus on positive qualities and attributes."*)

EXPLORING THE LISTENING COMMITMENTS

We found that these listening commitments were so radical that they required a great deal of work to embrace. Often other people have deep resistance to them, because these listening commitments require treating others as equals. In fact, listening skills are the behavioral evidence of equality in action.

The first commitment pledges you to listen with accuracy. You set yourself the high task of listening so thoroughly that you can restate or summarize what your partner has said without putting your "spin" on it. This listening commitment has changed people's relationships all by itself. For many people, being heard is so rare that when it happens, it shifts their whole way of being. On the listener's side, many people have never suspended their judgments and evaluations of other people's speaking long enough to actually hear what they are saying.

Many people require several intense hour-long learning

sessions to learn this skill. In the beginning, we ask people to practice their listening in short two-minute segments. In other words, we do not ask them to remember and summarize twenty minutes of conversation. Sometimes, in fact, we find that we must teach listening in only one-sentence segments. The careful attention is most worthwhile, though. When they get it, a great leap of energy and aliveness fills the room.

The second listening commitment, to hearing feelings, opens the possibility for a deeper level of attunement to what your partner is saying. Beneath the verbal message there is almost always an emotional message. Words and feelings must both be heard for useful communication to take place. For example, the speaker may be saying, "Are you going to the store this morning?" To accurately paraphrase these words, the listener might say something like "I hear you asking if I'm going to the store." But the emotional message might be anger, as in "I'm angry that you are going to leave me here with the children while you go to the store with that bimbo to buy more vodka." Or it might be despair, as in "I'm sad that you're going to work so soon after your coronary. I'm worried that you'll die and I'll be left alone." To fully paraphrase the original sentence, then, the listener would need to say something like "I hear you asking if I'm going to the store, and I also hear that you're angry (or sad or scared)." While the first depth of conscious listening—accurately paraphrasing the words—is very important, the second depth is often where people finally feel heard.

Emotions are a powerful gateway to spiritual development. Gary Zukav says: "Only through emotions can you encounter the force field of your own soul." When we can meet our feelings directly, and greet them as friends with a message, we make a great leap forward in our spiritual development. Not only do you learn that you're scared or angry or sad, you also pick up the distant glimmer of essence. All emotions melt into the soul. If you are scared and listen to your fear instead of hastening to be rid of it, you will find that the very sensations of fear dissolve and resolve into clear space.

The third commitment is to listen as an ally in the other person's full creative expression. At this depth you listen in such a way that you are "being for" the other person. Your attention is directed toward the other's essence and how it is expressed in the world. In its most basic form, third-depth listening is the ability to ask the other person, "What do you most want?" It includes the ability to listen in such a way that you draw people into deeper appreciations of their heart-desires.

Our experiences have shown us that these three listening commitments are extremely powerful but equally hard to master. The problem is that when we get scared, we tighten around our own point of view and wall others out. It is very hard to "be for" someone else when you are seeing that person as the enemy. It takes an act of high courage to let go of the contraction and embrace the other person as an ally.

The next five listening commitments deal with eliminating the filters that people habitually put on their listening. In our early days we called these listening shields, but now we have adopted a more benign and porous term, listening filters. In order to master the first three commitments of conscious listening, most of us need to remove one or more of the filters that our conditioning has placed on our listening.

At our seminars, we often harvest from the audience the filters they most commonly use in their relationships. We give them an example of a woman saying, "I've been feeling depressed. I don't feel like I'm using my potential. I'm thinking of going to medical school, but I'm forty-five and have three teenagers to raise." We ask people to imagine themselves in the role of her husband. Here are some of the listening filters that emerge:

Listening to criticize ("That's the most ridiculous idea I've ever heard.")

Listening to judge or evaluate ("I'm not sure that's a good idea.")

Listening to influence or control ("Don't even think of leaving your family to go to medical school. We need you right here where you belong.")

Listening to compare ("I put aside my education and my dreams to raise this family, so I don't think it's fair for you to go off and do what you want to do.")

Listening to fix ("Why don't you try working out at the gym for an hour a day—that depression would disappear quick as a wink.")

Another listening filter that is troublesome in close relationships is listening to support victimhood. This filter takes two main forms. One form is to encourage people to think of themselves as victims. In the medical school example, a victim-thinking friend might say, "You poor dear. You've put up with him for twenty years and now he won't give you a break. I don't know how a saint like you ever ended up with a lout like that." Some of us have friendship networks that include people who support us in being victims rather than in being effective in our lives. One of our therapy clients, a well-known entertainer who has portrayed many wronged women, uttered a memorable one-liner during a discussion of this issue. We were encouraging her to spend her time with friends who supported her effectiveness, and to stop hanging around with people who treated her as a victim. "Well," she said, "there goes my whole Rolodex."

In the second form of victimhood listening the listener compares their victimhood with the speaker's. This style is very popular in couples' therapy sessions. One partner will say, "I'm really angry that you didn't pick up the laundry," and the other will reply, "If I didn't work my tail off all day, you wouldn't have any laundry to pick up." The race to occupy the victim position is on, and there is never a winner. Even if you do end up portraying yourself as a bigger victim, you lose. Now and then a victim will hit the jackpot, perhaps by pouring hot coffee in their lap at a fast-food restaurant, but the race for victim never produces happiness.

The last listening commitment—listening to appreciate— is difficult to master. It requires that we live in a state of appreciation even under stress. In a famous story a Zen master is being pursued by a tiger. He comes to the edge of a cliff and is faced with the decision: jump or be eaten. He jumps, and as he falls, he passes the branch of a cherry tree, which he grabs. There he is, hanging over the abyss, tiger slavering above him, the void below. He sees a ripe cherry on the tree and, with his free hand, picks and eats it. Ah, he says with total enjoyment. The point of the story is that we need to learn to live in appreciation in each moment, even when the stress of life has got us hanging over the abyss.

In our own relationship we have done a great deal of work to learn to live in appreciation. It seems that each time we make a breakthrough to a higher level of this ability, the universe gives us a pop quiz to find out if we can practice the skill in the rigor of conflict. Sometimes we pass, and sometimes we fail. We find it downright maddening at times, given our long study of this problem, to find ourselves caught in its grip. Sometimes, in fact, our status as relationship experts gets in our way. Because of our intellectual knowledge, we forget to practice the basics of conscious listening, truth-telling, taking full responsibility, and keeping the flow of appreciation going all the time. When we forget, the real world is right there to remind us: No matter how far we've traveled, we must still take the path carefully, one step at a time.

THE FIRST LEVEL

The first level of conscious listening is to give a simple summary of what you have heard a speaker say. Until you have tried it a few times (or a few thousand times, in our personal case!), you may not appreciate what a challenge it is. We have seen people go through two or three rounds just fine, then completely lose their ability to listen on their next turn. You never know what is going to push the "stop listening" button in our brains (and we all seem to be equipped with that particular button). That's where the learning occurs, though. Don't make yourself wrong for not being able to give the summary. Just learn from each time you slip up— notice what triggered you to stop listening—and try again.

What follows are the simple instructions we use to teach the first level of conscious listening to therapy clients and workshop participants. We recommend that you begin by reading carefully the previous discussion of the listening commitments. If you are willing to embrace them, consciously and formally commit to them. Now you are ready to learn the first level of conscious listening.

Instructions

We will give the instructions verbatim as if we were speaking directly to two participants. You may want to get a third party to be your coach and timekeeper. If so, this person can read the directions to you as you practice them.

"Speaker, you will have one minute to say anything you want to say about your feelings or the relationship. Do your best to speak the deepest level of truth you can. You can expect us to stop you right on the minute, so both of you will know you're getting exactly the same amount of time. Later, you can do a free-form version of this without timekeeping, but we have found it easiest to learn in the beginning by watching the clock.

"Listener, your job will be to listen carefully, so you can paraphrase the content of what Speaker said.

"Speaker, go ahead. (*Speaker talks for a minute.*)

"Speaker, pause.

"Listener, summarize what you heard. Two phrases that are useful are 'I heard you say ———' and 'What I heard you say was ———.'"

(*Listener gives summary.*)

"Speaker, was that an accurate summary of what you said?"

(*If Speaker says yes, switch roles. If no*): "Speaker, say again the part you felt was missing. Listener, at the end of it, give a summary of what you heard."

(*Continue until Speaker okays the summary. If Speaker tries to add content that was not in the original minute, ask him or her to hold it until the next round.*)

THE SECOND LEVEL

The first level—listening for accuracy of content—forces the listener to separate the speaker's meaning from the meaning generated by the listener's own filters. The second level involves hearing the emotion under the words. One of our clients referred to the first level as "listening from the head"; the second level could be called "listening from the heart." At the second level we listen for the music that is running along under the lyrics.

Without the second level human relationships would be flat and one-dimensional. And without hearing the emotional undercurrents of communication, we would be doomed to miss out on the defining moments of intimacy. In our therapy practice we asked one couple whether they were committed to solving a certain problem. (This question often brings up the emotional level of communication very quickly.)

US: Are you committed to solving this problem?
NINA: Yeah.
JOHN: Sure.

On the surface—just seeing the words—you would think that both were committed. But the emotional tone told us a very different story. Her "Yeah" came out with an eye-roll of exasperation. It said, "Oh, right—like that's going to make a big difference!" His "Sure" was tinged with hostility and resignation.

As therapists, of course, we are trained to pick up on emotional nuances. Lovers often train themselves to tune out that very same level—or rather, they tune it out to their conscious minds. On a deeper level, they register all of each other's emotions and many other levels as well.

With this couple the emotions were crying out (to our ears), but the two of them seemed to be oblivious to the feeling-level of the communication.

US: John, tune in to the feelings underneath the way Nina said "Yeah." What do you hear there?

JOHN (*long pause*): I don't know.

US: Of the big three feelings—fear, anger, and sadness—which one did it sound more like? Did she sound scared or angry or sad?

JOHN (*another long pause*): I guess I'd have to say angry. Maybe sad too.

US: Let's check it out. Nina, as you tune in to your body-signals, do you feel angry or sad?

NINA (*starts to cry*): Yeah. All of the above. I feel angry that I've tried for so long without any success. I'm sad that I feel so alone.

US: How about John's feelings right now, Nina? Can you tune in to his "Sure" and say whether it was more like angry or sad or scared? Or more than one?

NINA: It would be mostly sadness, I guess. Maybe some anger too.

US: Is that accurate, John?

JOHN: Um-hm. Yeah, I can feel both of those.

US: Okay, so you're both feeling the same feelings.

(*There's a long pause as it dawns on them that they've been tuning out the very same feelings in each other that they've been feeling themselves.*)

US: You also both look scared too, from our perspective. Check inside and feel if that's accurate.

JOHN: Yeah, I'm scared. I don't want to be alone, either. That's been my big concern— I'll find that that's what I'm thinking about when I wake up in the morning.
NINA: Yeah, me too.
US: You're both scared about the same thing, too.

This is a classic example of something we see every day: Underneath the surface battles both partners are often feeling exactly the same emotions. John has been tuning out Nina's emotions because he does not want to feel them in himself. And vice versa.

Instructions

"Speaker, you will have a minute to say anything you want about your feelings or the relationship. After you have spoken for a minute, Listener will tune in to the emotional level of what you're saying. When you're ready, begin."

(*Speaker talks for a minute.*)

"Speaker, pause.

"Listener, tune in to the feeling or feelings you were hearing under the words. We'll focus on three of the most important feelings: fear, anger, and sadness. In hearing what Speaker said, did he or she sound more angry, scared, or sad? Or a combination?"

(*Listener replies.*)

"Speaker, is that an accurate summary of your feelings?"

(*Speaker replies. Go back and forth until the various feelings are accurately summarized, then switch roles.*)

THE THIRD LEVEL

Beneath the words and the feelings runs a third level: what the person wants and needs. A big sticking-point in communication, perhaps the biggest, is that we get so caught up in our own conscious and unconscious needs that we cannot hear what other people want and need. This practice is designed to remedy that problem.

Instructions

"Speaker, you will have a minute to say anything about your feelings or the relationship. When you're ready, begin."

(*Speaker talks for a minute.*)

"Speaker, pause.

"Listener, under the words and the feelings, what does Speaker most deeply want and need?"

(*Listener replies.*)

"Speaker, is that an accurate summary?"

(*If yes, switch roles. If not, ask Speaker to clarify the wants and needs that were not heard by Listener. Keep going until Speaker has okayed Listener's response.*)

You may find, as we have, that these conscious listening practices work miracles. If you find that they are not working for you, try them out with a third party keeping you on track. The only cause we've ever heard for the practices not working is that the partners got hooked by a contentious issue partway through and failed to follow the instructions. This has happened to us more than a few times, so don't be hard on yourself if this occurs. Remember, these practices involve lifelong learning. We have been doing them for fifteen years now, and every week we seem to learn how to do them a little bit better.

2/Making Soul-Commitments

❦

This essential practice is one you can do by yourself, as well as with a friend, colleague, family member, or romantic partner. We have found it equally valuable in the boardroom, the bedroom, and the family room. It is organized around two questions—in fact, two questions that are great gifts to ourselves and anyone we ask them of.

The first question is: *"What is really important to you?"*

You can use this question as a powerful problem-solving tool. For example, you could ask each other what is really important about:

- Leaving now to go to the party
- Having a certain amount of money in savings
- Disciplining the children

We all need to know what we really want. If we don't, how are we going to commit, body and soul, to any path of action? How can we enlist the support of others to help us get it? Asking what is most important—and listening to the answer—closes the information gap. You don't have to imagine what your partner wants or fill in the gap with inaccurate information that sends you spinning down the wrong path. Very few of us have ever had the total attention and support of another human being to bring our deepest dreams into reality.

One of our friends told us a story that brought the concept home forcefully. During her first marriage she asked her husband if something was going on, because she was feeling out of sync inside and out of touch with him. He denied that anything out of the ordinary was happening, denials that continued until he left an obvious clue that allowed her to catch him in his affair. Before she got that additional information, she had felt literally crazy inside, making up thoughts about what the problem might be, getting sick, missing appointments, feeling paranoid and irritable. Her illusions would quiet the craziness for a bit, but the rattle wouldn't settle. She said something very interesting about that time: "Once I recovered from [his] massive withhold [about the affair], I could see that I had been frightened of this very thing and had unconsciously colluded in the secret by not wanting to hear it."

When partners ask each other, "What is really important to you?" they commit to listening to the answer. You can then place your attention on just what you and your partner want, so that the information loops are kept open and circulating.

There are four useful areas about which to ask, "What is really important to you?":

- *Yourself:* your inner life, your relationship with yourself and who you are becoming

- *Interactions with others:* your relationships with others in your family, workplace, church, and other organizations, or in a particular meeting
- *The material world:* the realm of "stuff"; your wishes in the arena of cars, rugs, houses, jewelry
- *The larger world:* your relationship to the environment, to other cultures, to the reality we all share

The second question brings dreams into form: *"What can I do to help make that happen?"*

Your partner's response to this question can focus your actions and shape them in the direction that will most benefit both of you. People are often surprised by the common response to this question: "Your listening is what I most want; that's all—that's plenty." In many long-term relationships the support that partners experience from asking this question and listening to the answer provides all the jump start they need. Actions grow directly out of knowing what is most important.

In raising children, especially teenagers, these two questions are often the most effective way to become allies. Asking "What's important to you?" helped us to find out what Chris and Amanda actually wanted in their lives and from us. If we listened to them for a while, they would get down to wants that everyone could agree on—in contrast to our previous attempts to corral them into wanting what "was best for them" or what might be most convenient for us. Many conversations involved long discussions of what was currently important, whether it was getting the right material for an art project or understanding why people walk the way they do and what that means. For Chris, these conversations evolved into his career as a massage and movement specialist. For Amanda, they grew into a master's degree in fine arts from UCLA. We would take the time to support the question, then to see if we could support that course of action or empower them to create the result they wanted.

3 / The Essence-Meditations

❦

Questions are magical, because if a question is genuine, it takes us into the unknown. For this reason we have become strong advocates of asking questions to catalyze change and healing. Most of us grew up in an answer-oriented milieu, such as school, where getting the correct response was rewarded. On the spiritual path questions move into the foreground. Questions have the power to pull you into a future you can't currently imagine.

Our favorite teaching about questions comes from Rainer Maria Rilke's *Letters to a Young Poet:*

> I want to beg you, as much as I can, to be patient toward all that is unsolved in your heart and to try to love the *questions*

themselves like locked rooms and like books that are written in a very foreign tongue. Do not now seek the answers, which cannot be given you because you would not be able to live them. And the point is, to live everything. *Live* the questions now. Perhaps you will then gradually, without noticing it, live along some distant day into the answer.

ESSENCE-QUESTIONS

A number of questions generate the feeling of essence in people who ask them sincerely. A good time to float these questions through your mind is first thing in the morning, before you engage in daily activities. Then they become like beacons to orient the day. Another way to meditate on these questions is to post them around your environment—dashboard, mirror, computer screen—so you enter them into your consciousness throughout the day.

- What are two or three of your qualities, without which you wouldn't be you?
- What do you most love doing, such that if you didn't get to do it, life would have no meaning to you?
- If your relationship worked well, what would you do with the energy and time you have been expending in conflict?
- Imagine you are on your deathbed, and someone asks if your life has been a success. You answer yes. What four or five things have you experienced or accomplished that have made your life a success?
- If you could design your relationship any way you wanted to, how would you design it?
- Think about a recent relationship conflict—re-create it vividly in your mind. What would be the completely healed, positive outcome?
- If you knew you couldn't fail, what would you most want in your relationship?

- How can you best appreciate your feelings today?
- How can you play with your shadow today in a loving and friendly celebration?
- How can you use every experience to fuel aliveness in yourself and those around you?
- How can you express essence in a way that invites the expression of essence in those you meet today?
- How can you recognize and express who you are at your deepest, most expanded level in a way that invites celebration?

FOR PARTNERS

Here is a simple practice that produces strong feelings of essence. Most people find they have to stay with it for ten to fifteen minutes before the deep essence-feelings begin to build.

Face each other, and maintain eye contact. Take a few moments to just breathe and be with each other.

Take a moment to love yourself, then a moment to love your partner. Keep oscillating back and forth between giving yourself love and loving your partner.

With eye contact, take a moment to be *for* yourself, then focus on your partner and be *for* them, in your spirit and your heart, even if you're angry. Then focus on your experience and be *for* yourself, *for* your highest expression. Go back and forth, being for your partner, then for yourself.

Keep repeating the cycle until you feel the body-feelings of essence.

FOR INDIVIDUALS

Breathe gently and easily into your belly. Let yourself rest after the outbreath until your body is ready to take another inbreath, then ride the breath all the way in and out. Tune in to someplace in your body that is calling, and when breath comes, breathe into that place. On the outbreath let go in that place; just release as you breathe out. Pause again after each outbreath until your body is ready to breathe again, then breathe into any place that needs attention. Continue for two minutes.

Focus on a warm glow in your chest. Let your awareness rest gently on the warm glow, and keep returning to it. Nurture and be with the warm glow until you feel it more prominently. Close your eyes and get in touch with your own source of light. Be with that, and appreciate yourself for being your own source of love and light.

Love yourself for whatever you're feeling and thinking right now. Think of someone or something you absolutely know you love, and give yourself that same love.

4 / Balancing Power

❧

Relationships can occur only between equals. In every healthy relationship the power is equally balanced. To balance the power most efficiently, everyone should meet at the top by taking complete responsibility. When one person steps out of full responsibility for themselves or the relationship, a power struggle begins. Taking healthy responsibility is one of the most important steps you can take for your own self-esteem and for your relationships. A healthy understanding of responsibility can be very helpful in uncovering and expressing your spiritual self.

Here are some important things to remember about taking responsibility:

- Responsibility is best taken as a celebration rather than as a burden or a chore.
- Taking responsibility restores to you the power over your happiness that you have given to your parents, any authority, your partner, your moods, the weather, or anything else. It is the ultimate cure for self-esteem problems. It says, "We're equal, and I deserve to be here."
- Taking 100 percent responsibility for yourself means that you can acknowledge that others are 100 percent responsible for themselves.
- Take responsibility *now!* Don't worry about whether you created your parents or orchestrated your birth or have toothaches because you bit somebody in a past life. With these speculations we rob ourselves of the time and energy we need to take responsibility now. The same goes for blame. Your childhood is over. Instead of worrying about what your parents or somebody did to you, focus on what you would like to create now.
- Look around carefully in your life for any place you are operating as a victim. Are you perceiving yourself as the victim of another person, past or present? A victim of your body? The way the world is? Let it go: The way it is is the way it is.
- Taking responsibility does not mean blaming yourself. If you take responsibility for an old trauma, you just acknowledge that it happened and accept the feelings you felt and your interpretations of the experience.

RESPONSIBILITY MEDITATIONS

Practice these ideas by saying them in your mind and out loud:

- I am completely responsible for all my feelings.
- I am completely responsible for my well-being.
- I give other people responsibility for their feelings and actions.
- I take responsibility for making and keeping agreements. I take responsibility for handling the agreements I break.
- I take responsibility for expressing my spiritual essence in ways that make a difference in the world.

RESPONSIBILITY PRACTICE

Step One

Identify a major complaint in your life. Look for an issue or problem that has arisen three or more times without a satisfying resolution. It could be in your relationship with yourself, a romantic partner, a business associate, your children, or a friend. Take two minutes to just complain about it in your most unenlightened manner. Don't try to be nice or polite. You can write for two minutes or complain out loud. It's helpful to include words like "never," "always," "too (adjective)," "not enough." Give yourself permission to air the dirty laundry.

Step Two

Ask yourself: Are you willing to take 100 percent responsibility for clearing up this issue?

When you ask this question, your mind may argue, go blank,

or say, "I don't know how." Remember that the path appears *after* you take responsibility, not before. Just see if you are genuinely willing to step into healthy responsibility.

If you are willing to take 100 percent responsibility, designate a place on the floor that represents responsibility, and actually step into that place.

Step Three

When you're standing in your responsibility place, wonder about the following questions.

- Given your programming, why was it inevitable that this issue happened the way it did?
- What from the past does this remind you of?
- How do you keep this issue going in your life now?
- What did you learn from this issue that would have been difficult to learn in any other way?
- What positive potential did this issue release in you that would have been difficult to release in any other way?

5/Ending Control Struggles

❧

When we are feeling stuck, it is usually because we are focusing on things we cannot change or control. When we shift to focusing on things we can change and control, life smooths out very quickly.

Imagine that there are two files in your mind. If you are a computer person, you can visualize two computer files. If you're not, visualize two manila office files. Happiness comes from getting everything in your life in the right file. If you organize your two files correctly, you will feel an immediate surge of well-being in your body.

File number one is called "Things I Absolutely Can Change

or Control." The other is labeled "Things I Absolutely Cannot Change or Control." Many people exhaust their energy by putting things in the wrong file. In fact, the unpleasant feeling of drained exhaustion that many people feel is the direct result of worrying about things that are absolutely outside their control, and of avoiding thinking about things over which they have control. Typically, for example, therapy clients will come in feeling completely drained. It will turn out that they have been thinking about such things as:

- What other people think about them
- The problems of an adult child
- Whether their mate is sexually attracted to someone else
- The future
- The past

All of these things actually belong in the file called "Things I Absolutely Cannot Change or Control." Thinking about these things exhausts us and keeps us from thinking about issues completely within our control, such as:

- Whether we are doing what we want to be doing
- Whether we have communicated our feelings completely to our partner
- Whether we have told the child in question how we feel about his or her issue
- Whether we have taken an action step in the present that will contribute to the future or heal something in the past

All of these things are well within our power to change and control, but addressing them requires energy. That energy is drained by thinking about things outside our control. Think for a moment of the American obsession with weight. You may be one of the millions of people who struggle to control their weight but for whom the issue never seems to resolve itself. If you think you can control your weight, try an experiment. Go stand on your scale, and control your weight by losing five pounds. If you can do something in your mind that makes the scales register five pounds less, call us collect! The truth is, no one can control their weight.

Weight belongs in the "Things I Absolutely Cannot Change or Control" file. What *do* you have control over that might influence your weight? How much you eat and how much you exercise are behaviors that belong in the file "Things I Absolutely Can Change or Control." But if you're worrying about your weight or thinking about what you'll have for lunch in the middle of breakfast, you're misfiling. You're draining the energy it takes to change fundamental habits like eating and exercising.

As formidable as individual organizing is, correct filing gets even more complicated in relationships. In fact, it may be the basis for most power struggles. Many couples try to control something in their partner that they actually have no control over.

Here's an example of organizing the two files from a recent training.

We said to Debbie, "What's your big relationship complaint?"

She replied, "Trying to get my partner to tell the truth. Ever since I was a little girl, I've been obsessed with finding out what's really true and trying to dig it out of people. Frank just doesn't seem to understand how important this is to me!"

We suggested a radical (to Debbie) idea: "You've got Frank's truth-telling misfiled. Whether Frank tells the truth is not something you can control, is it?"

Debbie shot back, "I certainly try to, and sometimes I think it's working, my poking and prodding."

"Yes," we replied, "where did you learn to be a policewoman for truth-telling?"

Debbie laughed ruefully and said, "The truth was nonexistent in my family, and I became totally absorbed by the quest for truth. I even became a counselor"—the group laughed here—"and spend my days convincing people to tell the truth."

"How do you feel at the end of the day?"

"I'm just exhausted; I have nothing left."

"We've noticed that misfiling often starts with trying to do something now to correct something that *didn't* happen a long time ago. The problem is, nothing you do in the present can change the past. And focusing on the past depletes your ability to affect your life right now. So Debbie, take this opportunity to give Frank back complete control over his truth-telling. And make a distinction about that in your body. Actually place Frank and his telling the truth in the correct file, 'Things You Absolutely Cannot Change or Control.' "

Debbie took a few minutes to take deeper, diaphragmatic breaths and to unglue her shoulders and jaw, where she felt contracted when she tried to control Frank. After a bit her face turned pinker, and she started to smile. "If I don't try to get Frank to tell me the truth all the time, I'd have time to appreciate him, to ask for what I want, and to have more fun."

"Let's take a look at your responsibility in this issue. What do you withhold from Frank?"

Debbie flushed as she said, "I think Frank tries to control my eating. He brings home all the latest articles on fat studies and foods that are bad for you and good for you. I feel like I'm on a merry-go-round every week trying to reach the brass ring of perfect health, as Frank sees it. I haven't told him I keep stashes of Fritos and Milk Duds at work, where I can eat them whenever I want."

"So he's your health cop and you're his truth cop."

"Yeah, I guess that's our deal."

"We've noticed that truth-telling never changes on the level of doing or defending. It only works for you to be a space of truth. Then people want to tell the truth to you; you become safe to tell the truth to. So Debbie, would you be willing to be a space where people effortlessly tell the truth? Would you be willing to let go of any demand that they tell the truth?"

Debbie thought for just a few seconds and responded, "Yes!"

"Then, if people do tell the truth, you are fulfilling your commitment to be a space for truth-telling, and if they don't, it's a signal that you've slipped in your commitment, not that they are wrong."

By this time Debbie's face had relaxed and brightened. Someone in the group mentioned that she looked five years younger.

SORTING THE TWO FILES

Things I Cannot Change or Control	←Things to File→	Things I Can Change or Control
	Your feelings	
	Other people's feelings	
	The past	
	What hasn't happened yet	
	Other people's accomplishments	
	Choice	
	Action	

Choose one item from the column "Things to File." First, think about how you try to control this area, and tighten up your body and try to control it right now. Worry about it, and rehearse how you'll control it in the future; or practice harassing someone else as you tighten your body. Do this for a minute or two.

Now take a relaxed belly breath, and sigh through your open mouth as you breathe out. Take a moment to notice your body sensations. Is the residual tightness familiar? That rush you may have felt is adrenaline, a powerful and addictive substance that propels many people to continue misfiling. But those constant chemical bursts are ultimately exhausting, as Debbie noted. You might be surprised to discover what areas hold tension when you're trying to control the uncontrollable. For example, Kathlyn noticed "I hold tension in my forearms when I'm misfiling. I think I hold back the impulse to get in there and do my Supercompetent reorganizing thing."

Now take the items in "Things to File," and place them in the correct file. Write down the specific feeling, person, or event in "Things I Cannot Change or Control" or "Things I Can Change or Control." (Hint: There are only two items that belong in the right-hand column.) We suggest making yourself a map on the floor so you can step into the correct file and physically place the issue where it belongs. Make this a whole-body experiment. Write the issue in the correct column and step into the right file, or place a symbol of the issue in the correct place on the floor. Do whatever you can to let your whole body participate in refiling.

Next, redirect your efforts toward the most effective strategies to build up the file "Things I Can Change or Control." Take one issue that you've just filed correctly in the right-hand column and run through these three steps.

Make a new choice; think up a better idea. Think up the most positive result in the problem area. With Debbie, we suggested making herself a source of truth rather than a police officer. Here are some other examples:

- I celebrate my sexual feelings fully and express them with integrity.
- I enjoy the accomplishments of my colleagues and appreciate what I can learn from them.
- I have plenty of money to do whatever I need or want, and I enjoy what I have.
- Whatever I give my children enhances my creativity, vitality, and bank balance.
- I experience radiant health and abundant energy throughout the day.

Do your best to use present-tense, action verbs in your sentences.

Form a plan of action. If you want radiant health, schedule your exercise sessions in your appointment book along with all your other choices. Decide what steps need to be taken, whether it's a physical or weight training, and note the date on which you'll complete this step.

Make an agreement. Making agreements opens your creativity and completes the filing process. It's like the ending chord of the symphony that signals resolution. It's especially powerful to make an agreement with another person. Here are some examples:

- I agree to make requests about cleaning the kitchen rather than complaining to you.
- I agree to tell you whenever I have sexual fantasies about other people.
- I agree to take fifteen minutes each day to practice conscious listening.
- I agree to alternate car-pooling days with you for the kids' activities.

6 / Developing Appreciation

❧

M any relationship breakthroughs take place when people learn to appreciate. But few of us are skilled in this crucial area. How many hours of your formal education did you spend being trained to look at the student next to you and deliver appreciations? In most high schools such an activity would probably cause a riot. So most of us are kindergarteners when it comes to delivering gratitude. In therapy we often end a difficult session with a round of appreciation. "Okay," we'll say, "what is good about this relationship?" Or we ask a couple to face each other and take turns telling each other what they appreciate about each other.

We made a more concerted effort in this regard after reading some of John Gottman's research. As we mentioned earlier, he found that thriving relationships have at least a five-to-one ratio of appreciations to negative comments. In our own relationship we began to increase the number of conscious appreciations we delivered each day. We made it a point to deliver appreciations to the people who work with us and for us. Suddenly the workday began working more smoothly. Then we began opening our public talks with appreciations. Before a talk we would tune in to people we were feeling genuine appreciation for, then talk about those appreciations as we began. Once, in a talk at a large bookstore in Berkeley, someone came up afterward and told us we were the only speakers that had ever appreciated the staff for their contribution to the evening. How amazing! People had set up chairs, made coffee, and helped us in a dozen little ways. No one had ever appreciated them out loud during the talk! The world would be a better place indeed if we worked on getting the five-to-one ratio into each area of our lives.

In addition to actively appreciating the people in your life, continue to develop appreciation during contemplative time. The following is a journal activity that can be completed solo or shared out loud with a partner.

Complete the following sentences:

One positive thing I am aware of through my senses right now is _____.

Another positive thing I am aware of through my senses right now is _____.

One positive aspect of my life today is _____.

Another positive aspect of my life today is _____.

Think of a person you are in conflict with right now. One positive quality she or he has is _____.

Another positive quality she or he has is _____.

Make a list of daily activities or behaviors that people close to you do and that make your life sweeter or richer.

1. _____

2. _____

3. _____

Share your list today with the people involved.

Make a list of the people in your life whose contributions you appreciate. Make a plan to acknowledge those gifts in person or by phone, fax, e-mail, or letter.

ABOUT THE AUTHORS

KATHLYN HENDRICKS, PH.D., and GAY HENDRICKS, PH.D., are pioneers in the field of body-centered psychotherapy, nationally known teachers and seminar leaders, and co-authors of the bestselling *Conscious Loving* and *At the Speed of Life*. They have been partners in life and work for nearly twenty years and share two adult children and a grandchild. They currently live in Santa Barbara, California.

AUDIO, VIDEO, AND TRAINING RESOURCES
for Lifelong Learning and Professional Development

We offer a full range of resources for professionals and students of conscious relationships.

The Conscious Heart Video is available on VHS for $24.95, plus $5.50 shipping and handling. The video is a combination of demonstration, lecture, discussion, and activities for home practice.

The Conscious Heart Audio Program is available on cassette for $16.95, plus $4.50 shipping and handling.

Trainings are offered for professional certification and personal development. These are approximately one week in duration, and are offered primarily in Santa Barbara and Europe.

Information on these and other resources is available by writing to:

The Hendricks Institute
137 West Mission
Santa Barbara, CA
93101

or by calling

1-800-688-0772

Visit our comprehensive web site: http://www.hendricks.com